An Indian I Am

An Indian I Am

KK Muhammed

Published by
PRABHAT PRAKASHAN PVT. LTD.
4/19 Asaf Ali Road,
New Delhi-110 002 (INDIA)
e-mail: prabhatbooks@gmail.com

ISBN 978-93-5521-080-7
AN INDIAN I AM
by Shri KK Muhammed

Edition
2024

Concept of the book
Anish Kuttan

Basic translation
Dr Dileep Karanth

Price
₹ 400.00 (Rupees Four Hundred only)

Printed at
R-Tech Offset Printers, Delhi

Preface

The path I walked, the people I met, the tasks I accomplished—these are the things summarised in the book 'An *Indian I am.*' As an archaeologist, I had the rare privilege of working in more than ten different states, searching for the remains and relics of forgotten cultures. To dive deep into the fountain springs of Hinduism, Jainism, Buddhism, Islam and Christianity, drink deep from it and then fall asleep by the side of the same historic landscapes, where history was enacted—what a wonderful experience it has been! The historical monuments of great kings and emperors such as Bimbisara, Ashoka, Samudra Gupta, Harsha, Anang Pal Tomar, Prithvi Raj Chauhan, Iltutmish, Afonso de Albuquerque, Akbar, Shah Jahan, Clive and others are landmarks, commemorating important milestones in Indian history. The forts and palaces they built are reminiscent of rich and colourful history and an eloquent reminder of the pomp and panorama of a dim and distant past. To be a participant in the conservation and restoration of these landmarks in Indian history is, indeed the long-cherished dream of every student of history.

Isn't it a thrilling experience to be part of the exploration and excavation team that investigated at Ayodhya and that too under the legendary archaeologist Prof BB Lal? The sprawling mounds of Hasthinapura, the capital of the Pandavas and the plains of Mathura, the land of Sri Krishna have special meaning to an archaeologist. Despite being a suave diplomat and shrewd politician, Krishna could not bring the warring tribes on the same page. In Vrindhavan, Gokul and Radhakund, an art historian and archaeologist could still listen to the joyous notes of the divine flute of Krishna. The experience of walking in the footsteps of Mahavir Jain at Vaishali and Mahatma Buddha at Bodh Gaya is a dream come true for any student of history and archaeology.

The story of Chinese travellers such as Faxian, Xuanzang and Yijing, who walked thousands of miles, traversing treacherous tracks and braving the icy blizzards to reach India, exclusively to study Buddhism, inspired me.

When you help conserve their monuments or the monuments associated with them, you are entering into a partnership with these illustrious figures of human history. Who could have imagined that destiny would, one day, choose me to be a partner with Ashoka, Akbar and others? This is how I felt when I spearheaded many explorations, excavations, conservations and restoration projects in their capitals.

During this journey, I had to break the idols of some of the false human gods of Aligarh, who mercilessly used the sword of secularism and communism to stifle the voice of liberalism and free-thinking by branding them as communalists. Please do not get me wrong—this is not an attempt to denigrate communism, which has brought about revolutionary changes in the world's social structure. I have great regard for Communism and those hundreds of selfless revolutionaries who sacrificed everything to create a new world order. I chose to stand against those self-styled communists of Aligarh, who used it for blatant nepotism and favouritism.

As an archaeology student, I had to speak some unpleasant truths without yielding to the opinions of Hindu and Muslim communalists. My straightforward and forthright statements about Ayodhya were unpalatable to communist historians, who promoted minority communalism directly and indirectly. Muslim extremists of various hues and colours such as ISIS, ISI, Hizbul Mujahideen, or Taliban would be naturally against the book's content as I follow liberal views on many issues. Similarly, the statements of some ultra-Hindu organisations represented by the

VHP claiming the Taj Mahal as Tejo Mahalaya Shiva temple and the Qutub Minar as Vishnu-Dhwaj also had to be opposed based on sound historical records, manuscripts and architectural evolution principles of medieval India.

Jawaharlal Nehru's books *The Discovery of India* and *Glimpses of World History,* translated and published in Malayalam by the Mathrubhumi, gave a definite shape to my nebulous interest in archaeology and history. Later in life, I read these books in their original language, English. I also travelled to many of the places mentioned and watched *Bharat Ek Khoj*, a TV serial based on them. However, neither the English translation nor the TV serial could impact me as the Malayalam translations. I am unable to fathom the reason for it. Perhaps in my younger days, I looked at the historical landscape through rose-tinted glasses, which made them more attractive.

I am grateful to the renowned historian Professor MGS Narayanan, who has done me the favour of writing the foreword for this book. He could do it with ease and felicity, not only because he knew all the historical places mentioned in it but also because of some of the controversial characters I have referred to.

This book is respectfully dedicated to the memory of Shri Narayana Guru, who gave a clarion call for a society free of religion and caste. The call, given by the Guru, as if shot from the quiver of infallible wisdom, even now echoes at the doorstep of humankind. Its relevance comes into sharp focus whenever a Muslim fundamentalist attempts to bomb a temple; upper castes mercilessly beat up a Dalit, or a group of gau-rakshaks lynches a poor Muslim.

The first basic draft of the English translation of the book from the Hindi version was made by Dr Dileep Karanth, an academic teacher in Physics. However, I extensively rewrote this basic translation to reflect my inner feelings, as I had sourced the story from my own wounds. Along with it, the book was also revised by incorporating several issues that the Malayalam and Hindi versions did not cover.

Since some of the portions of the Hindi book were not clear to Dr. Karanth, he took help from Dr. Vanaja Menon who helped him from its Malayalam original. I am thankful to Dr. Vanaja Menon for her help and cooperation in preparing the first basic draft of the book 'An Indian I am'.

I am also grateful to Shri Anish Kuttan, who originally conceived such a book in Malayalam, which has now run into six editions within five years. The Hindi translation made by Dr O Vasavan of All India Radio, Calicut, has elicited unstinted appreciation from the Hindi-speaking areas. The Hindi book played a small role in presenting the real story of the Ayodhya excavation under Prof BB Lal and Dr BR Mani before the general public. I am grateful to Mrs Parvathi Menon, a Delhi based Film Maker, for going through the book and making many valuable comments. On the suggestion of Mrs Menon, a chapter on the 'Tragic Story of Queen Ketavan' was added. Thanks are also due to Mrs Geetha Badkaliya of Destination Heritage and Radhika Samuel for helping me with the finishing touches of the book.

The book has also been translated into Kannada by Shri Narasingha Rao, and the third edition is in the market. The second edition of the Telegu translation is expected to be released soon. Dr Srinivasa K Rao, an NRI based in Newyork, undertook the initiative for its Telugu version and he further proposes to get it translated to many major languages in the country. Right from the beginning, the small team associated with the book was very clear that the royalty from these books would be spent exclusively on charity works. Shri Narasingha Rao, the Kannada translator, himself goes to hospitals and other institutions to help the needy. Recently the Marathi translation made by Dr Sulabha Kore was published by Mehta publishing house. The Tamil translation made by Erode Rajan is expected to be released soon.

I would feel amply rewarded if the book can play a role, howsoever insignificant, in softening the sharp edges evident among various religious communities in the country. While the Muslim, Hindu and Communist fanatics ride roughshod, the free thinkers run for cover, as no political party supports them. This book stands for the suppressed voice of the liberals.

—KK Muhammed

Foreword

My friend KK Muhammed is one of India's most renowned archaeologists. It is a matter of pride for me that he is a Keralite, hailing from my district, Kozhikode. It is no mean achievement to have excellent theoretical and practical knowledge of a subject like archaeology. To put this knowledge to use in the service of the nation is an even greater accomplishment.

Without reservation, I wish to say that Muhammed is one of the few individuals in the field of archaeology who has combined in himself the qualities of scientific temper, courage and willingness to serve the downtrodden.

Being born in a traditional Muslim family in the small town of Koduvally could have been a disadvantage in the race for success in life, but Muhammed faced all adverse circumstances, converting every handicap into an advantage.

It is a matter of great regret that Kerala, which was once foremost in promoting inter-faith harmony, has become a centre for religiously inspired terrorism. Had it not been so, universities in Kerala or the state government would have only been too glad to welcome renowned archaeologists like Muhammed and put their talents to fair use.

I had heard of Muhammed and his exploits at Aligarh a long time ago. However, I had a chance to interact with him directly only in the early eighties, when I was an active member and an office-bearer of the Indian History Congress. During the annual session of the Congress in Bodh Gaya, Muhammed came up with a list of accusations against Irfan Habib, Professor of History at Aligarh Muslim University. Prof MP Sridharan, a few other friends and I came together and dissuaded Muhammed from pursuing his task. We ourselves did not have a very high opinion of Prof Habib and his communist group. At that time, our primary concern was that the convention should not be disturbed on account of Muhammed's work. The Indian History Congress, a voluntary organisation of historians, was a common platform for scholars of diverse points of view to interact. We thought that the criticisms against Prof Habib were a matter for his university to deal with and that the Indian History Congress was not the appropriate forum for such a discussion. Our efforts to calm Muhammed were successful to some extent.

Similar charges against Prof Habib and his communist group had been levelled by others too. We, too, had our share of grievances against him and the Marxist Party. With his narrow-minded politics and personal favouritism, Prof Habib had poisoned not only the field of history but also the cultural and public life of the current generation.

Prof Irfan Habib is a brilliant and resourceful man. A master of intrigue, he and his followers are known to use every possible trick in the dictionary in their efforts to paint their critics as communalists or *Hindutvavādīs*. Prof Habib himself is neither a Muslim nor a communalist, nor is he a man of religious belief. However, his followers worked day and night in the forum of the Indian History Congress and elsewhere for the success of Muslim communalism. The Babri Masjid issue was converted into a communal issue due to the stupidity of the *Hindutvavādīs* and the machinations of Communists. Muhammed has done an amazing service to expose the political intrigues of Communist historians at the Aligarh Muslim University through the medium of his memoirs. The next generation of historians and archaeologists will find them an excellent quarry to dig in.

Muhammed begins his autobiographical account with his reminiscences of his primary school teachers and the libraries in his village. They were the foundation for his successes in life. Many accomplishments can be arrived at on the strength of intelligence alone, but when intelligence is married to virtues such as patience, sincerity, sense of adventure and interest in public service, success in the real meaning of the word becomes possible. These qualities have now become a rarity in India. It is here that Muhammed stands out from the crowd. He has performed meritorious service in the field of archaeology, as the reader will notice from the pageant of events described in a simple and lucid language in his memoirs. His contribution to the area of medieval archaeology is outstanding.

The first milestone is the discovery of the *Ibadat Khana*, the Hall of Inter-Religious Discussion, where Akbar the Great assembled scholars from all religions. As it was the confluence of all religions, it was considered to be the nursery of Indian secularism. This discovery was made possible by a combination of factors such as wide reading, exhaustive field study and close personal connection with daily wage labourers of all kinds. Logical reasoning coupled with luck led to the discovery of the first Christian chapel of North India, built during the Mughal period. Instead of congratulating his former student on his extraordinary success, Prof Irfan Habib strained every nerve to run down the discovery and, in the process, was severely exposed. People who are acquainted with the professor can easily imagine what must have happened. Prof Habib is known to behave in this manner with all those who are outside his narrow circle. Sycophants like Makhan Lal encouraged Prof Irfan to adopt inimical and arbitrary ways. In his book, Muhammed has referred to people such as Makhan Lal, JP Joshi and Ramchandra Gaur, who are all well known to me. I can attest to the fact that there is nothing biased or exaggerated in what Muhammed has to say about them.

The next project that Muhammed undertook was restoring the site in Goa, where Kunjali Marakkar was killed. He was keen to carry out conservation of several churches, including that of Bom Jesus, where the body relic of St Xavier is kept. At the same time, Muhammed turned down the request to open some churches for worship for the simple reason that it was not legally permissible.

This has been a clear instance of Muhammed's balanced thinking and impartial views.

Through his kindness and interpersonal skills, he was successful in winning over the Naxalites operating in Chhattisgarh. Muhammed is respectful of diverse religious and political beliefs. If he had not been sincere, he would not have been able to make his mark. In the infamous Taj corridor case, Muhammed acted with diplomacy and alertness, contributing to stopping the building of the Taj heritage corridor—a dream project of Mayavati, the then Chief Minister of Uttar Pradesh.

He had to cross swords simultaneously with extremists of all hues—Hindu, Muslim and Communists. Muhammed has had the opportunity to restore hundreds of places of worship of different faiths, and he regards this privilege as his good fortune.

The most prominent of these accomplishments was the restoration of the Bateshwar temple complex, which is located in the dacoit-infested land of Chambal Valley. Everyone was afraid of the dacoits, even those living on the margins of society for centuries, following a culture of bloodshed, vengeance, killing and caste rivalry. Nearly two hundred temples had been turned into heaps of rubble by earthquakes. No one wanted to have anything to do with them. Muhammed established contact with the dacoits through an intermediary and renovated the temples at the risk of his own life. These temples now stand as a testimony to inter-faith harmony and as monuments to humanity. The famous Angkor Wat temple complex in Cambodia probably had been built on this model. Muhammed has undoubtedly earned a place of honour in Kailasa!

The leader of the dacoits was Nirbhay Singh Gujjar, a man of the Gurjar Pratihara dynasty of the 8-11th centuries, responsible for building these temples. Muhammed won him over by appealing to his dynastic pride in the works of his own ancestors. Thus these temples and their treasures were restored to their pristine glory. This achievement will have a tremendous positive impact on the immediate present and remain a source of inspiration for the future. Muhammed believes Nirbhaya Gujjar's change of heart is similar to that of the great poet Valmiki, who was once a dacoit before taking to composing the epic Ramayana. However, while many people appreciated this splendid accomplishment, it also provoked a backlash from some of the murkier elements of the bureaucracy. The illegal mining mafia killed an IPS officer by crushing him under a tractor. Fortunately, Muhammed's life was spared because of his connection with the dacoits and a timely transfer.

Life at the Archaeological Survey of India also brought Muhammed face to face with many happy experiences. When foreign dignitaries visited India, the task of showing them around the historical monuments was often entrusted to him. He got the opportunity to introduce Indian history to over thirty heads of state. During these tours, the visiting dignitaries would often ask questions, at times, tricky ones. These questions were posed by visiting presidents, ministers, ambassadors or their spouses. Keeping the historical truth in mind and the national interest was indeed a delicate balancing act to answer these questions!

Muhammed has described the visit of the Pakistani President to the Taj Mahal in his memoirs. He has also written about the visits by the President and First Lady of the United States, the German President and the Chinese Prime Minister. A perusal of these memoirs will give the reader a good idea of how effective an ambassador of Indian culture Muhammed has been!

Muhammed has described an unforgettable incident from the year 2010. Inspired by the maternal feelings of his wife Rabia, Muhammed began a school for the children of labourers hired by the ASI. With the school's expenses borne by him, Muhammed tried to impart education to the migrant labourers' children in the makeshift tents! Newspapers and television channels appreciated this gesture. When US President Barack Obama and Michelle Obama were in India, they met these children and appreciated his initiative. Muhammed can now look back on this incident with justifiable pride!

In this book, Muhammed writes about the most rewarding opportunities of his career. At Amarkantak in Madhya Pradesh, the source of the river Narmada, several eleventh century ruined temples were encroached upon by anti-social elements, some of whom were dressed in holy ochre robes! The government, as also the political parties, chose to look the other way. The ASI acquired the land, demolished the encroachments and liberated the temples. The matter soon went to court—a Muslim officer had acted against the established religious leaders and interfered in the temple affairs! The complaints went as far as the Central Government, and a Central Minister, Ambika Soni, summoned Muhammed.

Muhammed showed the said minister two photographs of the temple, one in a ruined and desolate state, when criminals took it over, and another, when it was freed of encroachments, restored and beautified with lush green landscape around it. A highly impressed minister expressed her satisfaction and informed him to deal with his opponents diplomatically.

Another great accomplishment during Muhammed's career was the careful restoration of the Bhojpur temple with its Mahashivalinga, which was constructed by Raja Bhoja–composer of the authoritative architectural text, Samarangana Sutradhara. This temple was damaged because of an accident followed by neglect for centuries. Once restored to its pristine glory, the temple management made it a point to invite this Muslim officer as their chief guest during the annual Shivaratri celebrations.

Muhammed is aggrieved that the ancient temple such as Guruvayoor and the mosques in Kerala is still in the grip of discrimination, where permission for entry is prohibited or restricted. Since he intends to settle down in Calicut, Kerala, after retirement, he can still do a great deal of good work in this domain.

Before retiring, Muhammed embarked on a significant programme. Under his guidance, a Replica Museum was established near the Siri Fort Auditorium in the capital, New Delhi. The Replica Museum is meant to house replicas of masterpieces of Indian art from different parts of the country. Although the government did not show much interest, thirty replicas of masterpieces of Indian art make it a centre of attraction. There was pressure from some quarters to take disciplinary action against Muhammed.

To stop youngsters from scribbling on the monuments, he launched a campaign by organising an 'oath-taking ceremony' in the premises of the monuments so that the visitors would not scribble on the monuments. This programme was initially started in Bihar but gradually spread to other states also. This became a popular movement as newspapers and channels supported it.

During his long career at the ASI, Muhammed has incurred the displeasure of his seniors from time to time. He was transferred at various times to Goa, Bihar, Uttar Pradesh, Chhattisgarh, Madhya Pradesh and Delhi, but he used each such transfer as a stepping stone to gain more experience in the field of archaeology. Just as foreign invasions and intrusions enriched the Indian culture, Muhammed was able to convert his handicaps into assets. He has now written his reminiscences, distilled in the crucible of experience. This memoir is nothing short of his manifesto.

I pray the Almighty grants Muhammed a long life and good health to keep up his excellent work, whether he gets support from the government or not. It will be in the country's interest if a private Institute of Archaeological Studies is established, based on Muhammed's ideals and philosophy, preferably in Kerala. I also hope these memoirs will be translated into Hindi and other languages.

I hope the readers of this book will come together to act on these suggestions and form a committee to bring them to fruition.

—Dr MGS Narayanan
Former Chairman & Secretary,
Indian Council for Historical Research (ICHR)

Contents

The World of Wide Reading

My school teachers and the village library are two important factors that shaped my life and personality. I belong to the *Mappila* Muslim Community. The *Mappila* community members are descendants from marriages of local women with Arab traders. The village being a Muslim majority area, my education began with the local *madrasa*. This madrasa was a traditional *one* with an old syllabus. At this time, another one with 'Al Madrasa,' under the Jamat-e-Islami, was opened with a new syllabus and teaching Urdu as an additional language. While in the traditional *madrasa*, one is forced to shave his head every fifteen days; in the latter, one could grow his hair and stylishly flaunt it in the village bazaar and school. This was an added attraction to many boys to join the new *madrasa*. They also trained us in other extracurricular activities such as sports and games.

The village primary school was founded by Pareekutty Adhikari and the high school by another philanthropist KV Moin Kutty Haji. Koduvally, once a sleepy little village and now a bustling town, is indebted to both for its entire development. Had they not established schools in those days, many of my generations would have become motor vehicle drivers or traders. Another philanthropist TK Pareekutty Haji took the initiative to open an orphanage in Koduvally and took care of the orphans in the neighbourhoods of Koduvally.

My parents were poor and worked hard as daily wage labourers. Over time, my father became a cleaner in a small lorry, then a driver and gradually worked his way to becoming its owner. This vehicle would supply rice and other articles from Calicut town to the nearby villages. As a result of his contact with road transport officers, he became a local agent for vehicle licenses and got the nickname 'Koduvally RTO'. But he was illiterate and could barely sign his name.

In those days (sixty years back), only a few families could afford two square meals a day. Having come from a poor background, my parents knew the pangs of hunger and what free food meant to famished and starving children. Hence, in the month of Muharram, which is the birth month of Prophet Muhammed, it was customary that *kanjhi*, a mixture of cooked rice and water, a poor man's lunch, was given for 100 children. Mother was particular that she should prepare it and serve it with her own hands. Similarly, every Friday, orphans from the surroundings were given their free lunch.

I started my *madrasa* education at the age of five. Since my mother wanted me to grow up to be a religious priest, she was not interested in me going to the village school. As the rest of my friends at the *madrasa* joined the village school and I was left alone in the *madrasa*, I resorted to a small innocuous trick. I approached my uncle and told him that my father had authorised him to help me join the school. That admission to the Mappilla Lower Primary school gave me an entry into the future big world. My teacher in the second standard was Abubackar Master, who looked every inch a Musliar (Islamic religious teacher). But he was the one who taught us stories from the Ramayana, the Mahabharata and other Hindu mythologies.

We listened to him in rapt attention when he narrated the heroic acts of Rama, Seetha and Lakshmana. We listened to the childish pranks of Krishna and Bhima with wide-open eyes. In my turn, I used to narrate these stories to my unfortunate friends who were not in Abubacker master's class. In the present surcharged atmosphere of the Hindu-Muslim divide, one cannot think of a teacher like Abubacker Master, who taught the Ramayana and the Mahabharata despite his typical Muslim appearance. Another teacher who made an indelible impression upon me was

Gangadharan master, who only wore Khadi, chewed betel and taught us about the Qutub Minar, Fatehpur Sikri, Taj Mahal and the Red Fort. Although he had never seen these monuments, he would speak about the *Diwan-i-Aam* and *Diwan-i-Khas* as if he had seen them in person. Another teacher, Susan Kurien, used to talk to her students only in English to teach them spoken English.

Shashidharan Master opened our world to the philosophy of Vivekananda and his electrifying speech at the World Conference of Religions in Chicago in 1894. Kasim master and Zainaba teacher took special classes for mathematics, as I was poor in the subject. It was Velayudhan master who made us conscious about our responsibility to society and groomed us as public speakers.

I owe everything to my school teachers for shaping my future. When I took round Pervez Musharraf, the Pakistan President, at the Taj Mahal in 2001 and Barack Obama at Humayun's Tomb, I remembered and paid my respects to them from the doorstep of the monuments as soon as the cavalcade of the VVIP departed. Similarly, when I was working at Ayodhya, Mathura, Hastinapura, etc., the names of these and many more teachers were uppermost in my mind. Let us recall Henry Adam, who said, "A teacher affects eternity; he can never tell where his influence stops."

For Muslim students, Malayalam was our first language up to the fifth standard, and after that, there was a switch over to Arabic. I had a special love for religion, history, philosophy, and social service from the very beginning. I also took an interest in the uplift of the downtrodden and people from the scheduled castes. In 1969, when I was in the 10th standard, a Dalit leader and Minister, O Koran, visited our village, and I was invited to address a gathering along with the Minister. With youthful energy, I spoke against the pernicious caste system quoting from Hindu scriptures and Mahatma Gandhi, which made an impression on the audience.

It was a new experience for the people from the scheduled castes that a man from the Muslim community addressed their meeting. Although Muslims did not oppose my participation in the forum, they gave me Harijan Muhammed's nickname. I freely participated in the marriages of all the lower class agricultural communities, which was a refreshing departure from the prevailing customs.

A small local library of the village also played an important role in shaping my thoughts and future. Although small, it had the Malayalam translations of some important books such as the *Glimpses of the World History* and the *Discovery of India* written by Pundit Jawaharlal Lal Nehru. Another book was on World Philosophy by Rahul Sankrityayan. All these books were too high for me, but the fact that I could feel and flip through occasional chapters gave me self-satisfaction. Sankrityayan, born in a Brahmin Pandey family, was an Arya Samaji, a Buddhist and then a Marxist. During my Bihar posting, learning about the large-scale conservation work taken up in Buddhist monuments, his wife, Dr Kamala Sankrityayan, came to meet me along with Dr OP Pandey.

The third book that attracted me was the one written by Umaya Nelloor Bala Krishnen about Bihar and Nalanda University. As these books dealt more on North India, especially Delhi, Agra, Bihar etc., the thought of continuing my studies in one of the North Indian universities started occupying my mind space. While working in Delhi, UP and Bihar, what I learned in these books were of immense use.

As I passed Arabic Lower while I was in school, which qualified me to get a job as an Arabic teacher, a few of my friends persuaded me to take up a job in the government, as there were several vacancies for Arabic teachers. But I refused to be enamoured by it, for I wanted to be a student of history and archaeology in a North Indian university closer to Delhi. I had started to dream. "The dreams have the power to push your whole world forward." Ralph Marston. I was on the right track.

While working in many historical places and guiding some of the heads of foreign countries, I have often looked back and seen that Arabic teacher or the *madrasa* Musliar, which I would have been, had I not aspired for something higher. Such trysts and twists come in the life of everybody, but if we continue to struggle without being enamoured of a lower position, nobody can stop us from reaching our coveted goal.

With time, my illiterate father diversified from a motor vehicle agent to a small contractor. After high school, he wanted me to pursue engineering to help him in his contract work. But I had no appetite for engineering whatsoever and found it absolutely unpalatable. So I decided not to follow the advice of my parents and teachers but follow my passion. Then again, history was the choice of back benchers. So what? History was my passion and something that could excite me. If I could get a job of my liking, it would amount to drawing a salary by following one's own hobby. Hence, with full excitement and passion, I enjoyed all my postings both in the Aligarh Muslim University and in the Archaeological Survey of India. Since I was following my love, I did not work in the traditional sense of the term, even a single day. Here my duty is my passion and my hobby. As Neil de Grasse Tyson, the American astrophysicist, said, "passion is what gets you through the hardest time that otherwise makes strong men weak or make you give up."

After passing out from high school, with the help of some old students, I got admission at the Aligarh Muslim University, which was closer to many of the historical places such as Delhi, Agra, Mathura, Fatehpur Sikri, etc. A change from South to North India shakes one up in food, dress, climate and language. I adjusted to the changes very quickly and started enjoying them. At Aligarh, the one thing that impressed me most was the extensive nine-storied library of Aligarh, which would be open up to 10 pm. The history of the Aligarh Muslim University (AMU) itself was a source of inspiration for a student of history. Its founder, Sir Syed Ahmed Khan, was the first Muslim modern thinker who demonstrated the courage to break away with the traditional thinking of the Muslim community. He had left an indelible impression of his magnetic personality on every brick of Sir Syed Hall where I was residing, as it was the nucleus of the university. About the contribution of AMU in reawakening the dormant Muslim community after 1857, RC Majumdar says, "It would be hardly an exaggeration to say that no single institution has done so much for any community as has this college done for the promotion of higher education and modern culture among the Muslims."

The History department had a pantheon of scholars such as Prof Nurul Hasan, KA Nizami and Irfan Habib. Prof Muhammed Habib, the father of Irfan Habib, who had retired by that time, came to give extension lectures. Since Prof Nurul Hasan was a Member of the Parliament, the Department of History had enjoyed special status.

One day, when it was announced that Dr Irfan Habib would be teaching us in the BA classes, all of us were overjoyed. It was, of course, an extraordinary privilege to be his student. All of us waited for the day with much expectation. But within half an hour, we were dissatisfied. His method of teaching was not at all impressive. Was it because we could not rise to the extraordinary standard of a PhD from Oxford? We started introspecting within ourselves. But I was one of the best students. Gradually, we started discussing among ourselves with much reservation. We realised that he fell far short of the teaching skills required to teach undergraduate students. He might be good for MA and research students, but when we discussed with some post graduate students, they refused to share our views.

At the post-graduate level, I was his student again, as I specialised in Medieval India. In student's politics, I was with the NSUI, which was affiliated with the Congress Party. Prof Irfan Habib cannot tolerate anybody working in any other student's union, while he is the lord protector of the Students Federation of India (SFI) affiliated with the Marxist Party of India. By this time, news of the student's critical assessment of his classes had also reached him. In the final MA examination, as David, another student scored more marks than me, he became the topper, and I was relegated to the second rank as per merit. Since David had left for JNU from among the internal students, I had the first claim for the PhD and the research scholarship. This claim was refused and given to Afzal Khan, who consistently scored lesser marks than me in MA, BA, and Pre-University.

For a teacher, political neutrality is indispensable for any credible engagements with students. When a teacher's actions start acquiring the unmistakable stamp of nepotism and favouritism and seeing research through the narrow prism of political ideology, it is not a place where a liberal thinker can pursue research work. Of course, for a Communist party sympathiser or a Students Federation of India (SFI) member, the Department of History of Aligarh was a haven, but not for those who have an independent opinion of their own. In their group, nobody could develop critical thinking or question their ideologies and decisions. There were a few such bonded researchers and workers with them. "A dead fish can float down a stream, but it takes a live one to swim upstream."- WC Fields.

In this situation, I decided to sail away from Aligarh and launch my boat catching the trade winds in my sails. I got admission for the Post-Graduate Diploma in Archaeology in the Archaeological Survey of India. Soon I realised that I had reached the right place, for the classes were exciting and also taught in the locations of various monuments all over the country. With seven cities, Delhi is a veritable treasure-trove for a student of archaeology and history. Like Rome, Delhi is overwhelmed by its own greatness. It was the third stage of my development and transformation.

□

The Discovery of *Ibadat Khana* (Hall of Inter-Religious Discussions) and My Aligarh Days

After securing a post-graduate diploma from the Archaeological Survey of India (ASI), I began my career at the Aligarh Muslim University as a Technical Assistant. Subsequently, I got promoted to the position of Assistant Archaeologist on an ad-hoc basis. By this time, Prof KA Nizami, who was earlier the Head of the History Department, the Vice-Chancellor and subsequently the Indian Ambassador to Syria, returned to Aligarh and replaced Dr Irfan Habib. It was Prof Nizami who had appointed me as an archaeologist. Had Dr Irfan Habib continued as Head of the Department, I would never have got an appointment at the Aligarh Muslim University, as I was not one of his party followers.

Due to his denial of justice to me, by initially refusing admission and scholarship for PhD, I had to leave Aligarh and seek admission for a course in the School of Archaeology in Delhi. By now, Dr Irfan Habib had converted the History Department of Aligarh University into a 'Land of Bonded Intellectuals,' in which free thought and speech had no role. The replacement of merit with mediocrity had become the hallmark of Aligarh during Dr Habib's period, and he did this with disquieting confidence as he knew that no one would challenge him. Afzal Khan, the recipient of the scholarship, was contrite and apologetic when he met me and said, "KK, it was your right, but I got it because of some other considerations. I am sorry."

During my second innings at Aligarh in the capacity of an archaeologist, I made several discoveries at Fatehpur Sikri, the most important of which was the discovery of the *Ibadat Khana* and the Christian chapel, both built by the Mughal Emperor Akbar the Great. *Ibadat Khana* was the place where Akbar had invited scholars from various religions and listened to the merits of each faith. As a result of these discussions, in 1582, he evolved a syncretic religion known as *Din-I-Ilahi*. Through this initiative, Emperor Akbar tried to bring the elements of different religions into one single harmonious whole. Since the *Ibadat Khana* was the nursery of Indian secularism, its excavation attracted much public attention as newspapers gave it comprehensive coverage.

Earlier, most of the scholars had located the *Ibadat Khana* among the standing monuments of Fatehpur Sikri but were widely differing in their identification. However, a traditional scholar, Saeed Ahmed Mararavi, identified a mound overgrown with a few trees between the Jama Masjid and Jodhabhai Mahal as the most likely site of the *Ibadat Khana*. But nobody took him seriously because he was not from the world of the educated English literati. After an extensive survey of the site, Prof Athar Abbas Rizvi and Vincent Flynn, two senior professors from an Australian university, agreed with Mararavi and cited original Persian sources in support of their claim. Despite this, many scholars did not agree with it and argued in favour of some of the standing structures at Fatehpur Sikri as the site of *Ibadat Khana*.

At this time, an excavation team under the general supervision of Prof KA Nizami and the directorship of Prof RC Gaur from Aligarh Muslim University reached Fatehpur Sikri for further research and excavation. The excavation of medieval cities such as Hampi in Karnataka, Champaner in Gujarat and Fatehpur Sikri in Uttar Pradesh was the brainchild of Prof Saiyid Nurul Hasan, Central Minister for Education, Social Welfare and Culture (1971–77). Prof Hasan had been a professor of history at the Aligarh Muslim University and was known for his urbanity, liberal thinking and sophistication, due to which everyone, including his critics, respected him.

I was a member of the Aligarh team along with Dr Jamal Muhammed Siddiqui and several supporting staff members. There was another team at work at Fatehpur Sikri under the directorship of the Superintending Archaeologist of the Archaeological Survey of India. The ASI and the Aligarh team had identified separate sites for research and excavation since Fatehpur was a sprawling area. So, every night I burned the midnight oil for consulting books and the daytime for exploring, excavating and identifying various mounds that are the great treasure troves of history. My personal rapport with the locals and labourers proved to be of immense help in getting information about the adjacent villages and the historical remains that was lying buried in the vicinity. Developing a close relationship with these downtrodden labourers and having a desire to help them in all possible ways was something I had inherited from my parents. I participated freely in all the festivals such as holy, shivaratri, id and bakrid. The combination of literary sources with exploration and excavation proved most helpful in locating various hidden structures. Labourers from the adjoining villages took me to those sites where archaeological remains were lying buried and undiscovered.

After four years of study and exploration, I was reasonably convinced that Mararavi's identification of the mound as the site of the *Ibadat Khana* was correct, and it was not the various standing structures suggested by other learned scholars. However, this required more archaeological proof to substantiate my presumption. Only an excavation of the site could be the final arbitrator in this case—it could either prove or disprove the *Ibadat Khana* theory.

While researching through the material, I came across a painting of the *Ibadat Khana* in the book of Arnold and Wilkinson housed in the Maulana Azad library of the Aligarh Muslim University. The original copy of this painting is in the Chester Beatty collection in Dublin. In this painting, the *Ibadat Khana* scene was painted by the court painter Nar Singh during the lifetime of

Emperor Akbar. Nothing was exciting about this painting, as it was a widely published one mostly known to scholars working on the subject. But, I looked at the painting through the eyes of an archaeologist working at the site. That made all the difference.

This painting depicted a compound wall, a few arches on the western side and a dome on the backside. It immediately struck me that this painting was somewhat similar to the compound and mound of the site of the *Ibadat Khana,* pointed out by Mararavi. After taking a photo copy of the image, I rushed to Fatehpur Sikri for an on-the-spot comparative study of both the painting and the actual mound along with its ruins. I was satisfied to see that the ruins broadly tallied with the Mughal painting. The compound wall, along with three broken arches and a dome behind the arches, still stood as shown in the illustration, though it was quite dilapidated. These three components (compound wall, broken arches and the dome behind the arches) initially gave me the brainwave about the site being the location of the *Ibadat Khana*.

In the centre of the painting, a pyramidal structure of three platforms is shown, where a religious debate seemed to be in

Archival photo in 1978-79, as I saw:
no. 1. arches, no. 2. boundary wall, no. 3. excavator, no. 4. *Ibadat Khana* mound with four metre earth and trees growing over it.

progress, with Akbar occupying the top platform while the others were sharing the middle and lower platforms. Was it not possible that the pyramidal structure shown in the painting, buried under the mound, covered with the earth of four hundred years and overgrown with trees? This question began to bother me day and night. Ten trees with their roots splintering the three platforms were growing over it at that time.

An archaeologist can, to some extent, depend upon his sixth sense. He is in search of the distinct survivals of the distant past. He develops an uncanny habit of engaging in a constant conversation with Mother Earth. As a result, his mind meanders through fascinating labyrinths, x-raying various recesses and layers before forming a tentative opinion of what he might unearth after an excavation of the site.

Like me, Prof AA Rizvi and Vincent Flynn had also walked over the mound several times. Indeed, both these eminent scholars must have seen the same widely published painting of the Mughal era. Many other scholars who had seen the painting also might have walked over them. Perhaps, one of them might be Prof Nurul Hasan, an authority on Mughal history who visited Fatehpur Sikri several times. But somewhere along the way, despite being so close to the discovery, they missed out on that connecting link and the 'eureka' moment of medieval archaeology. Marcel Proust rightly said, "The real voyage of discovery consists not in seeking new landscapes, but in having new eyes." But sometimes, even after having an archaeologist's trained eyes, one may miss the eureka moments. It has happened with Alexander Cunningham in the case of Harappa and Markham Kittoe with the identification of ancient Nalanda University. Finally, the credit for identifying the real significance of Harappa and Mohenjodaro and pushing back the history of India from the 6th century BCE to 2500 BCE went to John Marshall.

Similarly, Francis Buchanan Hamilton had discovered the conical and square mounds of Badgaon near Rajgir in 1811, and later, the same place was inspected by Markham Kittoe, but both of them missed the real significance of the site. Finally, Alexander

Cunningham could identify it based on two inscriptions as the well-known Nalanda University site. Fortunately, by this time, the travels of Xuanzang was also translated in to English which had given a graphic description about Nalanda. Some times, luck also plays a crucial part in it.

What was the material used for the roof of the pyramidal structure? Like the adjacent structures, it was made of lime concrete. In a weather-beaten state, the roof material was still lying, in several fragments, on the top of the mound at the site. A study of the pieces, including their composition and thickness, was essential for an imaginary reconstruction of the roof of the *Ibadat Khana*.

The platforms on which the participants and Emperor Akbar were sitting might have had stone pillars and brackets to support the roof. Fortunately, two such supporting brackets were lying just outside the southern side of the pyramidal mound. It was now possible to imagine the reconstruction of the *Ibadat Khana* based on the description given by the contemporary sources, the Mughal painting of the *Ibadat Khana* and above all, the materials lying at the site. An archaeologist should know the art of putting a tongue in every stone. That was what I was doing.

It was a moment of unbelievable excitement for me. "I am on the verge of the discovery of the *Ibadat Khana*," my inner soul whispered. This thrilling realisation caused the desolate ruins, covered with the earth of several centuries and overgrown with several trees, to hum and pulsate with life. At once, the magnitude of the mound multiplied several times. It started casting a magical spell on me, and I was filled with an overpowering curiosity and an urge for enquiry.

Through the maze of history, I could visualise Akbar, 'the most argumentative Indian,' (Amartya Sen), entering the Ibadat Khana hall and engaging in discussions with religious scholars of that age, drawn from all religious faiths. In this inter-religious debating hall sat the great Jain *guru* Hira Vijaya Suri, Vijaya Sena Suri and Shanthi Chandra, teaching the Emperor the sublime principles of Jainism. Dastur Meharji Rana from Navsari in Gujarat taught Akbar about Zoroastrianism, the Parsi religion, and *Ahura Mazda* and *Ahriman*. Devi and Purushotham, the two Hindu scholars, taught him about Hinduism from the very beginning. Under their influence, he had started marking his forehead with sacred vermillion like a Hindu devotee. Apart from *Ibadat Khana*, sometimes such discussions took place at other locations also. Akbar was profoundly influenced by the Sikh Gurus Amar Das (1552–1574), Ram Das (1574–1581) and Guru Arjun (1581–1606), although they had never participated in the religious discussions at the *Ibadat Khana*.

To this assembly had come the Christian Fathers, Rudolf Acquaviva from Italy and Antonio Monserrat from Spain, making the *Ibadat Khana* one of the most animated intellectual centres. Never before in history was a search for truth carried out by any ruler on such a large scale, especially one born as a refugee and technically an illiterate. Emperor Akbar was a man who could flaunt no literary credentials but still engage scholars in discussions on any subject with his photographic memory!

Wasn't the *Ibadat Khana* the meeting point and melting pot of divergent opinions on various subjects, especially religion? Was it not here, Akbar carefully listened to different religious views, questioned them in detail, but remained uncommitted? Was it not the outcome of the discussions at this place that led to the culmination of a new religion that came to be known as *Din-i-Ilahi*? Was this not the birthplace of Indian secularism, of which every Indian is rightly proud? As a result of the discussions at this place, the views and perceptions of this great Emperor underwent a miraculous change.

The short speech Akbar made on the occasion of the promulgation of *Din-i-Ilahi* still echoes at the doorstep of humankind. He said, "I perceive there are varying customs and beliefs of varying religious paths. For the teachings of Hindus, the Mussalmans, the Yazdanis (Parsis), the Jews and the Christians are all different. But the followers of each religion regard the institution of their own religion as better than those of any other. Not only so, they strive to convert the rest to their way of belief. If they refuse to be converted, they not only despise them but also regard them for this very reason as their enemies. And this causes me to raise many serious doubts and concerns" (Fr Monserrate). This speech constitutes the gist of Indian secularism.

Many thoughts crossed my mind while I walked on the desolate ruins of the *Ibadat Khana*. The fact that I was standing over the same mound, on the floors of which Akbar had spent many hours with scholars of various religions, further stirred in me an urge to excavate the spot. Every archaeologist in the '*eureka!*' moment of their discovery is reminded of the statement of Sir John Marshall, proclaiming the tentative discovery of the Indus valley civilization: "Not often archaeologists are as lucky as Schliemann at Tiryns and Mycenae.... It looks, however, at this moment, as if we were on the threshold of such a discovery in the plains of the Indus."

Prof KA Nizami and Prof KS Lal of Aligarh Muslim University and Delhi University came to the site and had a lengthy discussion. Prof Nizami, who was working on his book Akbar, quoted profusely from Persian sources and congratulated me for identifying the location. It was Prof Nizami, for the first time, discussed this discovery from an academic point of view in his book 'Akbar and Religion.' After detailed discussions, Prof KA Nizami and Prof RC Gaur approved the programme to excavate the mound. Dr Jamal Muhammed Siddiqui, Nasir Husain Zaidi and Husham Haider gave valuable inputs. Anis Alavi, Ghulam Mustafa, Muhammed Abid, Dr OP Srivastava, Sami Alam, Dr Qamar Usmani, Dr Giri Raj Singh Kushwaha, Zahid Hashmi and Sayyid Zameer Ahammed gave full support as they realised the importance of the discovery in which they were going to be one of the crucial players.

The excavation of an area of 5×5 square meters, done with meticulous care and precision, gradually exposed a part of a lower platform and a middle platform. The earth that had accumulated on the middle platform rose as high as my waist. The result was encouraging; hence, it was decided to extend the excavation north-south and east-west. But, before this was done, all the trees growing over different parts of the mound were cut down. The

Archival photo during the excavation:
no. 1. lower platform, no. 2. middle platform, no. 3. excavator standing on the middle platform, no. 4. earth and trees up to the chest of the excavator. Workers are using knives and brushes to remove the earth, no. 4. accumulated earth and trees over the top platform, yet to be excavated.

roots of the trees had penetrated the various platforms of the structure.

Further excavation exposed the top platform. To my surprise, the third platform was divided into two with a wall and an entrance door. (This dividing wall and the entrance door have extraordinary importance of their own, to which I would come back during the comparative study of the painting and the site).

Where were the steps shown in the painting, which enabled the participants to go to different platforms? This was bothering my mind when my eyes fell on a slightly raised accumulation of soil below the central part of the lower platform. This appeared to conceal within it the steps leading to the platforms. As expected, when it was excavated, the steps to facilitate access to the platforms lay exposed, as depicted in the Mughal painting. The painting was helping us to solve each seemingly tricky puzzle.

Archival photographs during the excavation before the find baulk: no. 1. east and south boundary wall, no. 2. steps, no. 3. lower platform, no. 4. middle platform, no. 5. front part of the top platform, no. 6. pillar base on which door frame stood and anti-chamber.

The third and top platform is divided into two, a front room and anti-chamber by a wall, and the pillar base on which the door post and lintel pillar stood is visible. The western and northern boundary walls can also be seen in this photograph.

Once the excavation was completed, it was time for the final leg of the comparative study of the painting with the excavated area. The painting showed the boundary wall, three arches and a dome behind. These structural features were already present there, and it was these components that gave the first clue to the possible identification of the *Ibadat Khana*. The painting clearly showed the steps leading to the platform, which, as described above, had been excavated. The painting also showed three platforms, of which the lower one was occupied by various participants, who were not identifiable. In the middle platform, both Abul Fazal and Abul Faizi are seen sitting close to Akbar. Father Rudolf Acquaviva (Italy) and

Father Antonio Monserrat (Spain) could be easily identified in the middle platforms with their overflowing black cloaks and caps.

On the top platform, Akbar is seen seated, presiding over the discussion. Thus the excavation exposed all three platforms and other structures, as shown in the painting.

The painting had some more secrets to reveal. The top platform where Akbar is seated is divided into two rooms with an entrance door dividing them. The excavation also revealed the remains of the dividing wall and the two stones on which the post and lintel of the door must have stood. As I have mentioned earlier, the excavation of this dividing wall and entrance door, as shown in the painting, is a testimony to the acute perception of the artist. At the top of the painting is inscribed a sentence from the *Akbar Nama book*, describing the presence of Christian priests: 'Padre Rudolf, one of the Nazarene sages, is seen making a point in the feats of intelligence.' This reference to Father Rudolf Acquaviva is very relevant to our discovery and sums up the whole story. As per scholars, this painting which was an unassailable proof of the identification of *Ibadat Khana* in stone and lime mortar, was made in the year 1602, three years before the death of Akbar. What more was required to prove that it was the site of the *Ibadat Khana*?

There are few Mughal paintings like this with 'architectural realism' that defines the seminal moments of Mughal history and help us identify sites and structures. Architectural realism in Mughal painting was due to the direct influence of European paintings combined with the development of portrait painting in Mughal studios. In portrait painting, one has to be remarkably accurate with the features of each individual so that one should not confuse Akbar with Jahangir or with other Mughal kings. This fastidiousness for details of individual parts enormously influenced the development of 'architectural realism in Mughal paintings.'

The painting of the *Ibadat Khana* matched the structure excavated at Fatehpur Sikri broadly. No doubt, it took two seasons' work (1981–1982, 1982–1983) to complete the entire excavation of the *Ibadat Khana*. The remarkable similarity of the Mughal painting with the excavated structural remains helped us resolve an elusive problem that had long defied a final solution. This excavation brought into sharp focus the potentiality of Mughal paintings as a powerful tool in medieval archaeology.

A comparative study of the photograph of the fully excavated structure with the *Ibadat Khana* painting given above enables a better appreciation of the subject.

The excavation of the first Christian chapel of North India was another important discovery made, based on the description given by Father Monserrate in his book, *Mongolicae Legationis Commentarius*. He had made a diary of the daily discussions with Akbar at the *Ibadat Khana* and the arrangements for their stay and worship. Soon after the arrival of the Fathers at Fatehpur Sikri, they were provided accommodation in a *caravan sarai* near Agra Gate before being shifted to another place near Hathya Pol (Elephant's Gate).

But on seeing the widespread sentiments against the Fathers, due to the popular perception that Akbar was on the verge of conversion to Christianity, the king became apprehensive of some Muslim fanatics trying to kill the Christian priests. As a precautionary measure, the Emperor got them shifted from Hathya Pol to a building outside the palace but closer to Akbar's bed-chamber in which entry was provided through a small door.

There are differences of opinions among scholars about the identification of this site also. Monserrate says that this structure, which was earlier used for the distillation of perfumes (Khushbu Khana), was modified into a small residence-cum-chapel. While Father Heras located it as Mariam's house, popularly known as Sunehra Makan, AA Rizvi and Vincent Flynn identified it on the northern side of the *Diwan-i-Aam*.

Differing from them, I closely followed the description given by Father Monserrate and preferred to identify a small mound near Akbar's bed-chamber but outside the inner boundary of the palace. It took another two seasons of careful fieldwork (1983–84, 1984–85) to complete the excavation of the Christian chapel. Meticulous excavation of the site exposed two rooms without any significant antiquities. Two rooms in Fatehpur Sikri does not mean anything; excavate any mound, and one is sure to get a few rooms. But it is the antiquities recovered from the site which provides the archaeologist with the necessary clues about the possible use of the site.

After I unearthed two rooms from this unpretentious mound, I invited the Archbishop of Agra, Dr Cecil D'Souza, to visit the site. Since they reached Fatehpur Sikri without informing me beforehand, I could not meet them as I had gone to Agra, but they were taken to the site by Nasir Husain Zaidi, Husham Haider and Anees Alavi. After seeing the two excavated rooms, the Archbishop had his reservations about the identification as the records in his possession showed that the chapel had three rooms. Mr Zaidi explained to him that we were only halfway through the excavation, and were expecting to find the third room on digging further down. Excavation is a slow process. As expected, on further excavation, within a few days, I could locate the third room also.

The Archbishop was happy when he came to know of it, but as an archaeologist, I was not yet fully satisfied, for I had yet to locate the distillation unit of perfumes and heating place. Father Monserrate had clearly stated in his book that it was the perfume house (*Khushbhu Khana*) that had been converted into a chapel.

Unfortunately, the place where I expected to find the furnace was filled with soil and well plastered with lime concrete. According to archaeological norms, no one should excavate below the plastered level unless one expects to find something very substantial. However, the entire excavation would have been futile in the absence of discovering the distillation unit and heating place as part of the three rooms.

We then decided to break open the plastered portion, where I expected the furnace and distillation unit to be present. To my great satisfaction, further digging exposed a furnace with an iron pan used for boiling flowers to distil perfumes. The encouraging result further prodded me to dig deeper down to reach the level of the heating place, where the fire must have been lit, either by using wood or sunbaked cow dung cakes as fuel. Here, an underground arched heating place was excavated, just below the furnace. These excavations proved that Father Antonio Monserrate was right to the minutest details.

The excavated three-room Christian Chapel at Fatehpur Sikri.

A field study conducted at Kannauj, where the conventional method of perfume distillation is still a small-scale industry, also proved the soundness of these arguments. A comparative study of a Mughal painting depicting distillation being done from *muraqa-i-gulshan*, made during the time of Jahangir and presently housed in the Tehran Museum, looked like the traditional arched heating place excavated at the site. Apart from this evidence, the perfume bottle (*zir-i-itradan*), excavated from the middle room, provided the clinching proof of the area being used as a perfume house (*khushbu khana*) before it was converted into a chapel. This perfume bottle was in many fragments when I excavated it. It was then patiently mended and pieced together to serve as a piece of irrefutable evidence to prove the authenticity of the excavated Christian chapel.

In addition to these two important discoveries, many other buried pages of history such as the bazaar, which traded in precious stones and other valuable items, the residential houses of ministers, stables, cells for hunting animals (*cheeta khana*), Gunga Mahal (dumb house) Pawan Chakki (wind mill) etc., were also excavated.

By this time, the University had demoted me from Assistant Archaeologist to Technical Assistant on the intervention of the Communist group. In an attempt to implicate me in another false case, a show-cause notice was issued to me stating that I had threatened some students from Kerala and why action should not be taken against me. When I sought the details of the fabricated allegation, there was no reply from the University. Later on, it was learnt that they could not proceed further as differences arose between the false witnesses and those who had got them prepared for it.

In another attempt to stop my academic work, an oral order was given to one of the library assistants that I should not be issued books from the department library (which is different from Central Library). If books were issued to me, I would use them to pave the way to some more astounding discoveries. Every month they were hearing the alarming news of the identification of the

Cheeta Khana, the stable, the house of Mir Akhur, pawan Chakki, Gunga Mahal (dumb house) and many other structures in Fatehpur Sikri. The construction of Gunga Mahal (dumb house) by Akbar was due to a difference of opinion between a section of Muslim scholars and Akbar. The Muslim scholars argued that if a newly born child is not instructed in any religion and not taught any language, they would follow 'nature's religion' and language, which according to them was Islam and Arabic. Although Akbar knew it very well that the newly born would not speak any language and follow any religion unless they were taught, in order to disprove the Mulla's arguments, he constructed an 'experimental house' away from the habitation where twenty newborn children were raised under trained nurses without giving any instruction in religion and language. After four years, when they were taken out, they all turned out to be dumb and, within a few months, died. As the structure was considered cursed due to the dumbness of the children and very high infant mortality rate, it got the name Dumb House (Gunga Mahal). I could discover it at Chudiyari, a village in the suburbs of Fatehpur Sikri, where the villagers still call it 'Gunga Mahal' without knowing its historical significance. The villagers were afraid of going nearby due to the belief that those who went nearby would turn out to be dumb.

A few of the important scholars who came to Fatehpur Sikri during this time were Dr Farhan Ahmed Nizami, the founder Director of the Oxford Centre for Islamic Studies, accompanied by another scholar from Oxford. I took them to all the excavated sites and explained the site in detail, followed by a lot of discussions. Another distinguished group of scholar couples who visited the site with a critical eye were prof Raymond Allchin and Bridget Allchin, authors of the Birth of Indian civilization, the Rise of Indian Civilization and The Archaeology of Early Historic South Asia. After detailed discussions at *Ibadat Khana* site, prof Raymond Allchin told me, "Muhammed, this is nothing short of 'Investigative Archaeology." He had one more piece of advice for me. "In India, mostly archaeologists write for scholars, but you should write for the general public also. Public archaeology is as important as archaeology for the specialists." Dr Geeti Sen, the author of the 'Paintings from the Akbar Nama, A visual chronicle of Mughal India and the former Chief Editor of India International Centre, was another distinguished scholar who was excited to see the excavated site of *Ibadat Khana*. Standing on the platform of the newly excavated *Ibadat Khana*, when I explained each part of the structure with the help of a copy of the painting in my hand Dr Sen was overjoyed.

The best way to keep me away from making any more discoveries was to stop me from getting the books issued. Although the issue of books was stopped, many were ready to help me in my academic pursuits by getting me the books I wanted.

Aligarh communists suffered from 'arachaeophobia' and were mortally afraid of archaeological discoveries, as it was something original, spectacular and could change the historical narratives. And at the same time, to add to their woes, it was a tool they could not understand, comprehend and wield. So they always resorted to the policy of 'condemnant quo non intellegunt' condemn that which they do not understand. They always suffered from an inferiority complex that none of their interpretations and books could compete with an archaeological discovery. Moreover, since archaeology provides demonstrable and tangible results, it could easily catch people's imagination and has an intrinsic news value of its own.

Even during the visit of the UGC committees and other expert bodies, although they hated archaeology, always showcased it to impress and get enhanced financial grants. Since the *Ibadat Khana* and the Christian Chapel enormously contributed to the shaping of Akbar's larger personality, the Aligarh Communist could not think of conceding the authorship of the discovery to anybody else and that too to an unyielding adversary who did not mince words and dance to their tunes. Hence, there was a deliberate and laboured effort to avoid mentioning my name. In the process, the Aligarh Communists, due to their preternatural hatred for Archaeology, dismantled the section of Archaeology, brick by brick, and now, it is a phantom of its former glory. Thus, the enlightened and comprehensive vision of Prof Nurul Hasan, an institutional builder and scholar, is awaiting a silent burial.

I continued in the demoted post for four years (1981–1985), while people far junior and less-qualified continued in higher posts enjoying all privileges and higher salaries. My fight and defeats reminded me of the statement of Babur when he lost everything "Is there a cruel turn of fortune's wheel unseen by me? Is there a pang, grief, my wounded heart has missed?"

The Aligarh communist historian's action proved to be a blessing in disguise and brought out my inner reservoir of energy to work hard and make my mark. The injustice meted out at their hands, and my bold resistance with the hope for a brighter future reminded me of another quotation, "Sometimes life does not give you something you want, not because you don't deserve it, but because you deserve more. You are meant for greater things."

The books on positive thinking and self-improvement that I used to read gave me the courage to deal with the demotion. Quotable quotes from such books helped me see the brighter side of life. Under normal circumstances, I would not have been able to work so hard and make such outstanding discoveries. The books on positive thinking also helped me immensely during my postings in the Archaeological Survey of India while dealing with dacoits, Naxals and criminals in various states. Inspiring quotations such as "Success is not final, and failure is not fatal. It is the courage to fight against it that counts" used to inspire me. Thus, in the negative sense of the term, I am thankful to Irfan Habib and the Aligarh Muslim University authorities for demoting me and for all the injustice meted out to me during my Aligarh days.

Like the gateway of a medieval fort, I still bear the bullet marks of rejection, demotion and false cases framed against me as a mark of my turbulent past. Some scars are worth retaining. My Aligarh wounds are a few such scars inflicted by the miscarriage of a 'revolutionary ideology' blatantly misused by an individual and his misguided followers.

The news of the discovery of the *Ibadat Khana* and the Christian chapel was published by the *Times of India* in 1984 with due importance as it was regarded as the nursery of Indian secularism. This news was repeated by many other English, Hindi and Urdu newspapers also. While this discovery created a sensation in academic circles and the public imagination, it naturally annoyed Dr Irfan Habib and the university authorities, who tried all kinds of tricks to run down the discovery. None of these had the desired effect. This outstanding discovery of *Ibadat Khana* in medieval archaeology by one who was demoted by the communist group and the university authorities was a sharp rap on their knuckles.

By this time, as per the rotation of the chairmanship system, Dr Irfan Habib became the Chairman of the Department of History, replacing Prof KA Nizami. During this period, an attempt was made to give credit for the discovery of the *Ibadat Khana* to Dr Viqar Siddiqui. Prof AA Rizvi of the Australian University wrote a very harsh letter against the purported claim of Dr Siddiqui that they had to disown him. Thus, this attempt failed miserably, ending in a whimper.

The next best thing was to refuse to acknowledge it as the *Ibadat Khana*. Who would dare to refute it if Dr Irfan Habib were to issue a statement that the alleged structure was not the *Ibadat Khana*? But he did not want to be seen as fighting against a non-entity. Why should he dignify this upstart by registering a protest? Why not harass him to such an extent that he would be forced to discard his own theory? If this had been accepted meekly, it would have amounted to a virtual suicide for an archaeologist.

As part of this modified plan, he sent a departmental peon, Idris Beg to call me from the Archaeology section where the excavated materials were on display. It was widely known that whenever he planned to lay a trap for anybody, like a strategist, he calculated the time and deployed his men at various places so that even if the unfortunate prey escaped from the first trap, he would be caught in the next one. While his men awaited me at the front gate, as deployed earlier, I reached the department through the back entrance, knocked at his door and asked him without an introduction: "Did you send for me?"

He looked at me angrily and remarked: "That is not *Ibadat Khana*."

"Which *Ibadat Khana* are you referring to?" I enquired.

"The one about which you published in the *Times of India* is not the *Ibadat Khana*."

"How can you say that? Are you an archaeologist?"

"I may not be as good an archaeologist as you are."

This sentence gave me enough ammunition to defend my turf and question his claim as an archaeologist. I remarked: "Sorry, you are not an archaeologist at all."

Dr Irfan Habib began to fumble for words before changing the track suddenly. Pushing a sheath of blank papers and pen towards me, he screamed: "Give it in writing that it is not the *Ibadat Khana*." That was another trick to coerce and force me down. But, I checkmated every hostile manoeuvring with diligence.

"Why should I give you in writing? Have you given me anything in writing?" It was my muscular retort.

All these sharp exchanges were made in a standing posture and in high decibel, which was audible to the outsiders, who were deployed at various places with clear instructions. If he loses an argument, it is time for him to create a scene to recover the lost ground. In such moments he would freely mix hysteria with histrionics. One should escape before that moment. And that too without tripping over the traps carefully laid out by him. When I felt he had nothing else to say, I walked out of the room, stronger in my resolve and banging the door behind me. I felt like Chhatrapathi Shivaji, who had escaped from the prison of Aurangzeb. But Shivaji had escaped concealed in a basket. And here I was walking out in the full blazing gaze of his followers.

Dr Habib's deployed men had heard the loud and sharp exchanges inside his room. They did not know how to react. Among them was Dr Shireen Moosvi, the principal advisor of Dr Irfan Habib. She seemed highly shocked and disillusioned at the turn of events. This was not what she was expecting.

After leaving his room, I calmly descended the steps, sporting a smile and sending a powerful message to his followers. Later, in the Department of History, I discussed with Prof RC Gaur, Prof Zaheeruddin Malik, Prof IH Siddiqui and a few others about what had transpired between Dr Irfan Habib and me. Prof Gaur was thrilled and complimented me for the bold step. In the evening, he invited me to his residence to hear a full replay of what had transpired. Soon word went around the university, and it also became a hot topic of discussion in the staff club. Dr Irfan Habib's image as the grandmaster of the ring had started crumbling down. All the chinks in his armour was exposed. He looked brittle and fragmented. The 'rejected person' has not only staged a comeback but also punched much above his weight.

I expected to receive a show-cause notice or a censure for my purportedly rude behaviour towards the soft spoken Chairman of the Department of History. But he did not do that; this meant that he had some other well-thought-out plan to deal with me. He was upgrading his arsenal. He might have told himself: "These are idealists who can neither be frightened nor purchased. You have to deal with such elements differently."

Reeling under the impact of the newspaper report on the *Ibadat Khana* and the recent confrontation with his prey, he now resorted to another gimmick to reduce the impact of my discovery. He propped up and showcased the work of Dr Iqtidar Alam Khan, one of his camp followers. For that, the best way was to organise an exhibition of the survey made by Dr Iqtidar Alam Khan in the Kennedy Hall of the university. This exhibition would have helped him combat the news value of the discovery of the *Ibadat Khana* and build a larger-than-life image of his group.

However, since it was a simple display of the standing Mughal *caravan serai* with a few photographs, it would not make much impact. Dr Irfan Habib then requested Prof RC Gaur to put up a few photographs of the excavations carried out at Fatehpur Sikri, simply to fill up space. Prof Gaur entrusted the work to me. This was the opportunity I had been waiting for.

I made the best use of the task entrusted, curating a fine exhibition of the *Ibadat Khana*, the Christian chapel and various other structures that had been excavated at Fatehpur Sikri. It was curated in a storytelling style, about how we had come across various mounds lying in desolate ruins before the excavation, unable to figure out what it was. Below the photographs, excerpts from sources such as the *Akbar Nama*, *Muntakhab-ut-Tawarikh* and various other sources were written to convey necessary information on the archaeological treasures concealed within the mound.

The next photograph showed how, on excavation, structures emerged slowly, still lying partly concealed under earth and debris accumulated over the centuries. It was enough to whet the curiosity of the inquisitive visitor and that of the ordinary person. Now the visitors were in suspended animation, holding their breath to see more of it.

In the final leg, the entire structure was shown emerging from the womb of the earth, completely transforming the site and unfolding the secret of the mounds. But now, the more significant challenge was to prove that this structure was none other than the *Ibadat Khana* or the Christian chapel. How were we going to do that?

For this, I took the help of Mughal paintings, sketches done by contemporary travellers and descriptions given in original sources. This method of storytelling of the excavated site created much excitement in the university as the news spread by word of mouth. Several professors and students visited the exhibition. I personally acted as a guide for the discerning visitors and showed them around. This guided tour naturally resulted in question-and-answer rounds by curious visitors.

Contrary to the expectations of the Marxist group, Iqtidar Alam Khan's exhibition on the '*caravan serai*' turned out to be a damp squib and did not attract any attention. It had no storyline, no discovery to flaunt, and nothing to catch the imagination. There was also no one to guide the visitors. Even if there had been anyone, the problem would have been what to explain to the viewer.

As an urgent remedial measure, Dr Irfan Habib deputed one of his research scholars, Nadeem Rizvi, to Kennedy Hall to guide Iqtidar Alam's '*serai*' exhibition and shore up their dwindling fortunes.

Nadeem came to me and sought my help to understand the excavation exercise at Fatehpur Sikri, especially the *Ibadat Khana* and the Christian chapel. He remarked that even my departmental opponents were also full of praise and admiration for the discovery of the *Ibadat Khana*. Although both Nadeem and I were on opposite sides of the political divide, we shared a warm friendship.

I narrated the story of the discovery, step by step, drawing from the sources and comparing them with the contours of the mound and the paintings of the *Ibadat Khana*.

He was completely taken by surprise, and I could see a sparkle in his eyes. He confessed: "KK Bhai, little did I imagine that the discovery of the *Ibadat Khana* and the chapel would be so brilliant." He took two more rounds of the Fatehpur Sikri exhibition, taking his own time. He was rehearsing what I had taught him as if it was his discovery and preparing himself to guide other visitors. He forgot that he had come on a completely different assignment. While he was still dazed and dazzled and savouring the discovery of the *Ibadat Khana*, a group of visitors came to see the exhibition. He requested me for permission to show them around, leapt towards them like a falcon and took them straight to the Fatehpur Sikri exhibition, without showing the '*caravan serai*' section, for which he had been deputed.

I thoroughly enjoyed this scene with concealed glee and the change of heart of the man, from the sidelines. He brought the visitors to me and introduced me as the discoverer of the *Ibadat Khana*. Then came Prof Azeem Qureshi from the Geography Department, and he was accompanied by his wife Rukhsana Qureshi. When he approached them directly without taking my permission, they excused themselves and said they had come at my invitation and expected me to take them around. That was a minor rebuff. Several learned professors from the arts and science departments came to see the exhibition.

Dr Shireen Moosvi, one of Dr Irfan Habib's closest associates, came with him to see the exhibition. He had visited the exhibition three times earlier also. Since I was not on talking terms with her, she was guided by Nasir Husain Zaidi and Husham Haider. The generally talkative lady was tight-lipped as she was given a description of the unfolding drama of the excavation from the beginning to the end. She was completely engrossed in the action drama of the excavation but was as silent as the sphinx.

The impact of the exhibition was so great that the closing date of the exhibition had to be extended on public demand. The extension of the exhibition was announced by Irfan Habib himself. The fact that many visitors from different departments unknowingly complimented Dr Irfan Habib and Shireen Moosvi for the discovery of the *Ibadat Khana,* rubbed salt to their festering wounds. Obviously, the carefully crafted move to bolster the image of the Marxist group had turned out to be an ill-fated misadventure. Dr Irfan Habib probably might have rued and cursed the momentary decision he had taken to put up a few photographs of Fatehpur Sikri. He would never repeat such a mistake. That 'South Indian' had turned everything to his own advantage. Thus, the poorly thought diversionary tactics had a disastrous end. (Please watch the documentary film titled "The Discovery of *Ibadat Khana*" on YouTube)

The person who enjoyed every moment of the news of this exhibition and the discomfiture of the powerful Marxist lobby, right in their own den, was none other than Prof Ram Chand Gaur. He had been involved in a running battle with Dr Irfan Habib and Iqtidar Alam Khan. The important reason for this was that there was a move by Dr Irfan to appoint Dr Iqtidar Alam Khan as a professor against the claims of Prof Gaur. The Communist group played their cards very close to their chest. As usual, each move was made very surreptitiously. But their arithmetical calculation went wrong when Prof KA Nizami, who was on leave, returned and joined as the Head of the Department, and Prof Gaur was appointed as the professor. This was a powerful blow for the Communist group. Apart from this, Prof Gaur's complaint against both of them was that they were constantly trying to paint him as an RSS agent in the university. The Communist group had also alleged that Prof Gaur had united all the Hindu staff members of

AMU when a Hindu-Muslim riot had broken out in Aligarh.

They also could not digest the fact that the Director of the Fatehpur Sikri excavation was Prof Gaur. To snatch away the directorship from Gaur and get appointed Dr Iqtidar Alam Khan in his place, the Communists had employed every ploy in their stock. When they failed in it, they floated a story that Prof Gaur wanted to change the narrative of the history of Fatehpur Sikri by surreptitiously planting Hindu idols at the site. The Communists were unaware of the fact that it wasn't possible to plant sculptures in the excavation, as a study of the section of the trench would instantly reveal whether the sculpture was planted or not. But ignorance of archaeology is bliss if you are an Aligarh Communist historian.

How could Iqtidar Alam Khan be the Director of the excavation without an archaeologist's necessary technical qualifications or field experience? Has he ever undergone the required training in archaeology or carried out any excavation? That was the question of Prof Gaur. The Archaeological Survey of India, which is the licensing authority for the excavation, would never grant permission for it under such an ill-qualified Person. But whether he was qualified or not, if he was an Aligarh Communist, the post belonged to him. Qualifications were necessary only for lesser mortals. If Aligarh Communists were against anybody, they would immediately declare that person an RSS protégé or follower of *Jamaat-i-Islami*, depending upon their religion.

Prof Gaur was declared to be an RSS agent and was hounded out. I always supported Prof Gaur and acted as a pillar of strength for him. He openly acknowledged it too. Prof Gaur was so much against the Communists of Aligarh that he would speak for hours against them. At the slightest provocation, he would pour forth criticisms against them like a possessed man and then there was no way to stop him. While Irfan Habib was maligning Prof Gaur as RSS man, Dr Habib, himself was getting the full support of the Sangh parivar from 1980 up to 1988, as he issued statements about the falling academic standards and students indiscipline of the AMU. The general psychology in the country is that anybody who speaks against the Benares Hindu university or Aligarh Muslim University and its falling academic standards would get immediate support from the opposite communities without looking into the issues involved and the intention and the track record of the person who has issued the statement. This psychological factor was misused and abused by Dr Irfan Habib to his maximum advantage. Unfortunately for the secular press, any person who speaks against the dominant community of an institution is progressive. Both these factors worked in his favour, and he used them to malign the University and oppose his ideological adversaries. The press needs to grow further to understand the operations of such elements in various institutions on a case to case basis.

Communism has brought about revolutionary changes in the socio-political, economic and cultural life of the people. Many early leaders had sacrificed their life, career and property for the welfare of the party and inspired a whole generation. But Dr Irfan Habib's Communism at the AMU was completely different. Here, there was neither freedom of thought nor expression; if anybody showed any signs of free-thinking, he was put under surveillance. Occasionally, one could hear the faint moans and groans of the teachers and young scholars, whose voices and careers were stifled by them. A few like me dared to revolt openly and even refused to pay the customary salutation to him when he was the chairman. It was open disobedience to his authority as the chairman and an end of the teacher-and-taught relationship. This passive resistance was something that he feared most. When this technique was employed in open meetings, his ego would be restless.

In 1985, in one of the interviews for the permanent post of Assistant Archaeologist/Dy Director, Dr Irfan Habib misguided the Vice-Chancellor Syed Hashim Ali against me. In the interview, as usual, I fared very well as I could answer all the questions, including those of Dr Irfan Habib, without any difficulty. The Vice-Chancellor found me as an outstanding candidate.

In the afternoon, there was one more interview for another post. Fearing that I had already made a good impression upon the

Vice-Chancellor and would carry the day, Dr Irfan Habib poisoned his ears by alleging that I was the force behind all the students' agitations that broke out in the university. Naturally, as an IAS officer, the Vice-Chancellor would be against such promoters of agitations on the campus.

When I appeared for the afternoon interview, the Vice-Chancellor was very angry with me for no reason at all and stated that he did not want anyone in the university who did not pay due respect to his teachers. As was expected, I calmly replied: "Sir, technically, Dr Irfan Habib has marked my presence and absence in the attendance register of the BA and MA classes. Beyond that, I refuse to acknowledge him as my teacher. Respect is commanded and not demanded."

Pulling down a teacher from the highest pedestal of the teacher and that too right in front of the higher authority is the biggest punishment a student could inflict. A teacher loses his credibility when his action is evaluated as sectarian and steeped in party politics. My assertion in the interview board against the uncrowned king of AMU and an all-powerful politician-teacher made the Vice-Chancellor realise that I held some strong grievances against Dr Irfan Habib.

I narrated before the board how a grave injustice had been meted out to me by granting scholarship and admission to the PhD course to Muhammed Afzal Khan due to his political leanings and to one who had consistently scored far lesser marks than I, in Pre-University (PUC), BA and MA.

I also brought to his notice another injustice done to me by refusing extension in the post of Assistant Archaeologist, which was then granted to Sami Alam, who was much junior and far less qualified than me, as he had no post-graduate diploma and original discoveries to his credit. He was so ill-qualified that the university had even refused to issue him an interview letter for the permanent position of the same post, for which he was earlier given an extension. "These are only a few examples of the blatant manipulations and favouritism in which Dr Irfan Habib had indulged in with impunity." The interview board was stunned into silence. Now, the interview board 'lent their full ears to me' and listened as the Romans listened to Mark Antony. (Julius Caesar)

I continued with my criticism: "In the month of May 1981, Dr Irfan Habib, in one of the complaints written to the then Vice-Chancellor, had implicated me in a student agitation. Fortunately, one day earlier, I had taken leave from the university and gone to Delhi to meet an official in the ministry, the security pass of which is still with me. I have brought all the documents with me as I knew Dr Irfan would resort to such gimmicks in the interview." That was another powerful punch. The carefully crafted ploy was crumbling right under his nose.

Regarding the question of salutation, I said: "This is a non-violent, passive resistance against a teacher whose methods I don't approve of." While I was presenting all the pieces of evidence like a lawyer, Dr Irfan looked pale and blank, running his fingers through his dishevelled hair. Neither Irfan Habib nor the Vice-Chancellor could foresee "*Baat nikalegi to fir duur talak jaayegi.*"

"Nobody knew if words go out....... it will spread too far.'

That pathetic sight of Dr Irfan Habib, sitting on the interview board, disappointed and disillusioned, is still vividly etched in my memory. He did not speak a single sentence nor try to defend himself. The news of my interview became the talk of the university for many days. According to Prof Abrar Mustafa, a Botany professor, such an interview had never taken place in the history of the university.

Smarting from the unexpected blow in front of the selection board, Dr Irfan Habib tried for a patch-up by asking for showing the minimum courtesy of wishing him whenever we met. Two young scholars of his group who had appreciated the worth of the discoveries made by me at Fatehpur Sikri had warned me to be cautious. He has an iron hand in his velvet gloves.

Once, after the patch-up, Dr Irfan Habib, Prof RC Gaur and Prof Som Prakash Verma came to see the excavation site at Fatehpur Sikri. Dr Irfan remarked that he was visiting Fatehpur Sikri after twenty-two years.

Standing on the very site of the *Ibadat Khana*, whose

identification he had refused to accept, asked me several questions; not a single question was directed to anybody else. He had come armed with Atillio Petrocelli's book on Fatehpur Sikri. In the book, the site of *Ibadat Khana* had been shown as a mound. As I had already gone through the book, I pointed out the mound in the book and said that it was this mound that we had excavated inch by inch to expose the *Ibadat Khana*.

From there, we took him to the Christian chapel. Again, all the questions were directed at me, and I continued quoting from Father Monserrate and *Muntakhab-ut-Tawarikh* of Abdul Qadir Badauni. After leading him from Akbar's bed-chamber to the palace walls, he was shown the door through which the Fathers (the priests) used to enter the inner palace. And then finally, he was taken to the chapel itself, the distillation oven and the heating place.

I showed him the photograph taken before starting the excavation. Prof Som Prakash Verma nodded his head from behind as he had recognised the worth of the discovery much earlier but could not dare utter a word before Dr Irfan Habib.

The entire day passed in moving from one excavated site to the other. Dr Irfan Habib did not say anything at the site–whether it was the *Ibadat Khana* or not. But he grudgingly admitted to Prof Gaur that no other structure in Fatehpur Sikri could have been the *Ibadat Khana*. Although he had an inbuilt hatred towards archaeology, he could now realise the potential of archaeology, even in the field of medieval history.

This site visit of Fatehpur Sikri and the discoveries of *Ibadat Khana*, the Church, the Gunga Mahal and several others should have triggered his mind about the enormous possibilities of archaeology in medieval history and the role archaeology could play in solving some of the problems in medieval archaeology. But he stopped short of realizing, acknowledging and harnessing archaeology in medieval history because of archaeo phobia. In case it is recognized, he might have thought many of the aspects of medieval history, like the economic history of medieval India in which he had specialised, would be relegated into the background, at least for the time being. But now sadly, he cannot also issue a decree (fatwa) against *Ibadat Khana* as he has verified it at the site. He was now caught in a cleft stick without being able to say anything, this way or that way.

When a group of college teachers from Bengal came to Aligarh for a refresher course in medieval history, Dr Irfan arranged their tour programme to Agra and Fatehpur Sikri with me and a senior Marxist historian, Prof Athar Ali, as guides.

After showing them the Taj Mahal and Agra Fort, they were taken to Fatehpur Sikri. In both places, they enjoyed special privileges as I accompanied them. When they were explained how the *Ibadat Khana* and the Christian chapel were located, excavated and identified with the help of literary sources, travelogues and various paintings, they were agog with excitement. It was a memorable experience for them. They admitted that never before had they experienced and enjoyed a historical site like this. The best part of it was that once I stopped in my explanation of the site, Prof Athar Ali would endorse me enthusiastically like an evangelical preacher repeating the same thing and sometimes adding a little bit from his side.

Once the college professors returned to Aligarh, they were full of admiration for me and shared their views with Dr Irfan Habib. He had no choice but to accept it in silence. He, however, was happy that the college professors had no inkling of my academic fight with him with regards to the discovery of *Ibadat Khana* and his earlier opinion about the site. Now, "the stone that the architect (builder) rejected has become the cornerstone."(Mark 12:10–11)

After this, there was a strange request from Dr Iqtidar Alam Khan, a close supporter of Irfan Habib, that I should help him in his survey of medieval structures. On an earlier occasion, he had visited the *Ibadat Khana,* and Nasir Husain Zaidi had explained it with the help of the *Akbar Nama* painting. This time, Mr Saeed-ul-Hasan, the photographer, and I accompanied him to Agra stayed in Fatehpur Sikri as a prelude to surveying Feroz Khan's tomb. I informed him that it had already been studied, and the article published by Dr R Nath was shown to him. He had not done his research well before starting the survey. He saw the *Ibadat Khana* and the chapel but very cleverly abstained from any discussion.

In 1986, Dr Irfan Habib became the Chairman of the Indian Council of Historical Research, with substantial powers to distribute scholarships to various history scholars. Within two years, Prof RC Gaur also became the Chairman of the Department of History as per the rotation of chairmanship.

Incredible as it may sound, the two teachers who held extremely diverse views now started coming together, forgetting their ideological mismatch and personal differences. Both of them went to the embarrassing extent of complimenting the achievements of each other. The mutual back-scratching was an obvious charade. This unprincipled overture from Dr Irfan Habib was an act of desperation, whereas, for Prof Gaur, it meant an increasing realisation of the position he could occupy in the ICHR. Once they began to do so, other professors in the department took to following their masters, forgetting everything they had spoken against each other. Lesser mortals immediately adjusted themselves to the changing times. Charles Darwin was right when he wrote, "It is not the strongest of species that survives, nor the most intelligent, but rather the most adaptable to change."

I was asked by Prof Gaur to join the group of Dr Habib, obviously as per the directions of the former, when both of us were returning from the Aligarh railway station after seeing off Dr KV Soundara Rajan. When the offer was made, I reminded him about his tirades against Irfan Habib and the hurdles he had created at various stages of his career, including the professorship and directorship of Fatehpur Sikri excavation. I specifically asked him: "Have you forgotten how they had tarnished your image and hounded you out, calling you an RSS man? It was I who had stood by you at that time and resisted all the sinister moves of Irfan Habib. You may be against Communism, but I am not. I am a good Communist. What I am against is the Communist coterie that Dr Irfan Habib has been trying to build up in the department." I refused to be one of his bonded intellectuals in the dumb house (Gunga Mahal) of AMU, as that would amount to contempt of my conscience.

I did not notice Dr Gaur's facial expression as I was seated behind him on his scooter. When we reached the department, we parted ways. We gradually drifted apart from each other.

In the meanwhile, the new alliance between Dr Irfan Habib and Prof Gaur brought Dr Makhan Lal from the Banaras Hindu University (BHU) as the new Deputy Director of Archaeology in AMU. I challenged this in court on legal grounds. The respondents in the case were not only Makhan Lal but also included Dr Irfan Habib and Prof Gaur. When Prof KK Sinha, the well-known Professor of Archaeology at Banaras Hindu University, came to know about the selection of Makhan Lal, he commented: "We are happy that he has gone from BHU, but within six months, he would turn Prof Gaur upside down."

I again resorted to my non-violent method of not saluting (greeting) Dr Irfan Habib. He regarded salutation from others as his birthright, regardless of whether he deserved it or not. If anyone refused to salute him, his complexion would change. Thus, the bugle was sounded for the next battle of Mahabharata at Aligarh.

Within a few days, Dr Makhan Lal became close to Dr Irfan Habib and Shireen Moosvi and started destabilising many old veterans from Dr Irfan's group. Prof Gaur also became suspicious of him. But now, he is unable to do anything. Dr Makhan Lal's undue interference in the archaeology section created much-unwanted friction, due to which there was a virtual revolt against him and the communist group. Naturally, I was a rallying point for them, and I indirectly taunted them by putting up a board saying, '*Satyameva Jayate*' on my table. As it was a virtue they were devoid of, it cut them where it hurt the most. They were irritated at the board as it pointed the finger at their character but did not have the guts to ask me to remove it. Moderates began to question the ideology and values of the so-called Communists in their own language.

The unholy alliance of the Communists and Makhan Lal resulted in the dismissal of Partha Pratibha Bose, a young archaeologist, from the service. Bose was a good Communist and an equally good archaeologist from Calcutta University. Dr Irfan Habib had selected him because of his political background, and also, he wanted to patronise someone who would compete with me. But contrary to his expectations, when Bose discovered the real nature of Aligarh communism, he drifted away from them. He also divulged a piece of interesting information that he had received from his sources at the National Museum—Dr Makhan Lal had been planted by the RSS lobby through Prof Gaur in the History Department of the AMU. In fact, Dr Irfan Habib had brought both Partha Pratibha Bose and then Dr Makkan Lal to AMU in a bid to rearrange the archaeological chessboard of Aligarh.

Neither Dr Makhan Lal nor Prof Gaur could forgive Bose for this indiscretion. As a result, Bose became the most vulnerable target as his probation period was not yet over. In fact, such classified piece of information should have set the alarm bell ringing. But the communists, in their phenomenal wisdom, chose to shoot the messenger. One day, while Bose was seated in the Archaeology section, he received his dismissal order from the University. It was within a few days of the birth of his son. "KK Saab, they have dismissed me from the service." Parth Prathiba Bose's frail cry still rings in my ears. But we all stood by him and helped him. Later on, he set up a small business in Aligarh.

Sajjad Haider, a dealing Assistant, and Faizul Rahman Haque, the storekeeper in the archaeology section, were also suspended. The differences went to such an extent that Sajjad filed a criminal case against Prof Athar Ali, a close confidant of Dr Irfan, for staging a physical attack on him. Later, Sajjad fought out the Employees Union election and emerged as a powerful union leader of the university by trouncing the nominee of the Communist group with a wide margin. When they tried to implicate Faizul Rahman Haque by forcing an employee to give false evidence against him, I forestalled the move by tape-recording the real story and exposing it before the inquiry committee. For the first time, like an investigative journalist, I had to tape-record an employee's voice to save another from the sinister motives and dismissal by Dr Habib. Both of them were reinstated and were awarded full arrears.

Although many of Dr Irfan's former loyalists in the archaeological section received show-cause notices, all of them continued to defy the autocratic behaviour of both Dr Irfan Habib and Makhan Lal. Mrs Nahid Khan and Ramjit, once staunch supporters of Habib, were now equally vociferous against him. Both of them were recipients of show-cause notices. It was through these two supporters Irfan Habib had invited members of the archaeology section to file their grievances. Initially, I refused to join them as I smelt a rat and trap in it and cautioned Nahid Khan. But she assured me that she had a detailed discussion with Dr Irfan Habib and has fixed up an appointment also. I just accompanied them. The discussion was not only smooth, but also he assured us to look at it sympathetically. In order to ease the tension of the moment, he peppered the discussion with phrases like butter cannot argue with the knife. Later, we sent a letter to him enlisting the points of discussion. Once he received our letter, he displayed his duplicity with all the undesirable indicators of his penal power and issued show-cause notices, hoping that all others would desert me at the eleventh hour as they were, earlier his ardent supporters. The means he used to trap me by using others was not only questionable but also deplorable. However, this arithmetical calculation also went wrong, and all of them stood solidly behind me. A buzz of discontentment and revulsion was now evident against him, even among his early followers like Nahid Khan and Ramjit. It was a mass resistance and disobedience movement by the Archaeological section against this group. The demeanour of defiance constituted rebellious behaviour. Dismissals, suspensions and show-cause notices had no deterrent effect envisaged. This turmoil was a symptom of a deeper malaise that an autocrat like Dr Habib could not fathom.

In fact, They were thirsting for my blood. Many carefully crafted attempts were made to trap me in any of the corners. By this time, my selection order in the Archaeological Survey of India had reached me, but I had kept it as a top-secret. The only armour under such circumstances was to keep out of gun shots. By sheer luck, somehow, my scalp was eluding them.

The best thing about the archaeology section was that its foundation was laid by Prof Nurul Hasan, an educationist with liberal values. One of the persons who shaped its early ethos was Hanif Hashmi, the father of Suhail Hashmi and Safdar Hashmi. A real Communist and a supporter of the downtrodden masses, Hashmi Saheb, as he was popularly known, was an inspiration for field workers such as Saeed-ul-Hasan, Naseem Haider, Nasir Husain Zaidi, Husham Haider, Anees Alavi and Naheed Khan. Although they had Left-liberal views, they did not belong to any organised group. The distancing of this Left-liberal group from Habib's opportunistic communism was another blow for him. He was no more the leader of the progressive groups. Liberals like me were questioning his credibility as a Communist right from the beginning.

At this juncture, the archaeology section received support from Matloob Ali Qureishi and Masood Agha, the office-bearers of AMU's Technical Association, which was earlier working under Dr Irfan's directives. They, too, had revolted, thereby cutting to size the man who had once enjoyed sweeping powers and seemed invincible. Matloob even brought out a monthly journal exposing many of Dr Irfan Habib's activities. As the university community widely read this, the communist group was much worried.

A few senior professors, such as Mahendra Dev Narayan Sahi, Rajkumar Trivedi, Satya Prakash Gupta, and Banwari Lal Bhadani, once staunch followers of Dr Irfan Habib, now openly revolted against him. Prof Gupta not only filed a legal case but also won the battle, and lived to become the Chairman of the History Department, much against the wishes of Dr Irfan Habib and Shireen Moosvi. Similarly, Prof Zameeruddin Siddiqui and Prof Mansoora Haider, associated with Prof Nurul Hasan, were also successful in becoming the Chairpersons, incurring the wrath of Dr Irfan Habib. Prof Tarique Ahmed, Banwari Lal Bhadani and Sayyid Shaihabuddin Iraqi all once his men, now showed the courage to revolt. Prof Liaquat Moini, associated with Ajmer Sharief, refused to submit before him.

While most of the Vice-Chancellors like Syed Hamid and Syed Hashim Ali were afraid of him as he had the capacity to foment trouble and declare them as communal, Mehmoodurrahman, IAS (1995–2000) and Lt. General Zameeruddin Shah (2012–2017) did not yield to any of the pressure tactics of the Communist group. It was impossible to tarnish them as Muslim fanatics as both of them enjoyed stronger secular credentials. Thus, during his period, a much chastised communist group, clipped of their power, looking forlorn and dejected, preferred to spend their time nursing their newly afflicted wounds. This turbulent period reminded me of the later periods of Aurangzeb when the Rajputs, Jats, Satnamis, Marathas, Sikhs and even minor vassals had openly revolted against him due to his religious fanaticism. Although I was not in the University during this period, I was getting all the information about what was happening in the department.

"Main akele hi chala tha janib i manzil magar
Log sath aate gae aur caravan banta gaya"

—Majrooh Sultan Puri

(When I started my journey, I was all alone
But as I progressed, many other caravans joined me and became a formidable force.)

My biggest hero in Aligarh is Prof Mahendra Pratap Singh, who never compromised his principles and continued to fight against Dr Irfan Habib like a Rajput warrior, reminding me of the statement: "The walls of Chittor crumbled, but not the spirit of the brave Rajput resistance."

When both the teaching and non-teaching employees turned against him, the stage-managed drama of 'murderous attacks on the secular professor,' which Dr Habib used to enact from time to time, also stopped paying the rich dividends. Earlier, it was Dr Habib's occasional practice that whenever he felt the university authorities didn't pay him much attention, the stage-managed 'murderous attack' on the 'secular professor' to gain attention and gain popularity would appear in the newspapers. But the unique technique of escaping unhurt, such murderous attacks of fundamentalists, would have put even the actor Amitabh Bachchan to shame!

Although Prof Gaur had changed the colour of his stripes and spots by joining the new camp, he found himself ill at ease. Basically, a good man whom material considerations had swayed, his heart did not permit him to do whatever he was instructed to do. He was also aware that some of the followers of Dr Irfan Habib were passing unsavoury comments about his changing loyalty. The internal contradictions and structural fault lines within the newly cobbled up group was also very evident. There was an apparent conflict between his conscience and the dictates of his new masters. One such order was the action he initiated against me.

The discovery of *Ibadat Khana* and the chapel had helped me get selected in the Archaeological Survey of India (ASI) as Deputy Superintending Archaeologist, for which I had applied through the proper channel, after serving for ten years (1978–1988) in the university. My selection was both a recognition of my discoveries and a stunning rebuff to the communists and the Aligarh Muslim University authorities.

According to the rules, I was entitled to seek 'lien', which would have enabled me to return to my substantive post at Aligarh if I did not want to continue in my new assignment. My appointment in the ASI was initially a great relief for them as it meant the removal of an eternal troublemaker bothering them in Aligarh. But they were also aware of the fact that once I joined the ASI, I would become more powerful and start breathing down their necks in some of the archaeological projects.

Hence, Dr Gaur was instructed to refuse me 'lien' unless I withdrew the legal case I had filed against Makhan Lal and the others. Left to himself, Dr Gaur would not have gone to that extent for he was very well aware of the support I had extended to him when he was in a '*chakravyuha*' and subjected to relentless attacks from Dr Irfan Habib. While there was none to help him in his hour of need, it was I who stood by him like a pillar of strength for many years. How could he have chopped off his own right hand at the instructions of his one time enemies? It was also under pressure that he had become an accessory in the dismissal of Partha Pratibha Bose from the university service just a few days after the birth of the latter's child. The show-cause notice to many of his subordinates in the archaeology section was served much against his will. He was not really as unkind and ruthless as the Communist group in whose hands he had now been reduced to a simple tool. Moreover, what KK Sinha, Professor of BHU, had said that within six months, Makhan Lal would hold him upside down was also haunting him.

His conscience was questioning and troubling him. There are serendipitous moments in life when one's conscience starts questioning one's actions. It is a moment for course correction for people with a conscience by taking a stand against an earlier action. Dr Gaur was caught in the vortex of a dilemma. A Latin proverb says, "Excusatio non petita, accusatio manifesta" A guilty conscience needs no accuser. He was wavering and vacillating. He had taken actions one after the other against his own nears and dears, following the instructions of his former enemies. This was a marriage of convenience in which he was never trusted by them, nor did he repose any trust in them. "O, Bhagvan, what a trial it is!"

On the day he wrote the negative comment on my application for not granting 'lien,' perhaps because of the acute psychological conflicts, he developed fever and other health complications. When it did not subside, he was rushed to the Aligarh Medical College and subsequently to the All India Medical Institute in Delhi. He was in a coma for many months, and even after a partial recovery, could not speak clearly. But all of us who received show-cause notices prayed for his speedy recovery as we knew that he was simply a powerless tool in the hands of the communist group. During the subsequent period, the story of the department of History would be the story of shifting loyalties and a gripping tale of betrayals.

Once the lien request was rejected, I took the hard decision of resigning from the university services, as I had 'nothing to lose except my rusted chains.' Of course, there would be a loss of a few thousands at the time of pension. Seething with revenge and blinded by fury, the Communist historian broke the wrong parts of mine. They broke my wings and forgot that I had claws.

I met Javed Usmani, IAS, the Registrar at AMU, who later became the Chief Secretary of Uttar Pradesh. When he came to know about my archaeological discoveries and selection to the ASI, he was sympathetic and approved my resignation despite all the pressures exerted by the Communist group.

Once Dr Habib was sure that 'Shiva' (Chatrapathi Shivaji) had again escaped from the prison, he hotly pursued me to the doors of the Archaeological Survey of India. He approached Dr JP Joshi, the Director-General of Archaeological Survey of India, with several complaints against me and requested him not to allow me to join the ASI, for I was a troublemaker and a *Jamaat-i-Islami* man. Dr Joshi told him that he knew me very well as a student, and the question of not allowing me to join the ASI did not arise, as my selection had been made through the UPSC and all the legal formalities had been completed. All through my UPSC interview, police verification and medical examination, I had to maintain a strict veil of secrecy as they were after me and suffered from an acute trust deficit. Under the circumstances, hide your strength and bid your time was the best policy.

As I had information from their own camps that Dr Habib in a desperate bid would approach Dr Joshi, in an equally pre-emptive move, I had requested Prof Mahendra Dev Narayan Sahi, the eminent archaeologist who was the Director-General's batchmate, to brief him about Aligarh politics and my running battle with Dr Habib. Prof Sahi himself was a victim of Dr Irfan Habib's betrayal. Later on, I also met Dr Joshi and explained everything about Aligarh politics before he could harm me. It was a battle of wits between David and Goliath.

"If you wanted to stop him, it should have been done at your level in the AMU," Dr Joshi told Dr Habib. On realizing that he was batting on a poor wicket, the disappointed ICHR Chairman made the last request that I should not be posted to the Agra Circle. He was afraid that if I were posted to Agra, I (whom he had stopped issuing books from the departmental library) would make some more discoveries at Fatehpur Sikri and make his life hell. The entire story was narrated to me by Dr Joshi himself. Following the request of Dr Habib, my first posting in the Archaeological Survey was not to Agra but Madras, far away from the political din and clatter of Aligarh. While in the Archaeological Survey of India also, this Communist group made two attempts to get me transferred from Agra and Delhi, as both the postings enjoyed considerable prestige, and I could easily trace out the authorship of the failed attempts to the same Aligarh forces from the pug marks, left by them on the wet ground.

Had se roj hi katara ke
Gujar jate hain,
Jane vah kaun hai
jo mujhko dua deta hai.

Every day I used to have frightening brushes with dangers. Little do I know, the prayers of who all have saved me from them.

Thus, after many twists and turns of fate and a 'tryst with destiny,' I reached Madras, my next port of call. Archaeological Survey was my home for the next twenty-two years. My posting in Madras instead of Agra, which was Habib's creation, posed another festering problem for him, as it threw both of us head over heels into the vortex of Ayodhya issue from two diametrically opposite poles. Sometimes we are blissfully unaware of how fate designs its fine meshes for us. Had I not been posted to Madras, there would have been no occasion for me to meet Iravatham Mahadevan, one of the liberal minds, and make my historic statement in Indian Express about the discovery of the temple remains below the Babri Masjid. My participation in this excavation under the legendary archaeologist Prof BB Lal and the consequent statement played a crucial role in combating the Communists and convincing the liberals about the veracity of the temple below the mosque and also the Honourable High Court and Supreme Court. (For details, please read the chapter on Ayodhya.

It did not end there. As my statement was considered fatal to the interest of the Aligarh Marxist + Babri group, they pressurised the ruling Government to take action against me, as my statement was against the Conduct Rules of a Central Government Servant. The Aligarh Marxists knew that it was easy to dismiss me from the service without serving a show-cause notice or suspension, as my confirmation letter after completing the probation period was not yet in my hand. It was a dangerous piece of information in the hands of a sworn enemy who was close on your heels. What they could not do at Aligarh, they were going to execute now silently. Sitting at a safer distance, they could now pull the trigger. It is said that even the devil does not know where the Aligarh Communists sharpen their knife. But sadly, in this case, what Aligarh Communits proposed God disposed of, with an enigmatic smile.

With the intervention of Iravatham Mahadevan and the Professors of Madras University, the proposed major punishment was reduced to a transfer from Madras to Goa. The news of the mild action against me punctured their euphoria and spoiled the celebration mood. I decided to turn this punishment transfer also into another archaeological discovery. A Bible quotation says, "A man wronged is more unyielding than a fortified city." Since hurt has no expiry date and every challenge and adversity contains within it the seeds of opportunity and growth," I felt that I was on the right track.

It was from Goa, the Christian Fathers Rudolf Acquaviva and Fr Monserrate had gone to Fatehpur Sikri to participate in the religious discussions at *Ibadat Khana*. Having failed to convert Emperor Akbar to Christianity, Fr Rudolf returned to Goa, and Akbar sent an escort for his safety in the Mughal kingdom. But in Portuguese Goa, at a place known as Concolim, they were brutally killed by an enraged mob. As they were killed at Concolim, they are known as Martyrs of Concolim in the Church history. When Akbar heard about the killing of Fr Rudolf, Akbar was grief-stricken and murmured, "Alas, Father! did I not tell you not to go away, but you would never listen to me." Since I had excavated *Ibadat Khana* and the Christian Chapel at Fatehpur Sikri, where the Fathers lived, I was sure the mortal remains of Father Rudolf would be preserved in one of the Churches. My earnest search yielded rich rewards.

One day while I was inspecting the antiquities kept in Se Cathedral along with fr Titonia Desoza, the Director of St Xavier Institute, we saw an old worn-out casket in one of the chapels. Curiosity drew us towards it. Blessed Martyrs of Concolim "BETOS MARTIRE DE CUNCOLIM" is clearly written over it. We looked at each other with joy and disbelief. I just wanted to ascertain whether the name of Fr Rudolf was also there. Excitement knew no bounds when we could see the name of Fr Rudolf Acquaviva in Latin "OSSA BTi RODOLFI ACQAVIVA ET QVATOR SOC RVM MARTYRUM E SOCIETATE JESU" (Bones of Blessed Rudolfi Acquaviva and four companion martyrs from the Society of Jesus) also written on it, 1691 km away from Fatehpur Sikri. That was an incredible moment in my life, and I saluted Dr Irfan Habib, in absentia, whom I refused to salute while at Aligarh, for facilitating my posting both in Madras and Goa.

Relic casket of Martyrs of Concolim, especially Fr Rudolf Acquaviva, at Se Cathedral, Goa.

My detailed article on the discovery of the Christian church at Fatehpur Sikri was published by Fr John Correia Afonso in

Indica, a research journal of the Heras Institute, St Xavier College. Soon, the Communists not only approached but also wrote to him against me and the discovery. Since I was living in old Goa looking after the conservation of old Goa churches, Fr Afonso contacted Fr Rego, the then Rector of Bom Jesus, to know about my academic and other credentials. Fr Rego gave such an excellent report that the scheme of the Communists again failed miserably. But, I did not know about it. Later on, when Fr Afonso came to Bom Jesus and had a long detailed discussion with me, he informed me about what had transpired between him and Fr Rego. Hats off: The Jesuit Fathers do their work silently. (please watch the documentary film "The Discovery of Christian chapel at Fatehpur Sikri" on YouTube.)

That was a necessary digression. Let us come back to Aligarh. As expected, both Irfan Habib and Makhan Lal fell apart at the World Archaeology Congress on various issues, especially over the subject of Ayodhya. Much before it, tension had started building up between the two astute and shrewd persons but, it was recorded low on the Richter scale. Soon, it erupted violently, engulfing the archaeologists and historians and turned out to be a virtual Bali-Sugriva battle between the two in the presence of scholars from different countries. Supporters of Irfan Habib and Makhan Lal argued fiercely and advanced menacingly. The official mike was used to provoke each other. Normally in such a situation, what Partha Prathiba Bose had said should have tormented Dr Habib, but it did not bother him. Both Dr Irfan and Makhan Lal are two sides of the same coin, using each other for their personal benefits.

For some time, it appeared as if Dr Makhan Lal was on a stronger wicket due to the then prevailing political configuration. He soon joined the Delhi Institute of Heritage and Research Management as its Director. In 2004, Dr Makhan Lal was suspended based on the complaints of girl students of the Institute.

Dr Nadeem Razavi, whom Dr Irfan had deputed to Kennedy Hall to guide Iqtidar Alam Khan's Sarai exhibition, remained in contact with me through letters. Whenever I was in Aligarh to take refresher classes for the teachers, he made it a point to attend my lectures and then discuss various aspects of medieval archaeology.

I remember him attending my talk on the *Ibadat Khana* at Aligarh while Prof Mansura Haider was the Chairman. In 2003, he attended another talk of mine with slides at Agra on the same subject and then visited Fatehpur Sikri along with Prof Azizuddin of Jamia Millia and me. Standing in the *Ibadat Khana* premises, we had a long discussion with the entire delegation on several aspects of the Hall of Interreligious Discussions.

After thirty years, he came out with his own bizarre and hilarious identification of the *Ibadat Khana,* which has become a butt of joke in the academic circle. It is a rectangular standing structure popularly identified as daftarkhana. The fact that it was endorsed by Dr Habib, due to his opposition to me was a grave reflection of the falling standards of the Aligarh Communist historians. Irfan Habib's seismically unstable opinion about the *Ibadat Khana*, ranging in the beginning from emphatic denial to endorsement and then going back to the earlier denial mode, provided us with enough stuff to discuss the quality of research work at Aligarh. The news that many of us have not only cold contempt but also strong revulsion for his changing opinions on *Ibadat Khana* made him jittery. As the *Ibadat Khana* of Nadeem was conceived not on solid archaeological proofs, it soon met with its tragic death like those unfortunate children in the 'Dumb House (Gunga Mahal) constructed by Akbar. Nobody takes their arguments seriously as it is supported on the scaffolding of personal enmity. Sadly, both the proposer and the seconder themselves have now stopped advocating for their *Ibadat Khana* as their much-touted theory met with infant mortality.

Over the years, archaeology, Fatehpur Sikri, *Ibadat Khana* and KK Muhammed had assumed a frightening proportion of psychological neurosis with them, which no one could exorcise. Their stand is that any structure in Fatehpur Sikri could be the *Ibadat Khana* except the one excavated by KK Muhammed—an improper response to a higher calling in history and archaeology.

How could one become an archaeologist without any training in archaeology or years of long, harsh fieldwork? This rope trick should be learned from Dr Nadeem. The *modus operandi* he had devised, developed and perfected is simple.

This meant identifying the places where earlier archaeologists had worked in the field for many years, braving the sun and the rain. Select the best technical staff who had worked with those archaeologists and gained enough insights about the site. Roam around the site along with them in the field for a day or two, and in the process, extract all the details of the earlier works. Get Prepared a few plans and elevations of the structures. Criticise and denigrate the original researchers and their understanding of the subject. And, lo and behold! A path-breaking new archaeological discovery is there for all the world to see. Present this extraordinary research work in the medieval section of the Indian History Congress, where nobody knows how archaeological excavations are conducted. I was cautioned against this kind of pseudo archaeology of Nadeem Rizvi by Dr Afzal Khan, who had once outsmarted me in the Ph. D and scholarship race. By now, he, too, had broken away from Dr Habib.

Lieutenant General Zameer Uddin Shah, the former Vice-Chancellor, wanted to showcase the rare sculptures collected by Sir Sayyid Ahmed Khan and also the antiquities excavated from various excavations carried by the AMU. He instructed Prof Ali Athar, the former Chairman, to take the initiative. In turn, he envisioned and set up an exhibition highlighting the rich collections of Hindu, Buddhist and Jain antiquities saved by Sir Syed Ahmed Khan and also of the later periods, including Fatehpur Sikri. Prof Ali Athar properly showcased the excavation of the *Ibadat Khana,* as it was one of the most important discoveries of the AMU.

When Nadeem Rizvi became the Chairman, his first act of vandalism was to remove the *Ibadat Khana* photographs and paintings and thus to remove the last remnants of KK Muhammed. I saw the perfume bottle (*Zir-i-Itardan*) lying in one place with no label. It was a piece of valuable evidence in proving the location of the first Christian chapel of North India. Not content with this vandalism, he in his enormous wisdom to immortalize his name as one of the archaeologists of AMU, has kept a few broken glazed pottery pieces in a showcase under his proud name. We should be thankful to him for not replacing the Hindu, Buddhist and Jain antiquities saved by Sir Syed Ahmed Khan with thrown away pottery pieces purportedly collected by him. Such pottery pieces are abundant in the *namaish* ground of Aligarh (Annual Aligarh Exhibition ground) once the Bengal and Khurja potters leave the site after holding their yearly exhibition.

His vandalism is reminiscent of the bizarre and outrageous actions of the BJP Government in Uttar Pradesh, in 2017 in dropping the name of Taj Mahal, one of the seven wonders of the world, from the tourist destinations of UP. However, Shri Yogi Adityanath, later on, as an atonement, visited the Taj Mahal and swept its floor.

Dr Nadeem Rizvi, who has no knowledge in the conservation of monuments, started flaunting his expertise in this subject also. It is a highly specialised branch where practitioners of conservation think twice before expressing their opinion. But Nadeem rushes in his sherwani and Aligarh cuts pyjama where conservation experts fear to tread on. In an attempt to tarnish me, he attributed the purportedly wrong conservation of the Santrashi Masjid and the royal stable at Fatehpur Sikri, as carried out by me.

In the first instance, both the works were technical, and he had no domain competence to speak on the subject. Even conservation experts speak on such subjects, only after considerable study. But that did not stop Dr Nadeem Rizvi from coming out with his flawed and immature opinion. Moreover, it was Dr PBS Sanger, who had taken up the conservation of Santrashi Masjid while he was the Superintending Archaeologist. Similarly, Dr Dayalan Duraiswamy initiated the conservation of the royal stable at Fatehpur Sikri in 2004–05. I had nothing to do with either of the alleged works, but that did not prevent Nadeem from rushing in his sherwani from making a false allegation against me and displaying the monumental mockery of his expertise in conservation.

I was in one of the archaeology meetings when Dr Shireen Moosvi took up the issue of Santrashi Masjid. She was highly embarrassed and uneasy when she saw me in the meeting, as she knew that I would reply back on the same coin. But I was not supposed to speak on the issue as it was not my work. However, when Dr PBS Sanger presented a befitting oral reply, justifying the conservation work of Santrashi Masjid, Dr Moosvi sank into her seat in embarrassment. She could not even raise a single counter-question. But, a fully tense Dr Moosavi was relieved that I did not stand up to reply to that question.

Dr Nadeem Rizvi repeated 'the tale of two lies' to gullible audiences at many Indian History conferences and seminars to tarnish my reputation. Indian History Congress venue provides them a conducive atmosphere for such self-styled archaeologists as the audience is blissfully unaware of archaeological conservations. One could have treated them as the inadvertent mistake of a simple medieval historian in his 'great leap forward' to transform himself into an archaeologist. But it was not so. Dr Nadeem Rizvi has learned the art of telling white and dazzling lies as part of his career promotion.

This dubious craft of Nadeem reminds one of a similar attempt made by Pakistan at the UN in 2017 when they displayed the photographs of the victims of Palestine violence in a bid to highlight the alleged Indian army excesses in Kashmir. The remark made by Paulomy Tripathy, the Indian representative at the UN, that "a fake picture to push a completely false narrative" is equally applicable in the case of Nadeem also.

Both Nadeem and Dr Irfan resorted to telling barefaced lies in the case of Ayodhya also, but in the process, they were caught in a cleft stick and badly exposed. I have written in detail about this in the chapter on Ayodhya. (For more information, please read the chapter on Ayodhya)

Even after I departed from Aligarh, I continued to be the biggest thorn in the flesh of Dr Habib. Whenever I went to Aligarh on the invitation of various departments to speak about the discovery of the *Ibadat Khana,* the archaeology of Buddhist sites, or the conservation of Bateshwar temples, Dr Irfan's secret service would be very active in reporting about my route map–where I was going, whom I was meeting, etc.

If the Wiki pages have listed my name in terms of popularity among the 96 notable Alumni of Aligarh Muslim University, the credit goes to Dr Irfan Habib, again, in the negative sense of the word. When I accompanied President Parvez Musharraf of Pakistan to the Taj Mahal and Barack Obama to Humayun's Tomb, it was given wide coverage by newspapers and television channels. These were the worst days in Aligarh's Communist group's life, as the person they had refused scholarship, demoted and tried to implicate in false cases walked like a colossus right in front of their eyes. My selection as one of the Padmashri Awardees in 2019 was another body blow to them. The man whom they had demoted and tried to implicate in false cases is now a Padmashri.

My PowerPoint presentations on various aspects of archaeology was another source of grief for them. These exciting presentations were in sharp contrast to their dry-and-drab lectures. Hence, calculated attempts were made by the bonded intellectuals of Dr Irfan to stall them. They were successful only in the Jawaharlal Nehru University (JNU), where my lecture was cancelled due to Marxist pressure. However, the lecture halls at the India International Centre, India Habitat Centre, Indira Gandhi National Centre for Arts, Nehru Museum, Jamia Millia and various colleges of the Delhi University were filled to the capacity.

Thus, looking back to my life and struggle at Aligarh, it sounds like a page from 'Alif Laila.' Not because they tell us such islands of fairy tales and unethical practices exist in various Universities, but they tell us that one can successfully emerge out from their clutches, beat them in their games and also make one's mark. (doctored version of Neil Gaiman)

"It matters not how strait the gate
How charged with punishment the scroll
I am the master of my fate
I am the captain of my soul" —William Earnst.

With this chapter on *Ibadat Khana* and Aligarh Muslim University, I am now half relieved for "There is no greater agony than bearing an untold story within you." Mayo Angelo.

□

Ayodhya Excavation—Some Historical Facts

This autobiography of mine would be incomplete if I were to exclude this important chapter of my life. It is not my intention to hurt anyone's feelings, nor do I wish to provoke anyone's emotions. My humble request is that this chapter may please be taken in the true spirit in which it is written.

In the year 1990, a raging debate lashed across the country about the original owner of Ayodhya. Few individuals who were gifted with farsightedness could see through the future maze of history and the frightening form it was going to assume. When it took a monstrous shape, there were sincere attempts from moderate Hindus and Muslims to solve the problem amicably by handing over the mosque to construct the Rama temple. But Marxist historians and their supporters saw it as a very good occasion to 'make hay while the sun shines.' For them, it was a rare opportunity to perpetuate their authority on the Indian Council of Historical Research (ICHR), which would enable them to dole out its largesse to the obliging camp followers. The Chairman of ICHR, Dr Irfan Habib, who was the main brain behind the Marxist historians, openly supported the Babri Masjid Action Committee and had many meetings with them and their experts in ICHR. A few people like Prof MGS Narayanan, the then Member Secretary of ICHR, cautioned him about the dangerous implications of such meetings with the Babri Masjid Action Committee. But a man of strong likes and dislikes, Irfan Habib, brushed aside all such sound suggestions. Possessed with an authoritarian streak, Irfan believed in the practice of 'either you follow me blindly, or you are my enemy,' and rode roughshod over other's sober suggestions. As I knew Irfan Habib and his ruthless ways from my Aligarh days, I spoke to Prof MGS Narayanan that he would soon be declared a Hindu fanatic and RSS man. In those days, Dr Habib was the sole manufacturer and distributor of 'communal tags.' But the hilarious part of this branding exercise was that the moment an earlier 'die-hard fanatic' realigned with Irfan Habib and his coterie, he would immediately be hailed and anointed as a 'principled secularist.' If anybody, without knowing the dangerous consequences of such a step, expressed his opinion, he would not only be hounded out but also an army of hydra-headed warriors would spring to life to cut off his anti-proletariat head. Realising the importance of 'the survival of the fittest,' many in the Department of History, AMU, ICHR and various universities had perfected their navigational skill, in switching over the groups, depending on the time and tide.

However, many years before, in 1976–77, I had the privilege of participating in the excavation headed by Prof BB Lal at Ayodhya. Prof Lal was the former Director-General of the Archaeological Survey of India, who opted for voluntary retirement at a relatively young age from the prestigious post, exclusively for research and study. After a brief stint in Gwalior University, he took up the Directorship at the famous Indian Institute of Advanced Study, Shimla (IIAS), as per the friendly persuasions of some of his educationist friends. While serving there, he formulated a proposal known as 'Projects of Archaeological Survey of Ramayana Sites.' Before this, he had completed the Project of the Mahabharata sites, excavated Hastinapura, and other sites associated with the Mahabharata. His theories and conclusions were so refreshing and convincing that it lit up the entire archaeological activity in India and is still holding ground.

The team of Prof Lal at Ayodhya consisted of officials of the Archaeological Survey of India (ASI), the Indian Institute of Advanced Studies (IIAS) Shimla and twelve members of the School of Archaeology. We were housed in an inn that was constructed just by the side of the mosque and stayed there for two months excavating the site. As usual, before taking up the excavation, an exploration of the surrounding area is carried out to contextualise the excavation. During this exercise, we went to the inner part of the Babri Mosque to study the structure and its topography. Although Puja rituals were in progress, and the multitudes were thronging the site, the *mehrab* part of the mosque was under lock and key, and a policeman was standing guard of it. When we told them that we were from the excavation team, the gate was opened for our research work.

A student of art and architecture, based on style and motifs, can broadly date the architectural work of each century or dynasty, which is known as typological dating. On inspection, it was found that the pillars used for the mosque were actually temple pillars with typical Hindu motifs of the 11th–12th centuries. There were twelve pillars made of black basalt with the lower part engraved with purna kalasha Hindu motifs. In temple art, *Purna kalasha* is one of the *Ashtamangala chinhas* eight auspicious symbols. This has been extensively used in ancient Indian art and architecture. Even now, whenever a Hindu Acharya is received, he is welcomed with a *purna kalasha*. The whole Quwwat-ul-Islam complex by the side of the Qutub Minar is full of such reused temple pillars with *purna kalasha* motifs carved on them. In the said complex, there is an Arabic inscription on the front side of the mosque, expressly declaring that parts of twenty-seven temples have been used for the construction of the mosque. The same thing is mentioned in Tajul Masir, a book written by Hasan Nizami, a contemporary historian of the period.

In the Babri Mosque, apart from the pillars, a defaced Hindu sculpture was also seen embedded in one of the walls. When the actual excavation started behind the western and southern part of the mosque, several brick bases were exposed, obviously to stabilise the ground and support the pillars. It was now clear that the mosque was built over the remains of a Hindu temple by reusing the black basalt pillars. The fact that the brick bases were slightly larger than the circumference of the reused pillars further strengthened this assumption.

But Prof Lal was not excavating Ayodhya to ascertain whether there was a temple below the controversial mosque or not. He was looking at the historical landscape of the ancient period from the dispassionate view of an archaeologist. He wanted to know the cultural sequence of the Ramayana sites and compare them with the Mahabharata sites which he had already excavated, and evolve an acceptable scientific chronology for future generations. So he did not highlight the pillars and brick bases, as he did not wish to create an unnecessary controversy.

It is regretful to say that some of the Left historians of JNU, with the active connivance of Aligarh Marxist historians, came forward in November 1989, in a small publication titled '*The Political Abuse of History: Babri Masjid-Ram Janambhumi* dispute—An analysis by twenty-five historians' to support the Babri Masjid Action Committee. Had it been a pure historical study, it would have been the right step in the right direction. But here, everything is being done with a clear motive of helping the Babri Masjid Action Committee. They raised questions about Rama, his historicity, the Ayodhya site and asserted that it became prominent only after the Ramanandi sect settled in the area after the 18th century. With the apparent motive of misguiding the public, they argued that the excavation conducted by Prof Lal had not exposed any temple remains at all. The sad part of the story was that these historians who passed the 'last judgment' about Ayodhya were neither archaeologists nor had visited the site while the excavation was in progress. It sowed the seeds of a long civil war, and the nation paid heavily for the calculated misdeeds of the Marxist historians.

Not content with it, in another attempt to bring more claimants to the Babri site, drive wedges among other religious communities and vitiate the atmosphere, they also pointed out that the place was holier for the Buddhist and the Jains much before the Hindus. This well-thought-out move, they anticipated, would be a brilliant shot to divide the communities into Hindu, Muslim, Buddhist and Jain fighting groups. But unfortunately for the Marxists, both the Buddhists and the Jain communities refused to bite the bait and largely ignored it. Hence, that proved to be a failed Chinese strategic missile. They also laboured hard to prove that even in the 15th and 16th centuries, Ayodhya was more a prominent centre of Shaivism than the cult of Rama. So strange was their argument that there was no mention of the demolition of the temple before the 19th century.

The prominent leaders of this group were Professors S Gopal, Romila Thaper, Bipan Chandra, RS Sharma, Irfan Habib, Athar Ali, DN Jha and Suraj Bhan at various points in time. As part of a design to create confusion, they said that the Babri Mosque was built on 'virgin land' below which there were no previous structures at all. This statement, made more in bravado, without knowing archaeology and the site, later on, boomeranged on them when many structural remains were encountered below the mosque, one after the other. Irfan Habib even refused to accept that the reused pillars in the Babri Masjid were sufficient evidence that the mosque stood on the temple site. As part of their dilatory tactics, he said the pillars in the Masjid could belong to a Jain or Shiva temple from somewhere else and had nothing to do with the Sri Rama temple at Janamsthan.

Using their wide connection with the journalistic fraternity, this group embarked on a publishing spree to prove that the excavation carried out by Prof Lal had not exposed any temple remains. Normally averse to such publicity stunts and statements, Prof Lal was pained at the way non-archaeologists were passing their false comments on archaeological subjects without any domain competence. But much against his nature, this time, Prof Lal came out against such street smart trade union historians and openly said about the pillars and brick bases he had excavated at the Babri site. This was an unexpected bombshell both for the Marxist historians and friendly English journalistic fraternity, as they thought that Prof Lal would not come out so openly against such formidable formations.

While the controversy between the two groups was at its height, Iravatham Mahadevan, a senior IAS officer and well-known scholar on the Harappan script, came up with a very sober suggestion in *The Indian Express*. He submitted, if there were controversies between two groups about the existence of temple remains at the Babri site, the issue could be settled by excavating the site once more. But he strongly condemned the proposal to demolish the Babri Masjid by VHP, to right a historical wrong that had taken place hundreds of years back. What a perfectly balanced and impartial opinion! I liked his sensible approach. Since I was posted at that time in Madras as Deputy Superintending Archaeologist and knew him very well, I wrote him a personal letter congratulating him for his principled stand and the impatient plea not to destroy a historical structure (Babri Mosque) for righting a historical wrong. I elaborated that there was a temple below the Babri Mosque, as I was a participant in the excavation project under Prof BB Lal. I wrote: "I can reiterate it with greater authority, for I was the only Muslim who had participated in the Ayodhya excavation in 1976–77 under Prof Lal...." Further, I said: "Ayodhya is as holy to Hindus as Mecca and Madinah are to Muslims. Muslims should respect the sentiments of millions of their Hindu brethren and voluntarily hand over the structure for constructing the Rama temple."

At that time, the social and religious atmosphere was simmering at the boiling point because of the combined action of the Marxist historians and hardliner Muslims. Both Hindus and Muslims had drawn into their watertight compartments. Some moderates in both groups were trying to evolve a compromise formula. The Vishwa Hindu Parishad had tightened its grip on the Ram Janmabhumi. Many liberal Muslims, especially those who were unattached and non-denominational to any group, were ready to defuse the crisis by handing over the site to Hindus. Some Muslim liberals even argued with Muslim hardliners that if Muslims relinquish their claim to Babri Masjid, BJP would be left with no issues in the next election. If this moderate trend of thought had progressed further, the entire Mandir-Masjid problem could have been solved amicably. That would have changed the entire socio-religious arithmetic and created a soft space for Muslims in the Hindu heart. Hindus themselves would have come forward to solve many of the problems from which the Muslim community was still suffering. But the Communist historians headed by Irfan Habib raised the Great Wall of China between Hindus and Muslims and foiled every attempt to find a solution to a burning problem.

As soon as Mahadevan received my letter, he came to my office of the Archaeological Survey of India in Fort St George in Madras and requested permission to publish it. Being a senior government servant, he knew very well that it would be against the Conduct Rules of a Government servant to issue a press statement on such a sensitive subject. I took him to Dr B Narasimhaia, the Superintending Archaeologist and Head of Office at Madras. Fortunately, it was the same Dr Narsimhaia, the General Supervisor of the Ayodhya excavation, who coordinated everything under Prof BB Lal while the brick bases were exposed. It was sure that no government would permit such a statement under the present condition, as the government would then be held responsible for further consequences.

We calmly deliberated the pros and cons of such a statement in public domains. The immediate action would be suspension from the government service. In my case, the risk involved was double, as I had not yet received my confirmation letter after completing the probation period. I could be dismissed from the government service in the present vulnerable position, even without being served with a show-cause notice. The Aligarh historians headed by Irfan Habib, with whom I was having a running battle while I was in Aligarh, would undoubtedly use this opportunity to pressurise the government to take action against me. Venom, vengeance and vendetta are the pronounced qualities of the Aligarh Marxist group. Images of a dark future started hovering before my eyes. After prolonged deliberations, it was felt that the truth should not be suppressed, and I decided to publish it. An inner voice said that I had double duty in this case as I was the only Muslim who participated in the excavation. My silence should not be equated with acquiescence and perhaps complicity. Thus, I took a conscious decision that I should listen to my inner voice, come what may.

Thus my statement that there was temple remains below the Babri mosque, published in *The Indian Express* on 15–12–1990, fell like the second bombshell on the arguments of Aligarh and JNU historians. It naturally unleashed a political storm and totally silenced the Marxists as they could not challenge it. Since it was from the only Muslim who had participated in the excavation, seen the temple remains during the excavation and was serving in the Archaeological Survey of India as Deputy Superintendent Archaeologist, it carried more conviction. On the other hand, the Marxist historians were neither archaeologists nor had visited the site while the excavation was in progress. Since both Mahadevan and I were strongly against the demolition agenda of VHP, moderates perceived it as a sober and saner voice. To leave no room for any suspicion, my full address was also published by *The Indian Express.* While the statement was music to the ears of some, the Marxists fretted and fumed as they had been badly exposed. But as decided earlier, I kept aloof from both Hindu and Muslim extremists. Many threatening calls came over the phone. Congratulatory calls, far exceeded. And as decided, they were all met with one line 'thank you.'

Within a few days after the publication, RC Tripathy, Secretary of Culture and MC Joshi, the Director-General Archaeological Survey of India, came to Madras to organise a UNESCO-sponsored International Seminar on the Silk Route. The participants, a judicious combination of academics, explorers and journalists from different parts of the world, had come in a special royal ship that belonged to the Sultan of Oman. Since the local convener of the seminar Dr Narasimhaia had to go to Cambodia, heading an Indian conservation team, the entire responsibility of conducting the seminar was entrusted to me and my senior colleague Dr KT Narasimhan. Although the burden was thrust upon us midstream, we were able to complete it successfully, and thus elicited unstinted appreciation from the UNESCO seminar members, the Ministry of Culture and the Archaeological Survey of India.

When all the programmes were over, on the day of the

ceremonial dinner, Shri Tripathy and Dr MC Joshi took me to a corner and profusely complimented for the flawless conduct of the seminar and then added: "If that professor (Irfan Habib) were here, after seeing your performance, he would have hung his head in shame." Dr Joshi then narrated my life and struggle at Aligarh to Shri Tripathy.

A little later, Dr Joshi said, "We are going to take you to task for your controversial press statement in favour of the Ayodhya temple. How could you make such a statement on a very sensitive issue without taking the mandatory permission from the government? All of us knew the truth but did not speak about it as it is a political issue and not an archaeological one. I will suspend you right now." The same Dr Joshi, who appreciated me earlier, was a changed man now. "Sir," I replied. "I was aware that permission would not have been granted had I sought for it. I made an honest statement in the interest of the country. Then I quoted the well-known Sanskrit hymn from the Bhagavat Gita "*Loka Samgrahame Vapi Sambashyan Kartu Marhasi.*" (Just for the sake of educating the people and for the public's welfare, you should do your duty.) The hymn annoyed Shri Tripathiji, who said, "I am a Brahmin from Allahabad. Are you teaching me Sanskrit? I will suspend you right now."

I replied calmly with another hymn, "*Swa Dharme Nidhanam Sreya*" (In the fulfilment of one's Dharma, even death is welcome.) The last hymn had the desired effect on Shri Tripathiji. "Well, Mr Muhammed, your unswerving resolve is commendable. It should have been spoken by an Archaeologist. You are an archaeologist. It should have been spoken by a Muslim archaeologist. You are a Muslim archaeologist. But I am under pressure to take action against you."

"I understand, sir. But it was after weighing all the pros and cons, I have given the statement."

"Why did you give your full name, designation and address to the press?" Dr Joshi angrily asked. "I could have explained it away that it was some other Muhammed. But your full address has left me no manoeuvring space."

"But sir, if I had not given my full address, its authenticity would have been doubted. I did not want to make it ambiguous and open to interpretation." For a moment, they looked at each other. Although they kept a grim face, they really appreciated my stand and honestly wanted to help me. They had to cut short the discussion as it was time for the Hon'ble Governor, the Chief Guest, to depart. Both of them left abruptly as they were called to see off the Governor and other dignitaries.

When Mahadevan heard about the proposed action, he immediately swung into action. As an IAS officer, he was much senior to Shri RC Tripathy and as a scholar respected by Dr Joshi. Moreover, he was the most influential Chief Editor of the widely read Tamil newspaper *Dinamani*. He personally met both of them and had long discussions. Owing to his intervention and a host of others from Madras University, especially Prof KV Raman, the proposed suspension was commuted to transfer from Madras to Goa. As both the officials were sympathetic to me, I was asked by Dr Joshi to immediately join at Goa and report so that he could file an action taken report in case of anything cropped up.

In Goa, on 6 December 1992, while I was discussing the conservation of the Bom Jesus Church with its Rector Father Rego, the news of the destruction of the Babri Mosque came as a shock to all of us, who believed in the secular values of the country. Many moderates like Mahadevan and the entire archaeological fraternity grieved the destruction of the historical structure by Hindu fanatics. We could have saved this monument and transplanted it to some other place had both the groups come to some understanding. But the adamant attitude of the Babri Action Committee aided and abetted by Marxist historians had driven the Hindu fanatics to a scorch earth policy that they decided to destroy it to the last brick.

One of the important antiquities that came to light after the demolition of the Babri mosque was a revealing stone plaque with Devanagari inscription. It was embedded in one of the walls of the mosque. It tumbled down while the demolition was in progress. Prof Ajai Mitra Shastri, a specialist in Epigraphy and Numismatics, identified it as Vishnu Hari Shila inscription, written in chaste classical Nagari script of the eleventh and twelfth century AD. He read it as: "That this temple, built with heaps of stone and beautified with a golden spire, was constructed in the temple city of Ayodhya, situated in Saketa Mandala. Vishnu is the destroyer of Bali and dasanana (ten-headed Ravana)." When the Hon'ble Court referred it to Dr KV Ramesh, the former Chief Epigraphist of India, he also dated it to 12th century on the paleographic ground and found the name of Govindachandra of Gahadvala dynasty, who ruled from 1114–1145. This inscription was another unassailable proof of the existence of the temple before the Babri Mosque.

As soon as the details about inscription came out, the Marxist historians got together, and their traditional game of confusing the general public started. They all came with various opinions, although none was epigraphists. So what? How would it stop them from passing their learned arguments? The initial attempt was to discredit it as a fake inscription planted by the VHP. When that did not find any takers, they resorted to another gimmick. A Marxist historian, D Mandal, said that the inscription might or might not be a fake one and if it was a right inscription, it did not speak about the temple at the Babri site, but it should be looked for somewhere else in Ayodhya. What a fertile brain he has! Yet another diversionary tactic! More was to come from Sitaram Roy, another scholar from their group, who dated it to the 18th century. But when he was confronted with its decipherment by two living authorities on epigraphy, Dr Ajai Mitra Shastri and Dr KV Ramesh, he meekly admitted that he had neither seen the full photograph of the inscription nor did he know about its decipherment. Thus, their bold posture and strident stand without knowing the subject ended in a whimper.

Initially, Irfan Habib declared that it was an inscription which originally belonged to some private collection but had been cleverly planted by the VHP to misguide the public. When that argument did not attract traction, he revised his opinion and asserted that it was not from the private collection but the '*Treta ka Thakur*' inscription from the Lucknow Museum, stolen and planted at the demolition site by the VHP, to hoodwink the general public. But, unfortunately for Irfan Habib, a clarification from the Lucknow Museum authorities that the '*Treta ka Thakur*' inscription, alleged to have been asserted by Irfan Habib, as stolen and planted by the VHP, was in their safe custody, completely exposed the Professor Emeritus of AMU. This Professor is in the habit of resorting to such gimmicks with impunity.

On 18 June 1992, while the land in front of Babri Masjid was levelled up, several architectural members associated with temples such as *amalaka* and *chadya jala* were encountered. While *chadya jala* is used for constructing the shikhara, the *amalaka* is the crowning member of the temple, just below the *kalasha*. With the help of these two parts, it is possible to reconstruct the upper part of a North Indian temple. The list prepared and submitted to the Hon'ble Court by Dr Rakesh Tiwari, Director, Uttar Pradesh State Archaeology, included 263 antiquities associated with the Hindu temples. With every passing day, strong evidence, in favour of the temple, below the Masjid was coming out, which naturally embarrassed the Marxist historians.

A GPR Survey (Ground Penetrating Radar Survey) conducted by Tojo Vikas International, a Canadian company, on 17 March 2003, indicated that there were ancient structures below the mosque. This caused much anxiety in the dovecot of the Marxist group. What is the nature and size of the structures below the mosque? Only an excavation would reveal. The Aligarh historians were now restless because they had earlier declared that the Babri mosque was built on 'virgin land' and there was nothing below it. But now, the GPR Survey was proving them wrong.

The direction of the Hon'ble High Court on 5 March 2003 to the Archaeological Survey of India to excavate the site and determine whether there was any temple below the Babri Masjid came as another rude shock to the Marxist group. On 10 March 2003, Irfan Habib and others realising the fact that the excavation would expose them fully, tried to make one feebler attempt to stop the excavation at any cost on various flimsy grounds. In their panic reaction, they questioned the ability and impartiality of the ASI to conduct such a scientific excavation. Indirectly, he was painting all the archaeologists of the Archaeological Survey of India as Hindu chauvinists. The medieval historian, who had no training in archaeology, had the arrogance to question the competence of the Archaeological Survey of India, the country's premier institution.

Now, they wanted to stop the excavation at any cost. The inevitable was happening closer than what they had expected. Generally, the Aligarh Marxists and I are at daggers drawn. In their frustration and as a last attempt, they pressed Saiyid Zaheer Husain Jafri, a former student of Irfan Habib and now Professor Delhi University, to talk to me to find out ways to get the excavation stopped. At that time, I was posted in Agra as Superintending Archaeologist. When Jafry contacted me over the phone, I informed him that nobody could stop it, as the excavation was as per the directions of the Hon'ble High Court. I further told him that in the excavations under Prof Lal, I was there in the team and had seen the temple remains under the mosque. Reminding him about my press statement to this effect in 1990, I requested him to join in settling a problem that had been troubling the nation for the last many years. When Dr Jafry found me firm in my stand, he did not continue the discussion further. It appeared to me that he was speaking to me as per the instruction of some other person. This panic reaction was an implicit admission of the possibility of getting Hindu structures below the mosque.

According to Dr Meenakshi Jain, the Professor of History at Gargi College, it was quite a U-turn and a complete reversal from the earlier stand of the Marxist group. Earlier, their stand was that the mosque was built on virgin and vacant land. If the excavations of the site would bring out temple remains below the mosque, which now seemed to be inevitable, it would further seal the fate of Marxist historians. Hence, they started shifting the goalposts according to their convenience.

As per the court order, the Archaeological Survey undertook the excavation under the veteran Archaeologist, Dr BR Mani, assisted by an able team of archaeologists and technical staff. The team excavated 90 trenches between 12 March and 7 August 2003.

Dr BR Mani, known for the meticulous care and precision with which he excavates, has written under what adverse conditions he and his team had to work.

While the excavation was very well in progress, a Director from the ASI, who claimed closeness to VHP, repeatedly made many failed attempts to install him as the Director of the excavation replacing Dr BR Mani. The fact that the Minstry of Culture and Mrs Gauri Chatterje, the Directo General, Archaeological Survey of India saw through the game and refused to be guided by the extreme rightists, is a testimony to the integrity of the ASI. If that person was appointed as the Director of the Ayodhya excavation, it would have created further controversies.

The excavation under Dr BR Mani exposed more than fifty brick bases in seventeen rows, suggesting that the demolished temple was not ordinary but a huge one. It may be recalled that during the excavation of BB Lal, only a few temple brick bases were exposed. The huge structure excavated by BR Mani ran in the North-South and East-West direction, with a minimum dimension of 50×30m. The temple brick bases in the central part could not be exposed, as Ram Lalla was enshrined there. However, recently in May 2020, while the ground was being levelled, several temple pillars, idols and Shivalinga were again reported after transplanting Ram Lalla, confirming the earlier discovery. The five feet Shivalinga, seven pillars of black stone and broken idols, further strengthened the arguments in favour of the temple.

The *makara parnala*, (crocodile-faced gargoyle) for draining out *Abhisheka jala* (sacred water poured over the deity) exclusively used in temple architecture was another conclusive proof in favour of the existence of an earlier temple. Several other temple architectural members also emerged one after the other from the excavated trenches. Carved architectural members with foliage patterns, *amalaka*, door jamb with semicircular pilaster, broken octagonal shaft of black schist pillar, lotus motif, and circular shrine having the *parnala* were all irrefutable evidence of the presence of a temple below the mosque.

The way the Marxist historians opposed the ASI report

submitted by Prof Lal and Dr BR Mani not only showed their lack of experience in understanding the archaeological strata but also a malicious mindset, which enjoys sadistic pleasure in creating trouble with selfish motives. They went to the extent of saying that the brick bases were not original ones but fabricated by the ASI officials. The simple question was, how could one fabricate, while everything was being recorded with videography, under the surveillance of independent judicial members appointed by the Honourable Court? Besides the Judicial Members, the Babri Masjid Action Committee Members and their experts and lawyers were also overseeing everything very minutely. If fabrication was going on, why didn't they stop it at that time? As a measure of extraordinary precaution to make the excavation free from all types of manipulations, 52 Muslims were included in the team of the 131 labourers. When all such precautionary measures were in place, how does one manipulate the data? Such malicious accusations were a reflection of an afflicted mindset.

It is amusing to note that one of their experts, D Mandal said that the brick bases excavated by Prof BB Lal, was not brick bases (1976–77) but a long wall, which was cut and shaped by Prof Lal to look like brick bases. Had it been a wall, a simple look at the section of the trench would have revealed whether it was a wall or brick bases. This shows the shocking lack of experience of Babri Masjid experts in interpreting the sections of the trenches. In every excavation, the first lesson of archaeology is to train an apprentice, to read the section of an excavated trench. The skill of an archaeologist depends upon his expertise to read it. An experienced archaeologist reads the section of an excavated trench like a book. By misreading sections of excavation trenches, D Mandal brought disgrace to the Institution in which he was working and misguided further discussions on the subject. Dr Suraj Bhan, another Marxist archaeologist, realising the folly of his comrade, admitted it as brick bases but diluted its significance by interpreting it as the brick bases of a cowshed.

The unholy nexus of Marxist historians and few journalists of English newspapers helped muddy the water and fomented trouble. The method of operation of the nexus has been recalled with alarm by Prof BB Lal in his book *Rama, His Historicity, Mandir and Setu*. Once, while Prof Lal had gone to sleep, he was woken up by Dr Suraj Bhan of the said group, asking him to show the drawing of the pillar bases at Ayodhya. When he was told the drawings were under the custody of the ASI, which would be available in the morning the next day, this Professor was annoyed and left the place immediately. The next day, what Prof Lal read in the newspaper was a statement by the same professor that while the pillar bases in the Janmabhumi area did exist, these belonged to a cowshed! One should marvel at the flight of imagination of these historians! The second excavation under Dr BR Mani in 2003 has exposed more than fifty pillar bases in 17 rows. How would do they explain the fifty pillar bases of the latest excavation of Ayodhya?

Once Dr Suraj Bhan came to me with the same ploy and trick while I was working in Bhopal. He told me that he had come to attend some meetings with the state Archaeology and thought of utilising the spare time to see some of the excavated materials of Sanchi kept in the reserve collection. He said that he was in a hurry as he had only one hour at his disposal. I told him that the material was in Sanchi and it would take one hour to reach there. I further expressed my inability to show him the material, as the reserve collection required permission from the Delhi Headquarters of the ASI as it was under the Museum branch. Annoyed at my reaction, he started flaunting his position as a Member of the Central Advisory Board of Archaeology and therefore, he didn't require any such permission. I said that CABA Membership was meant for something else, and that did not entitle him any privileges with regards to the antiquities under the reserve collection of the Museum. He threatened me that he would make a complaint against me to the Director-General and also speak to the Press in Bhopal. My assertion that I could call the press persons then and there to my office to facilitate him to talk to them forced him to leave my room in a huff. I immediately pressed all the buttons to alert the Press. He neither complained to the Director-General nor spoke to the Press. Perhaps, somebody had advised him that I enjoyed an excellent relationship with the Press in Bhopal. Better counsel had prevailed.

The discovery of a circular temple of the 10th century with a *parnala* on the north for draining out the *abhisheka jala* was interpreted by Babri experts as a Buddhist *stupa* without knowing the fact that *stupas* are solid structures, whereas this was a circular temple with a hollow space in the centre like the Shiva temples of Chandreh, Masaun and Indore, all of which are in Madhya Pradesh. Similar temples made of brick are found in Kurari and Tindauli in Fatehpur District. Most of the Chausat Yogini temples like Dudhai in Jhansi, Mitauli in Morena and Bheraghat in Jabalpur are also circular temples. I had carried out many conservation works in the last two temples, and both are now pilgrimage and tourist centres.

Moreover, Babri experts were unaware of the fact that the parnala is never part of a *stupa* but an essential part of a temple. And that too, this *parnala* was oriented towards North, as is mandated by Hindu temple architecture. Wherever the holy rivers take a turn towards the north, that place is considered holy in Hinduism. Holy places like Gangotri, Yamunotri, Hardwar, Lakshman Jhula, Prayag, Kashi, etc., are prominent places where the Ganga and the Yamuna take a turn towards the north and it is known as *Uttara Vahini*. Unable to find support from any corner in the face of unassailable evidence coming from scholars like Dr BR Mani, another last-ditch attempt was to prove that the unearthed circular structure was a Muslim shrine. Everything that ended in the mosque was the best form of excavation for them.

The ASI interpreted the discovery of a wall, and three niches at the site as temples remain based on associated finds of terracotta images, which the Babri group claimed as the *qanati* mosque or *idgah* mosque. When it was pointed out during the cross-examination that the Babri Action Committee had not made any claim for the *idgah* and had asserted then that the Babri mosque was standing on virgin land, the Aligarh experts had no other way but to cut a sorry figure. Dr Meenakshi Jain sums up the embarrassing condition of Babri experts in her book, *Rama &*

Ayodhya, "The court took cognizance of the shifting stance of the pro-Babri archaeologists. Initially, they claimed that the disputed structure was constructed on a spot that was neither a place of worship nor the site of a previous Hindu religious structure, nor was there any evidence to associate it with the birthplace of Lord Rama. However, as the excavation progressed, a marked change in the approach of the plaintiffs became evident. Some archaeologists, appearing on behalf of the plaintiffs (Babri Masjid Action Committee) tried to "set up a new case" that there appeared to be an Islamic structure beneath the disputed structure. (pages 869–3870, para 3809) Meenakshi Jain, *Rama & Ayodhya*, pp 220–221). It was one of the strongest judicial indictments on the integrity of an academic group.

The excavation also brought out a number of terracotta figures of humans, animals, *kirthimukhas*, divine couples, lady figures, figures of cobras, horses, elephants, tortoises and crocodiles, etc. (62 human figures and 131 animal figures and a carved *yakshi*). In short, all the items recovered from the excavation site conclusively proved that there was a temple at the Babri site before the construction of the mosque. Keeping any such figures in the mosque is prohibited in Islam. How do they then explain the presence of such terracotta images and sculptures in such large numbers in the premises of a mosque? The archaeological evidence presented by the Archaeological Survey of India in favour of the temple was so overwhelming that the Honourable High Court was left with no other choice but to give the entire disputed land to the temple. Yet, in a spirit of accommodating all the contending parties, the Honourable Court, in its order dated 30 September 2010, divided the property and tried to find a solution to the nagging problem.

But the Honourable High Court's order did not satisfy any of the contending parties, and the dispute was further taken up in the Honourable Supreme Court for a solution. In an attempt to find an answer, the court started hearing the case on a day-to-day basis. Frantic efforts were going on to find out a solution outside the court, and a committee headed by Justice FMI Kallifulla, Shri Shri Ravi Shankar and Advocate Sriram Panchu was constituted by the Honourable Court. One-day Advocate Panchu contacted me to get my reaction about the possibility of allowing *namaz* in a few of the non-living mosques of Lucknow and Delhi as part of a negotiated settlement of Ayodhya. I politely told him that such an action would open Pandora`s box in the whole country and there would be demand from various communities to open monuments for prayers and *pujas*. In a few monuments like the Qutub Minar, Bhojshala, etc., there would be fights between communities as they were temples converted into mosques. There are many such sites converted as mosques in the country. Similarly, there could be problems in Ajanta, Ellora, Elephanta and many other monuments also. Shri Panchu realised the seriousness of the problem.

In October 2019, when the final days of the arguments were drawing to a close, I knew that the Marxist historians headed by Irfan Habib would come out with some Press statement to create confusion. Having known, fought and emerged successfully from all the traps carefully laid out by them at Aligarh, I could gauge what their next step would be. Outsmarting them at their own old game, I gave a statement to Kumar Shakti Shekhar of the *Times of India*, on 1st October 2019, describing in detail the temple remains that I had seen in 1976–77 excavation and the large volume of evidence provided by the excavation conducted under Dr BR Mani in 2003.

Meanwhile, a concerted attempt was in progress to paint the excavation report, presented by Dr BR Mani, as being communally prejudiced, and therefore, it should not be accepted. Their earlier stand was that the ASI was not competent enough to excavate Ayodhya. But now, the communal virus was unabashedly injected by them to vitiate the entire atmosphere. Once communalism is set in motion, it would spread dangerously in an ever-widening circle, engulfing everything.

In my statement, I defended the excavation report fully and said that the report is not an ordinary report, which the court could reject, but it was a 'court commissioner's report' as the ASI had excavated as per the order of the Honourable High Court. Hence, the report should be accepted in totality.

I also argued that four Muslim officers of the Archaeological

Survey of India, namely, Dr Ghulam Sayyidain Khwaja, Director, Arabic and Persian Epigraphy, Dr Atiqul Rahman Siddiqui, Former Superintending Archaeologist, Agra, Dr Afsar Adil Hashmi, Former Deputy Superintending Archaeologist, Bhopal and Dr Zulfiqar Ali, Superintending Archaeologist, Chandigarh were co-authors of the excavation report submitted by Dr BR Mani. The storm it unleashed in the religious, political and social spheres were phenomenal. This unknown fact, known to officers of Archaeological Survey of India only, took the wind out of the sails of the Communist rhetoric and the accompanying communal propaganda. Now it was clear to them that it was a lost cause, and their communal propaganda would not whip up the communal frenzy as expected.

It was a new revelation for liberals and Muslim intellectuals that the report was co-authored by four Muslim archaeologists. Several people telephoned me to verify the facts. The Aligarh Communists, for the first time, came to know that their communal rhetoric was not yielding the earlier dividends. The Muslim intelligentsia started seeing through its nefarious and divisive games.

Soon there were meetings of Muslim intelligentsia in Lucknow under the aegis of the organisations such as Muslims for Peace headed by Kamal Khan, a senior journalist based in Lucknow. They were actively supported by Lt General Zameer Uddin Shah, the former Dy Chief of the Army and former Vice-Chancellor of Aligarh Muslim University. At the forefront of the team was Anis Ansari, IAS, Padma Shri Mansoor Hasan and many retired bureaucrats, soldiers, lawyers, journalists, doctors and businessmen. The Central Sunni Waqf Board Chairman, Zafar Farooqui, also solidly stood with those who wanted to hand over the mosque to the Hindus. Many members of the Waqf Board like Abrar Ahammed, Muhammed Junaid Siddiqui and Adnan Ferruk Sha also openly came out in favour of handing over the entire site for the temple construction. In the All India Muslim Personal Law Board, Maulana Salman Nadvi, the distinguished scholar from Nadva, pleaded with the rest of the members to behave in the right spirit of Islam. He had discussions with Shri Shri Ravi Shankar, the great spiritual leader of international repute. Although Maulana Salman Nadvi was expelled and hounded out by extremist Muslims, he firmly stood his ground. By quoting Islamic scriptures, he justified the gifting of the land for the temple. In many of his interviews, Maulana Nadvi has described how sincerely he tried to convince the Babri Action Committee members to gift the land for temple construction.

Right from the very beginning, the enlightened Shia community was in favour of the temple, which was led by Maulana Qalbe Jawwad Saheb, an eminent scholar of outstanding repute. Wasim Rizvi, the former, four-time President of Shia Waqf Board, was very vocal in articulating the opinion of the Shia community in favour of the temple.

Divested of the support of the moderate Muslims, the Aligarh Marxist historians now had the support of the extremist Muslims only. They were now desperate to cling on to it with some ploys and gimmicks. Although defeated in their own game, I was sure that they would make one more attempt to hit me from the back by resorting to low-level tactics, for which they were notorious and had over the years earned a dubious distinction.

Thus, as a rejoinder to my interview in *The Times of India*, on 12 October, another statement was made by Dr Nadeem Rizvi, Chairman of the Department of history, AMU that KK Muhammed was not a member of the excavation team headed by Prof Lal in 1976–77. He said that before making this statement, he had scrutinised my documents in AMU, and I was in Aligarh Muslim University in 1976–77. While serving the AMU, how could I participate in an excavation conducted by Prof Lal?

I was in the School of Archaeology when I participated in the excavation at Ayodhya under Prof Lal in 1976–77. It was not me alone, but the field training of the whole batch of the School of Archaeology 1976–77 was at Ayodhya. I joined the Aligarh Muslim University, the Archaeology section, as a Technical Assistant in the month of August 1978. This is a matter of records, and anyone can get all this information under the Right to Information (RTI) also. But by manipulating, mixing and confusing data, Dr Rizvi, who had earlier on two occasions also resorted to such substandard tricks, tried to argue that I was not a member of the excavation team of Prof Lal. Unfortunately, the dignity of the teaching profession is sometimes seriously undermined by the presence of such persons in academic institutions. As per journalistic ethics, *The Times of India* should have sought my clarification before publishing such a defamatory statement against me. In a clear-cut violation of all moral and journalistic ethics, *The Times of India* tried to give credence to the view that I was not part of the excavation in 1976–77 under Prof Lal.

Prof Lal was not in India as he had gone to America. I contacted him via email with the help of Neera Mishra of Draupadi Trust and apprised him of the content of the combined efforts of *The Times of India* and Marxist historians. Prof Lal immediately wrote back to Kumar Shakti Shekhar, who filed my original story that KK Muhammed was very well a member of his excavation team in 1976–77. Shakti Shekhar, as part of his research work, contacted the living members of the team under Prof BB Lal, such as Raj Nath Kaw, the Chief Photographer, ASI, Ashok Kumar Pandey, the former Superintending Archaeologist and Rama Kant Chaturvedi, the former Director of the Municipal Museum, Gwalior. All of them confirmed my presence throughout the excavation in detail and spoke about the various aspects of the Ayodhya excavation. Although Shakti Shekhar contacted Jayaram Ramesh, the former Union Minister, as his wife Jayashri Jayaram was also a member of the team, at Ayodhya site, Shri Jayaram Ramesh informed Kumar Shakti Shekhar that Jayashri passed away a few months earlier. I met Jayaram Ramesh only once in a dinner meeting hosted by Srilankan Embassy. The moment I introduced myself as Jayashri's classmate, the meeting became informal, and at home, he spoke to Jayashri about my meeting with him. Later on when he went to Vaishali, a heritage site associated with Buddha in Bihar, he specifically enquired about me.

Madhyamam, a newspaper in Kerala associated with the Jamaat-i-Islami, published the version of the Aligarh Marxists with all the frills. Apart from Nadeem Rizvi's version, it also published a separate independent version from Irfan Habib himself. In a bizarre statement, dated, 14.10.2019 he categorically asserted that KK Muhammed had no association with Ayodhya at all, what to talk of participating in the excavation. This canard was totally ignored by the Malayalam media, including *Deshabhimani*, the official Marxist newspaper, as they were familiar with me.

One of the persons who attested to my participation at the Ayodhya excavation was Rajnath Kaw, who, besides being the photographer, was a seasoned archaeologist and a writer on archaeological subjects. It was he who taught me how to delineate and mark layers in scientifically excavated trenches and write the daily reports. Raj Nath Kaw is the father of the well known investigative journalist Sanjay Kaw of the Statesman, who had sneaked incognito to the camps of the Karsevaks of Ayodhya in 1992 December with a fake identity card. Sanjay, a young man from Kashmir, was interrogated at many places to prove his identity. Posing as a Pandit who had to discontinue his Engineering due to insurgency in the Kashmir Valley, he smartly managed and diligently collected all the information, while most of the journalists were confined to Shan e Avadh hotel and was the first to predict the impending demolition of the Babri mosque in The Statesman, on 4th December, two days before it happened on 6th December 1992. It was exclusively on the basis of Sanjay Kaw's report, SB Chavan, the Home Minister, rejected the contention of the BJP in the Parliament that the demolition of the Babri masjid was not pre-planned. When Dipen Gosh (CPI_M), a Member of the Parliament, asked when you read Sanjay's report, SB Chavan candidly confessed that it was after 6th (The Statesman, 22.12.1992) Where the Central administration and intelligence failed, and the state was giving solemn assurance, Sanjay made a realistic report from the battleground, risking his life. Later on, Sanjay was a prosecution witness against Shri LK Advani, Murali Manohar Joshy, Uma Bharati, Vinay Katyar and many other Sangh Parivar leaders in the CBI case and an independent witness in front of the Liberhan Commission.

Had I made any false statement about my participation in

the excavation, as stated by medieval historians of Aligarh, an uncompromising Sanjay would have been the first to file another investigative report against me. Sanjay suffered heavily at the hands of Kashmiri Muslim extremists, badly beaten by the police and was fortunate to reach Delhi with his certificates. Still, unlike me, Sanjay does not harbour any ill will against his tormentors. Naturally, most of the Kashmiri pandits, then, leading a despicable life in refugee camps of Delhi, might not have looked kindly to their prodigal son.

Once I asked Sanjay how could he be so objective and dispassionate, despite being suffered at the hands of Muslim extremists. He disarmed me by saying that you did your duty as a professional archaeologist, and I did my duty as a professional journalist. But I felt sorry for the medieval historians of Aligarh who were bereft of any such ethics, moral principles and professionalism. Recently while discussing a wide range of subjects, Sanjay told me that he better understood the anguish and agony of Afghan refugees in various camps.

Raj Nath Kaw sold his house in Kashmir for a paltry amount, not in distress sale but to help a suffering Muslim family. Sometimes, even amidst the bombshells and gunfires, we hear stories of triumph of humanitarian considerations over barbarity.

What I have written above is a grave reflection of the intellectual degeneration to which Irfan Habib, a Professor Emeritus of a Central University and Nadeem Rizvi, the Chairman of the Centre of Advanced Study, History, has gone down. It shows very clearly that Dr Irfan Habib could not upgrade himself even after becoming a Professor of Emeritus. What kind of history are they going to teach the next generation? Dr Nadeem Rizvi has perfected the art of telling false stories and using foul language, for which he was earlier suspended by LT Gen Zamir Uddin Shah, the then Vice-Chancellor of the Aligarh Muslim University. Elder brother of Nasir Uddin Shah, he was another Vice-chancellor who could not be intimidated by the Communists and did not care for the secular certificate of the Aligarh Communists.

The rebuttal of Prof Lal stating that I was a member of the

excavation team at Ayodhya, once more exposed both Irfan Habib and his dear student Rizvi, now the Chairman of the Department of History. But the sad part of the story is that the Ministry of HRD and the Aligarh Muslim University took no action against both these historians.

When the judgment of Ayodhya came on 11 November 2019, the whole country heaved a sigh of relief, as it was the most perfect and balanced judgment one could ever think of under the then prevailing circumstances. If any part of the disputed area was given to the Muslim community, that would have proved to be an ever festering sore thumb. Instead, much more land than what they had claimed was given to them so that they could develop the area in a bigger way. But it was doomsday for Communist historians of Aligarh and their supporters. News coming from the Department of History, Aligarh, informed me that the Marxist historians were utterly shattered. Broken-hearted and frustrated, they were running up and down in the Department. Frantic consultations were going on to decide the next plan of action. The fact that the Muslim community has fully accepted the judgment served as a dampener and warning for them. Finally, good counsel prevailed upon the fence-sitters, and the Muslims finally accepted the land given to them.

The Aligarh Communists resorted to every method to stop finding a final solution to Ayodhya issue. They tried to provoke every section of the community. It was easy for them to operate as there were a number of well oiled organisational networks with them. But, still, this time Humpty Dumpty had a great fall. But I am doubtful "whether all the perfumes Arabia can sweeten their hands" in the case of Ayodhya.

□

My Stand against Hindutva Activists

While standing against Muslim communalists and pseudo-secularists, I also had to fight with a BJP MLA, Jawahar Prasad, who had encroached into the mausoleum of Shershah Suri, a protected monument of the Government of India, at Sasaram in Bihar. A man of little education, Jawahar Prasad had become the MLA of Sasaram, in the aftermath of the Hindu Muslim communal riot that broke out in the city. As he won the election continuously for the second time in the wake of communal riots for *Ram Janmabhumi*, he grew into a law unto himself. In a brazen display of arrogance and muscle power, he encroached upon the mausoleum of Shershah Suri and started constructing many structures around the temple. Since 1977, the ASI had filed sixteen complaints, but the district administration and the police took no action, as they were also supporting such illegal activities. In 2000, the MLA tried to enlarge the construction, hoping that the present Bihar ASI Chief, a Muslim, would not muster the courage to object to it, as the Central Government was under the BJP.

Contrary to his expectations, I immediately took up the issue with the district administration but found the District Magistrate in dread of the powerful MLA. He instead advised me to steer clear of the MLA, as he enjoyed much muscle power in the area and political clout in the Centre. Since the District Administration and police were not supporting, there was little I could do, except filing the routine complaints, as my predecessors used to do. Meanwhile, the MLA personally trespassed into the government office at Sasaram, beat up ASI Officer Sarvan Kumar, and tried to throw him from the terrace of the office. Luckily for Sarvan Kumar, the staff members standing below could save him. The MLA was such a terror that neither the Medical Officer treated him nor were the police ready to file an FIR. Later on, after my intervention, the police filed a case.

A few days after that, the District Magistrate rang me up to request Sarvan Kumar's transfer as his continued stay in Sasaram could cause a communal flare-up. I knew that this proposal was as per the demand of Jawahar Prasad. I replied that Sarvan Kumar was discharging his duties as a government officer, and it was the MLA who was responsible for all the problems. Not only was the request of the DM rejected, but I also filed another case against the MLA in the Tribunal of SC and ST, as Sarvan Kumar was a member of Scheduled Caste. Since the situation was getting worse with every passing day, I wrote a letter to the Chief Secretary, VS Dubey, complaining about the illegal temple and non-cooperation of the district administration. Later on, I met the Chief Secretary and apprised him about the seriousness of the issue. As the Chief Secretary also did not take any positive action and the temple construction was in progress, after exhausting all the administrative remedies, I approached the Honorable High Court, Patna, requesting a stay against the illegal temple construction and removal of the same from the protected area. We put up a brave fight, and our Adv. SN Patak of the Patna High Court diligently followed the case, that the Hon. Court granted the stay and directed the district administration to implement the court direction.

This was a mortal blow for Jawahar Prasad, the state administration, the District Collector and the BJP. For the first time, the prestige of Jawahar Prasad was in tatters, and he could feel earth sinking under his feet. His political opponents made full use of it, and Prasad and the BJP miserably lost the next election from Sasaram. When Prasad was breathing fire and brimstone and whipping up communal frenzy against me, my friends in Sasaram were busy distributing the xerox copies of Panchjanya, an RSS magazine, which had explained my statement about the Ayodhya issue. This caused further erosion in the support base of Jawahar Prasad. Later on, I wrote a letter to Sushil Kumar Modi, the opposition leader of BJP, in Bihar Assembly against Jawahar Prasad and his illegal acts in the Shershah tomb.

The news that the illegal temple construction had been stopped at Sasaram, during the BJP's rule spread widely as many newspapers and periodicals covered them. Syed Shihabuddin, one of the active members of Babri Masjid Action Committee, wrote a letter to the Culture and Tourism Minister Anand Kumar, appreciating the principled stand taken by the ASI. The letter was forwarded to me by Komal Anand, IAS, the Director-General of the ASI. In my reply to Syed Shihabuddin, while thanking him for appreciating the work, I also touched upon the Ayodhya issue, as he was the main brain behind the Babri Masjid Action Committee. I wrote to him that I had participated in the excavation under Prof Lal and seen the temple remains and pillars beneath the mosque. I further pleaded with him to take cognizance of the reality and settle the issue by handing over the structure to the Hindu community. The last portion of the letter written on 27–10–2000, reads: "Since the Muslim opinion is changing in the right direction, it is your duty, Hon'ble Sir, to give a further forward push to it and take it to its logical conclusion so that Islam is painted in its true colours and we make a united India. Fondly, I do hope, and fervently I do pray that you would rise to your historical responsibility and change the course of history with your bold and constructive decision to create a new united India."

A few days later, I received his reply that a meeting of the community leaders, which was scheduled to meet shortly, would discuss the issue that I had raised, and I would be informed accordingly. The meeting did take place, and Syed Shihabuddin's letter came stating that no one supported the idea of giving up the Babri mosque to Hindus. After some time, he called me over the phone and requested to meet him, as he was coming to Patna. We had a long talk about the Babri issue, the temple below it, etc. When he quoted D Mandal and Suraj Bhan about the brick bases, I informed him that they did not have much experience in the field of archaeology and further cautioned that any further excavation would bring out many more temple remains. If this could be settled at this juncture by gifting the land to the Hindus, it would save Indian Muslims from facing an embarrassing situation. It appeared to me that he was in favour of a settlement but still under extreme pressure from the fellow Babri group and the Aligarh historians. While taking leave of him, I told him, "All the officials who supported me in putting a halt to Jawahar Prasad were Hindus. My Advocate SN Patak who fought this case and took it to a successful end, is a Brahmin." I could see from his face that he was undergoing some kind of inner questioning of his own conscience. But even after knowing everything, unable to take an independent and categorical stand. If this was the condition of a highly educated Indian Foreign Service Officer and an ex-MP, what could we expect from the ordinary Muslims? And my last sentence that all my supporters were Hindus in Sasaram issue was a sharp barb at him.

Once I had an occasion to go to Salalah in Oman as part of an excavation team led by Dr Michel Janson of the Achaean University, Germany. Our task was to excavate Al Balid, a medieval trade port, as a precursor to developing it as a tourist centre. In the hotel where we were staying, the Keralite staff members easily recognised me as the only Asian and Keralite. During the discussion, they invited me for delivering a talk to their members associated with SIMI (Student Islamic Movement of India). Some of their leaders knew about my opinion about the Ayodhya. Most of them were from Thalasseri and Kannur areas. I welcomed their invitation to speak and be part of the question-and-answer session, provided they ensure discipline and respect for persons with the opposite view. They not only agreed but also promised to maintain discipline.

I began my session citing examples of religious toleration from early Islamic history towards non-Muslims and profusely quoted from the Quran. Having mistaken me as a supporter of the Ayodhya issue, they never expected the recitation of Quranic *ayats* from me. I spoke at length about my participation at the Ayodhya excavation and the existence of temple remains by the side of the mosque. I also told them that Ayodhya was as important for Hindus as Mecca and Madinah were for Muslims. And then asked them how they would have felt if Mecca and Madinah were destroyed by some other communities and constructed their places of worship over it? Obviously, you cannot even imagine such a calamity. Such a situation would have created hundreds of *Jihadis* and thousands of suicide squads from among the Muslims. Do you expect Hindus, the majority community of the country, to live in permanent discomfiture, ignominy and insult? Was the Babri Masjid in any way associated with Prophet Muhammed? Had it been so, we could have justified the Muslim stand. Was it associated with the pious Caliphs, the second most important persons in Islam? Was it associated with any *Sahabees* (the companions of Prophet Muhammed) of Islam? Was it in any way connected with the *Auliyas* of Islam like Khawaja Moinuddin Chishti of Ajmer or Hazrat Nizamuddin Auliya of Delhi? Had it been so, I, too, would have stood with them. For Muslims, it is just another ordinary mosque associated with King Babur. For the Hindus, it is one of the holiest places associated with Hinduism. Ayodhya, Mathura and Kashi are the places that have provided the warp and woof of Hinduism. Why should Muslims be adamant about keeping such holy places of Hindus and making it an eternal festering sore thumb? Muslims should have voluntarily handed it over to Hindus for constructing the Shri Rama temple.

I narrated a painful incident from my school days when the Baitul Muqaddis in Jerusalem, the third holiest place for Muslims, was captured by Israel in the Arab-Israel War in 1967. Dejected and disappointed at the loss, all the Muslims of my village had assembled at the Jami Mosque in Koduvally and tearfully prayed to Allah for the reconquest of the place. The entire Islamic world was in disarray and tears. The anguish and agony the Hindus feel at the thought of Ayodhya, Mathura, and Kashi are comparable to that pain Muslims had gone through in 1967. It is like silent grief that bleeds inwardly. Whenever a Hindu sees such a mosque standing in the place of a destroyed holy place of his own, his soul writhes in pain like an impaled worm when it is forced down on a fish hook. I stayed in Ayodhya for two months. Every day thousands were thronging there just to have a *darshan* of Ram Lalla. Most of them were coming from far-off parts of the country on foot without proper clothes and footwear to guard against the hot sun and the biting cold. It was only faith that was sustaining them. Couldn't we respect their religious faith and belief? Couldn't we heal their aching hearts?

On hearing my words, the entire audience plunged into pin-drop silence and reflection. I continued my speech. "After Independence, Muslims were given a separate country. In that religiously polarised and surcharged atmosphere, it could have been easy for Hindus to get India declared as a Hindu country. There were concerted efforts from some Hindu organisations for making a Hindu India. However, Gandhi, Nehru, Patel and Azad were highly eminent leaders who could not think of anything less than that of a secular country. Even after giving the Muslims a separate country, India has been declared a secular democratic state with full citizenship for the Muslims. Do you have another example of this kind in world history? All this came at a great price. Bapu, the half-naked *Fakir* dressed in a loincloth, like the ancient Rishis, had to pay with his lifeblood. Even when he fell down to the bullet of a religiously mad man and as life ebbed out, the last words the Mahatma recited were "Hey Ram." Hindus are pleading for the Birthplace of that Ram whose name that apostle of non-violence had murmured at his last minute.

I stopped for a while and then resumed asking a question: Don't you think India's greatest plus point is that we have a secular country? I further asked, "Do you think India would have been a secular country had it been a Muslim majority country? I got no response from the audience." Never, had India been a Muslim majority country; it would never have been a secular country. That is the greatness of Hinduism and its broad-mindedness. We have to acknowledge this all-encompassing spirit of Hinduism. Whether you believe in God or don't believe, you are a Hindu. People from every religion must learn to respect the religion of the other person. Religion is an accident of fate. We follow our own respective religions because of indoctrination from childhood. People should appreciate the historical realities and cultivate a mutual understanding of the religion of the other person. If we cultivate this feeling, then only India will be a real secular country. I call it reverse thinking. Let Hindus look at the problems of Muslims from the standpoint of Muslims and vice versa. If we develop this line of thinking, many of our problems will automatically find a solution. But adjustment and elasticity are required more from Muslims than from Hindus. Hindus have demonstrated their ability to swim together. Muslims should modify their thinking that their's is the only right religion and apart from them, all others would go to hell." When I spoke this much, a question arose from somewhere in the audience. If we give up these three places, will the VHP not raise a demand for giving up 3000 mosques? I replied: "I am talking about a compromise formula. No unreasonable demand would be endorsed by the Hindu community themselves. Even today, organisations like Vishwa Hindu Parishad, Bajrang Dal, Ram Sena, etc., have not found general acceptance among Hindus. Hindus from various walks of life will come forward to oppose such outlandish claims. They would not even allow Muslims to get involved in it. The Hindu community itself would fight for Muslims. That is the greatness of Hinduism.

After the speech was over, I had the impression that the audience largely agreed with me to relinquish the Muslims' claim and amicably solve the problems. But they did not say anything openly. After the talk, some of the senior members took me to a separate room and asked me: "Why do you not present the facts exactly like this in front of persons like Syed Shahabuddin or other Babri Masjid leaders?" I replied: "I don't personally know

Shahabuddin Saheb nor anybody in the Babri Masjid Action Committee." However, within a few months of this meeting, the temple issue at the Mausoleum of Shershah Suri gave me an opportunity to write to him and discuss with him.

In Kunnamangalam near Calicut, I had met a few Welfare Party members associated with the Jamaat-i-Islami. They were engaged in the task of building houses for poor people. In the list of beneficiaries, I found the name of a Hindu woman Sushma. I wholeheartedly congratulated them for this kind of social service without caring for religion and also gave financial assistance to their scheme. They invited me to speak on the Ayodhya issue in one of their welfare committee meetings. Here also I repeated what I had spoken at Salalah in Oman. They listened to what I said in rapt attention and perhaps agreed also with me. I expected a question-and-answer session, but the organisers did not want it. But I was sure that the Welfare Party sympathisers had moved away from the belligerent attitude of other organisations, and younger Muslims have started developing a sympathetic attitude towards the Ayodhya issue. I felt that there should have been more such engagements with the Muslim youth. Indeed, one may not be able to convert them but at least can set them thinking. Individual perception in this meeting was also in favour of handing over the mosque to Hindus. But they would not say anything openly as they are all brainwashed and conditioned by periodic party meetings. What is laudable, however, is that they have started thinking freely. Later on, I heard that some visionary Muslims in Jamaat-i-Islami and Muslim League were also contemplating the idea of gifting the land to the Hindus, although they would never come out openly for fear of being thrown out of the community.

Both these discussions at Salalah and in Calicut with the hard-liners show how they have shown resilience by shifting from their earlier rigid stand on the *mandir* issue. I was in Aligarh from August 1978 to August 1988 as an employee. There also the general feeling was towards finding a solution by gifting the land. But their only fear was that it should not open Pandora's

Box for the VHP's endless list. The Muslim fear, in this case, is quite genuine, and I fully understand it. The best expression of this Muslim feeling was represented by Maulana Abul Hasan Ali Nadvi, popularly known as Ali Mia, the then Chief of the Muslim Personal Board and the Islamic seminary Dar-ul-Uloom Nadva. A man of encyclopedic learning, he was the greatest Islamic scholar of the time. There was an understanding between Ali Mia and Rajiv Gandhi that Rajiv Gandhi would reverse the judgment on the well-known Shah Bano case in return for a tacit understanding for the unlocking of the Ayodhya temple and the consequent foundation-laying ceremony for a new temple. Arif Muhammed Khan, a Minister in Rajiv Gandhi's Ministry, who resigned because of his principled stand, has spoken about this unwritten deal on several occasions. But later on, to the dismay of all well-meaning Muslims, after the Shah Bano case was reversed, the Muslim leaders did not support Ali Mia in amicably solving the problem of Ayodhya. In his autobiography, Ali Mia blamed the Babri leadership for provoking Hindu revivalism and described their movement as leading Muslims on the path of 'collective suicide.' It was the Aligarh Communist historians who paved the way for the 'collective suicide' of the Muslims by supporting and guiding the Babri Masjid Action Committee.

In Agra also, I took such a stand against Hindu extremists. One day while I was inspecting the western part of the Taj Mahal along with Dr Shyam Singh, the Chief Horticulturist and Arkhit Pradhan, the Assistant Archaeologist, there, we saw an illegal extension of a temple and a lot of building materials heaped up near a 19th century temple. This temple was within the protected area of the Archaeological Survey of India. Since the temple was there earlier, there was nothing wrong with it. But they had already constructed an extension to it, which was illegal. The building material heaped up was for further enlarging it. Immediately, I reported the matter to the Commissioner and Collector, and a team was constituted to demolish the extended portion forthwith. Extreme Hindu groups tried their level best to get it stopped as it was the BJP that was ruling at the Centre in 2003. I went to the demolition site along with SP Singh, Rakesh Tiwari and photographer Srivastava, all staff members of the ASI. From the state administration, the Additional District Magistrate Tripathy was there, and he had provided enough police protection at the site. Within an hour, we demolished the extended portion of the temple, while VHP was burning my effigy at Purani Chawk in Agra. The protesters spared the Commissioner and the District Magistrate, and their real target of the attack was me. A few months earlier, the group had attacked the office of the Archaeological Survey of India at 24 Mall Road and damaged furniture, etc. Here also, although I was the main target, had a providential escape as I had gone out for some official work a few minutes before they reached. This action against Hindu extremists was also taken while the BJP was ruling at the Centre.

In 2002, a Parliamentary Committee for Tourism and Culture came to Agra for inspection. One of the members, Shri Banatwala, a senior Muslim League member, was very much prejudiced against the Archaeological Survey of India and asked a pointed question about the percentage of expenditure spent on medieval monuments, a euphemism for Islamic monuments. When I explained to him that 90 per cent of the funds were being utilised on medieval monuments as there were no roads to some of the temple sites, it was a revelation for him. When I narrated in a private conversation the action taken against illegal temples in Sasaram and demolition of the extended part of a temple in Agra, he looked at me in disbelief and told me: "Nowadays nobody musters the courage to take such drastic action against religious structures." When I took strong action against the illegally extended temple by the side of the Taj Mahal, it was the intelligence officers of Agra who told VHP youths that they were demonstrating against a wrong person as it was he who stood in favour of the Ayodhya Temple. I could take such strong actions against illegal temples, both at Sasaram and at Agra, while BJP was ruling at the Centre because of strong secular credentials. In

Agra also, both the press and the public stood behind me.

What Indian Muslims are lacking and what they require is self-introspection and broad-mindedness. They should willingly accept the entire history of India as their own history. And Indian heroes like Shri Rama and Shri Krishna as their own heroes, just as Rustam and Sohrab are Persian heroes for entire Iran, although both were non- Muslims. Shri Rama and Shri Krishna need not be accepted as religious leaders but as national cultural icons of the country. They should also learn from the Muslims of Malaysia and Indonesia, who still celebrate the Ramayana and the Mahabharata with gusto, zeal and fervour, as they consider the epics to be part of their heritage and cultural legacy. Recently, when I participated in the World Ramayana Conference at Jabalpur, special troupes came from Indonesia to stage a performance of Javanese Ramayana. They told me that they give national importance to the Ramayana in Indonesia, and the 'Ramayana Kakawin' was written in the 9th century. The Malaysian Ramayana, 'Hikayat Seri Rama' was written in the 14th century. In Indonesia, the national emblem is Garuda, the vehicle of Vishnu, and their airline is also named after Garuda, the vehicle of Lord Vishnu. Similarly, Indonesia, where 87.2 per cent of the population are Muslims, has no mental reservation in inscribing Lord Ganesh on the currency of the country. Indonesia, a country with only a 1.7 per cent Hindu population, has 'Arjuna Vijaya statue' at the well-known Jakarta square, and Lord Hanuman is the official mascot of the Military Intelligence wing. It would be surprising to note that Bandung Institute of Technology, the most prestigious academic centre, has Lord Ganesh as its logo.

As Islam was born among Bedouins of Mecca with no rich culture to boast of, they adopted a lot from the neighbouring highly developed civilisations. Islam, during the period of expansion to Persia, Syria, Egypt, Spain, Central Asia, South Asia and India, has adopted many local traditions. The entire Islamic art and architecture, of which we are so rightfully proud today, is nothing but a total adoption from Sassanian Persia, Byzantine Syria and

Egypt as they were the developed cultures around the nascent Islamic region. With time, Islam adopted profusely from Central Asia and India. The great Sufi saints such as Khawaja Moin-ud-Din Chishti of Ajmir, Khawaja Bakhtiyar Kaki, Nizamuddin Auliya, Amir Khusro and Muhammad Ghaus, liberally assimilated from Hindu thoughts and yogic practices. This coming together of Hinduism and Islam into one single harmonious knot has elicited admiration from Sir Johns Marshall: "Seldom in the history of mankind has the spectacle been witnessed of two civilisations, so vast and so strongly developed, yet so radically similar, as the Muhammadan and Hindu meeting and mingling together."

But this unity process has suffered irreparable damage for various reasons, especially over the fight on the Ayodhya and Babri issue. The Marxist historians of Aligarh, for their narrow personal gains, have further aggravated it.

Muslims indeed have their own grievances about frequent communal riots in which many Muslims have been brutally killed. While admitting the fact that they have been on the receiving end in all these violent communal clashes, they have never stopped a while to think that many of these clashes could have been averted if they had behaved a little more responsibly? The terrible riots of Gujarat also flared up killing many Muslims, as a result of the burning of the Hindu pilgrims who were returning from Ayodhya. In such a situation, a reaction was inevitable. Of course, it was not an equal and opposite reaction. It far exceeded it. But that was the reprisal of a majority community, who had exhausted all its ways due to a chain of conflicts, and the most important being Ayodhya itself. Muslims drove the Hindus against the wall, where they were left with no other option except to turn around and fight back for self-respect and religion. But, it is to the credit of the Hindu community that all those who condemned such unjustifiable reprisals were also Hindus and Hindu intellectuals.

The lynching of persons such as Mohammed Akhlak and Pahlu Khan, and others have terrorised the Muslim community. But all those who condemned such inhuman activities and firmly stood with the Muslim community were also Hindus. Businessmen such as Shri Narayan Murthy of Infosys, Raghu Ram Rajan former Governor of the Reserve Bank of India boldly protested against it. Many intellectuals returned their awards and decorations as a mark of their protest against the rising intolerance. Sanjiv Rajendra Bhat, the IPS officer, has been dismissed from service. Teesta Setalvad was slapped with many cases. Such a bold stand by Hindus against their own co-religionists can happen only in India. But it is worthwhile to ponder whether Dr Irfan Habib, the historian behind the Babri Masjid Action Committee, ever returned his awards? He has never done it. And if he ever does it, that would be a miracle. Why?

How many Muslims stood up for the persecuted Hindus when Hindus were persecuted and atrocities were perpetrated against Hindu women in Pakistan and Bangladesh? How many Muslim leaders stood in support of Kashmiri Hindus when they were mercilessly killed and driven out of their own land? Many of them are still living in tents in various parts of the country. Kashmiri Hindus are refugees in their own homeland.

For Indian Muslims, it is the gift of Allah that the majority community are broad-minded Hindus. What would have been the fate of Indian Muslims had some other communities been the majority community in India? Just look at China, where more than ten lakhs Uighur Muslims have been imprisoned in detention camps. In Myanmar, more than ten lakh Muslim Rohingyas are stateless refugees. The Sri Lankan Sinhalese Buddhist nationalists have been against Muslims for a long time, especially after killing 257 people on the Easter Sunday bombing. On the whole, in Europe and America, why is there a general hatred against Muslims? Is something fundamentally wrong with the Muslims and the way they conduct themselves?

The syllabus in Islamic institutions, which was initially meant for an Islamic country should be revised according to the need of the hour. Muslims should realize the fact that they are living not in an Islamic country but in a multireligious country where several compromise formulas have to be evolved for peaceful coexistence. Islam itself needs to be reinvented and reinterpreted in the light of the Quran. Presently, it is the extremist organisations like ISIS, Al Qaida, Taliban, the Lashkar-e-Taiba, and a host of others who are interpreting the Quran through their inhuman killings and bloody wars. What is happening in Afghanistan is an eye-opener for Indian Muslims. Their senseless violence against women and children have shocked humanity. The fierce-looking Taliban's and a number of other extremist Islamic organisations with their barbarian mindset have hijacked real peaceful Islam.

In Hinduism, nobody can ex-communicate a person for his faith and belief. A Hindu is a Hindu, irrespective of the fact whether he goes to the temple or not. It does not matter whether he believes in God or not. It is one of the most tolerant and catholic religions in the world. A Hindu generally cannot be a fundamentalist except in a few exceptional cases. Muslims should realise the importance of such a tolerant religion and greatly value the presence of this large-hearted community as brothers in progress.

Let us understand and appreciate the religion of others. Also, the religion of those who do not believe in any religion and God at all. Let there be a Brahma Dutt in every Muhammed and Muhammed in every Brahma Dutt. Let us recall Poet Rabindranath Tagore...

"Where the world has not been
Broken into fragments by
Narrow domestic walls;
Into that heaven of freedom
My father let my country awake."

□

Goa: The First Medieval European City outside Europe

Thus, my second posting in the Archaeological Survey of India was to Goa as a punishment transfer due to the controversial statement on the Ayodhya excavation. I was under instruction to immediately join the Goa circle and report back to Delhi. I immediately joined the Goa circle without losing time and was happy that no strong action was initiated. Goa occupies a unique position in the history of India and Europe. Being the first European city outside Europe in the medieval period, it was also the meeting point of the East and West. The Portuguese modelled the evolving Goa after Lisbon, the capital of Portugal. A Portuguese proverb says,"Quem viu Goa excusa de ver Lisoba" (those who have seen Goa need not see Lisbon).

In the middle of this busy worldly life, unaffected by the temporal world, stood eighty churches with their high towers. As this was the period of the Counter-Reformation, various Christian orders such as Franciscans, Carmelites, Jesuits, Dominicans and Augustinians competed with one another in constructing churches and convents. Architecturally, these spiritual asylums were a distillation of Indian and Latin temper brought to a brilliant culmination under Portuguese masters. After the conquest of Goa on 25 November 1510, Afonso de Albuquerque started laying the foundation for the Portuguese Asiatic Empire in Goa. Merchants and traders flocked to it from the East and West. Horses came from the Persian Gulf, ivory and gold from Mozambique, cotton from Gujarat, indigo from Agra, pepper from Malabar, cinnamon from Ceylon, and silk from China. Goa in the 16th century had a population of 2.25 lakh, rivalling that of London and Antwerp.

St Xavier moved through these bazaars with his little bells fervently appealing to the people to save their souls by converting to Christianity. Every Sunday, three thousand students from the college of St Paul came to the Basilica of Bom Jesus carrying crosses and flags and chanting hymns all along the road. Louis de Camoes, the greatest poet of the Portuguese language, lived in Goa during the years 1561–67, working on his classic poem Lusiads. Garcia de Orta compiled his treaty on botany while living in Goa. Historians such as Gasper Correa and Diogo de Couta also lived in Goa. The first printing press was introduced in Goa in the college of St Paul in the year 1565.

Few monuments in Goa such as Se Cathedral (1562–1619), Bom Jesus (1594–1605), St Cajetan (1665), St Francis Assisi (1517 and rebuilt in 1661), St Catherine (1510), the Vice Roy's Arch (1599), St Paul (1542), St Augustine (1597–1602), etc., have been protected by the Archaeological Survey of India. But the vast portions of land and ruins in between them and outside it is unprotected. Many places such as Reberia Grande, Rebeira das Gales, Cais de Santa Catherina, Al fandaga, Bangacal, Arch of Conception, Tronco, Casa do Contuse, Cruz de Milageres and St Lazarus, etc., although unprotected, were integral parts of the first European city outside Europe, i.e. Goa. Realising the importance of these unprotected vestiges, I felt that an attempt should be made to protect them as part of the larger European heritage in India. A heritage zone, much bigger than the protected area, encompassing the unprotected remains, was envisaged for this exclusive purpose.

Although the heritage zone proposal was sent to the state government and Archaeological Survey of India, the officials failed to grasp its significance. Many real estate groups, who had purchased the land near Old Goa, were working overtime to undo any heritage zone initiative. There were few heritage activists such as Percival Norona, Dr Nanda Kumar Kamat, Fr Rego and Dom

Martin, who untiringly worked for getting the Old Goa declared a heritage zone. But forces on the other side were more powerful, and every effort was soundly defeated. Recently in January 2020, when I visited the site, hundreds of new constructions had come up within the core area of the proposed heritage zone, never to be retrieved again.

The most important and holiest Church in Goa is Basilica Bom Jesus, where the body relics of St Xavier is kept. Thousands of devotees visit every year during the feast of the Saint. Even otherwise, Goa is an international tourist centre because of the old churches, beaches, and the state's greenery. Here, conservation works were taken up in 1964 and then in 1983. On the later occasion, Mrs Gandhi herself took a personal interest in the conservation work. But subsequently, it suffered cracks due to the earthquake of 1993.

Immediately, it was stitched by using iron girders at regular intervals and strengthening them with steel dowels. The moss and lichen that had grown over the Bom Jesus were removed by misting technology and then soft scrubbing it with nylon brushes. As an abundant precaution, the pressure (2 ksc) and the volume of water (6 lts/hr/per nozzle) were kept at a low key so that the stone was not damaged. After washing and drying, a fungicidal coating was applied on the surface in order to arrest any growth. The whole work was undertaken by ACC cement under the close guidance of Ravindra Gundu Rao, who later became a well-known conservation architect.

The marble mausoleum of St Xavier, sculpted by the famous artist Giovanni Batista Foggini (1653–1737) and assembled in 1698, had suffered damage over the years. But getting the right artist who was competent enough to carry out the delicate work was a problem. The Italian Government came forward and deputed a few Florentine artists to carry out the specialised work. Thus, the work was carried out under the joint auspices of the Archaeological Survey of India and the Italian government.

A huge crack at St Cajetan, just below the dome, was also repaired based on the same principle. Repairing the horizontal crack on the entire length was the most challenging job. Horizontal and vertical cracks were a common problem in Goa, for the Portuguese engineers used huge stones even on the roof, which inevitably developed cracks when the binding materials gradually disintegrated, weakening the entire structure. St Paul, built in 1542 and rebuilt in 1560, had also suffered from the same problem. As a solution to it, arched buttresses were erected to support them from outside. Similar arches were provided at Bom Jesus and St Monica also.

The medieval city of Goa was a land of churches and convents. Every November, devotees arrive to worship at Bom Jesus Church. Every ten years, the holy relics are transferred to the nearby Se Cathedral Church, where it is kept for veneration for forty days. On such occasions, the responsibility of the mega event is shared by the Church, the Archaeological Survey of India and the state administration. In 1994, the Church Committee was headed by Fr Rego and the Monument Committee by me. I had completed all the conservation work much ahead of the due date. Since both of us shared certain values and were personally very close, I was invited to attend the religious ceremony along with my family, during which the holy relics were transferred from Bom Jesus to Se Cathedral.

St Augustin (1597–1602) had fallen down and turned into ruins with a number of trees growing over it. The excavation of it had started during the period of AK Sharma with the active assistance of Dr SK Joshi, a veteran archaeologist and Dr Ajit Kumar. When I joined the Goa Circle of the ASI in 1991, I could excavate the main part of the church and the part that had housed the magnificent library, etc. But our attempt to discover the grave of Queen Ketavan, whose relics were brought by the Augustinian Fathers from Shiraz and then buried in St Augustin, could not be successful. I spent almost six years excavating various parts of St Augustin in search of the relics of Queen Ketavan. My successor Dr JVJ Rao and Dr Narasimhan also spent another seven years in search of the relics. However, after relentless pursuits, the credit to discover this important relic was shared by Dr Nizamuddin Tahir, assisted by Dr Abhijit Ambekar and Rohini Ambekar for which Dr Tahir and his team was felicitated by the Georgian government. This was indeed an important international recognition. Part of the relics was given by the Government of India to the Georgian Government in July 2021 as a permanent loan.

In an outburst of misplaced nationalism, some Goan youth organisation had damaged the statue of Louis Camoeus, which imparted a European aura to old Goa. Dr KV Rao ably assisted by Dr Nambi Rajan pieced them together and displayed them in the Old Goa Museum. Similarly, the statue of Albuquerque, the founder of the Portuguese empire, lying in the store of the museum was also repaired and exhibited by them. Many of the museums have beautiful antiquities in their possession. Innovative, out-of-the-box thinking and dynamic action can go a long way in giving a new lease of life to showcasing our rich heritage, as demonstrated by Dr KV Rao and Dr Nambi Rajan.

Old Goa has many historical structures that are very important but technically unprotected either by the ASI or the state government. How to save them before the next rain was a problem bothering my mind. For such structures, the 'Adopt A Heritage' scheme was envisaged by employing the students as 'non-conventional energy' without any financial burden on the government treasury. This way, I was able to conserve the arch of conception where Kunjali Marakkar, the Naval Chief of the Zamorin, the King of Calicut, was executed by the Portuguese. Kunjali relentlessly fought against the Portuguese and inflicted many crushing defeats on them in several battles.

Kunjali was such a terror for the Portuguese that the entire population of Goa had assembled near the Viceroy's Palace and the Arch of Conception to see the execution. His head was chopped off, and then his body was quartered and gibbetted at various places in Goa. When I saw this arch, a number of trees had grown over it, as no conservation work was ever undertaken. It was in such a perilous condition that during the next rain, it would have fallen down. As it was not a protected one, no fund could be utilised over it. In this situation, with the help of Sajjan Kumar Bhatkar, the NSS volunteers of Dempe college were approached, and they agreed to take up the cleaning work. The trained ASI workers completed the technical work as they were specialised in it. This way, by using the students as non-conventional energy, I could save some of the historic structures. Thus, the unique idea of 'Adopt a Heritage,' through the voluntary labour of the students as non-conventional energy for the monuments was floated in Goa. Impressed by the idea, *Nav Hind Times*, a leading daily of Goa, not only reported it but also wrote an editorial appreciating the innovative initiative.

A commendable work of the ASI in Goa was the transplantation of Kurdi Mahadev Shiva temple in Salaulim. Uncared for years, it was overgrown with vegetation. In order to save it from submergence when a newly proposed dam would come up, it was decided to transplant it from its original place to a distance of 18 km away. When I joined Goa, after documenting it, the temple was dismantled and transported to the proposed site. But reconstruction, the most crucial work, was yet to be taken up. As many of the markings on the stone were faded, perceiving it as a risky work, reconstruction was postponed. Normally, such reconstruction works should be taken up immediately as any delay would result in the fading of numbers causing problems during the reconstruction. As there was no point in crying over the spilt milk, a decision was taken to reconstruct it. A good and dedicated team of workers under Ganghdhar Korgaunkar, Dr Gopal Rao and Rangaswami was constituted to accomplish the task.

The poor labourers worked at the site, away from their families for the whole year, and round the clock to complete the work. Since they were staying at the site, working hours was not a problem, and overtime allowance was granted. Thus, within a period of one and half years, the transplantation of Kurdi Mahadev temple was completed to the satisfaction of all the stakeholders. This was the third transplantation of a monument in India. The labourers who had worked with me were the happiest. They had a lurking fear that since they were responsible for dismantling the temple, they would be answerable to God if they were to die without the reconstruction being completed. Narayana Swami from Tamil Nadu, the head of the labourers, approached me to take up the reconstruction and offered his voluntary services. This was the kind of implicit faith and devotion many of the labourers had towards Kurdi Mahadev temple. Today the transplanted temple stands on the bank of the Salulim water reservoir, in the lap of nature surrounded by lush green landscape. Once they returned to Old Goa, they all went and lighted candles at Bom Jesus Church in Goa at the altar of St Xavier. I also arranged a thanksgiving all religious Mass at Bom Jesus Church.

As a reward for this outstanding and similar other works in Old Goa, all the daily wage workers who had completed many years at Old Goa were appointed as government employees before my transfer from Goa.

Nagarjunikonda (1960–1966) and Shri Shailam (1979–85) were the only two transplantations that were undertaken in India before Kurdi Mahadev. In 1964–68, the Abu Simbal in Egypt was similarly transplanted by an international team under UNESCO. In this huge project, fifty countries had joined together to provide technical and financial help to Egypt. It was out of this joined effort by various countries that the idea of World Heritage Monuments emerged. The concept of World Heritage Monuments declares that the most outstanding cultural and natural heritages in the world do not belong to an individual nation, but are the property of humankind as a whole.

In the meanwhile, some priests and people in Goa wanted to start prayer services in churches where prayer had been discontinued. According to the rules of the ASI, when a religious site is taken over, if prayer or puja was practised in a given monument, only that would be permitted to continue. Permission is not granted to any community to introduce new puja or worship, irrespective of the religion to which the site belongs. For example, in Ajanta, Ellora, Mahabalipuram, Aihole, Pattadakkal, Badami, etc., there is no ongoing puja, and thus they are regarded as non-living monuments.

When the Brihadeeshvara Temple and the Taj Mahal were declared protected monuments by the ASI, there used to be a tradition of worship in those places, and so they were continued, with some regulations. However, at the mosques inside Agra Fort and the Red Fort, there was no worship when the ASI took over them and hence permission was not subsequently granted for worship at those sites. In Old Goa, only Bom Jesus and Se Cathedral were under worship when they were taken over by the ASI.

Thus, the demand by few persons to open churches such as Francis Assisi, St Cajetan, Lady Rosary, etc., could not be acceded. If the rule was violated in Goa for the Christian community, there would be similar demands from other communities to open Agra Fort, Ajanta, Ellora, Elephanta and many other monuments. When I explained our position to the church authorities, most of the people agreed. However, some recalcitrant elements disagreed, and it became a hot issue in the local press. I remained firm in my position.

At that time, Rama Kant Khalap, an important political figure from the Gomantak party of Goa, was the Law Minister under Shri Deve Gowda. The Church authorities approached both of them and exerted pressure. Another group complained to Romesh Bhandari, the Goa Governor, misinforming him that I had stopped prayer at Se Cathedral. Shri Bhandari called me to Raj Bhawan to enquire about the details of it. I explained to him that prayer was prohibited in St Francis Assisi, St Cajetan and Lady Rosary, the non-living churches and not in Se Cathedral. He realised the seriousness of the issue as he had faced a similar problem in Delhi while he was the Lt Governor of Delhi. In Delhi, the demand was from the Muslim community to open several non-living mosques for prayer. The then Prime Minister Indira Gandhi stood her ground and did not allow prayer in any of the mosques. If Mrs Gandhi had allowed prayers in these mosques, the question was who should be allowed in the Qutub Minar, where the earlier temples were converted to mosques. Hindus also had led many agitations in Qutub Minar for similar privileges to do puja in the Qutub Minar.

In 2009, this issue again erupted in Delhi, during the chief ministership of Sheila Dikshit. At that time, as I was the Superintending Archaeologist of the ASI in Delhi, I had to bear the brunt from the Muslim community. The Muslims had forcibly started worshipping in four mosques. As discussions and persuasion did not yield any result from the Muslim community, massive deployment of police had to be resorted to thwart any attempt to create violence. My explanation was that if permission was granted at one place, it would have to be granted at all the places. In the struggle against the Muslim extremists in Delhi, I received the greatest support from Suhail Hashmi and from Hindi and English newspapers, especially the *Hindustan Times*.

In Goa, in a meeting of priests called by the Archbishop, Father Rego, the Rector of Bom Jesus Church, made a forceful speech endorsing my stand. In addition to a section of Church officials, several Goan intellectuals such as Dr Nandakumar Kamat, Dr Dhume, Sajjan Bhatkar, and the famous artist Mario Miranda spoke out in my favour. The independent journalist, Mario Cabral, who had taken a first-hand look at the unprecedented restoration work at the Church complexes, also lent me his support. Another famous Goan artist, Dom Martin whose painting is displayed at the Bom Jesus Church, had always stood by me.

The section that wanted to offer prayers were keen to prove that they were smarter and in the process, collected signatures from unsuspecting students of various colleges and schools against me and sent it to the Prime Minister's Office in Delhi. Some of the schools were from Kerala, as was evident from their names and initials, very peculiar to Kerala. When my explanation was sought, I wrote that all these signatures were through the schools of Kerala, who had nothing to do with Goan monuments, as part of an organised movement. The Central Government decided to depute BP Singh, the Secretary of Culture, to visit Goa, investigate and submit a report. Normally, a visit to Goa starts at Bom Jesus as it is the most important church. But in a move to outsmart me, some persons who had come from INTACH, Delhi, and closer to the opposition group took him to the Lady Rosary Church, which they thought had undergone very little conservation. But I had carried out the conservation work of the Church and refurbished it, as it was from here that Afonso de Albuquerque had started the conquest of Goa and thereby the entire Asiatic empire.

After inspecting the Church, BP Singh's first question was: "Is it a living church or non-living church?" "It is a non-living church, sir," I replied. "Despite being a non-living church, you have preserved it remarkably well. But I had heard many negative stories against its poor maintenance," he added. This sentence disarmed the group which was insisting on converting non-living monuments into living ones. Then we proceeded to Bom Jesus, Se Cathedral and other churches also. The Rectors of Bom Jesus and Se Cathedral also gave a very good report about the maintenance by the ASI. Fr Saquira of Se Cathedral had given a press statement which said: "Never before was the conservation work as good as it was during Muhammed's period." BP Singh was staying with the Governor. As I had an excellent relation with the Governor, he also gave a good account of me. Thus the programme of the forces who wanted all the churches to be opened up for prayer fizzled out. What they had demanded was not something on which the government could give a concession to any community. My stand was vindicated by the report prepared by BP Singh, which explained the matter in all its seriousness.

□

The Tragic Story of Queen Ketevan of Georgia

In the year 1991, as soon as I had taken charge of the monuments of Goa, I went to Bom Jesus Church, where the sacred relics of St Francis Xavier was enshrined and duly paid my veneration. It was followed by a visit of the Se Cathedral, St Francis Assisi church and all other churches. My last port of call was the St Augustin Church. I stood in front of the ancient monument stunned and silent. The left tower, rising to a height of 150 ft, had already fallen down in 1931. Although badly battered and severely bruised, half of the right tower had survived, posing a challenge to archaeologists, architects and engineers. The half-broken tower was now standing precariously, dragging on with its melancholic existence.

In 1572, the Augustinian Fathers had reached Goa and built a small church at the present site. Later on, a magnificent structure was erected (1597–1602) within the same complex. However, this was abandoned in 1834 as a result of the then Portuguese Government's ban on all the Christian orders. Consequently, all the fathers had to flee from there, saving whatever they could carry with them. Since there was none to maintain it, the roof of the large nave collapsed in 1935.

According to Denis L Cottineau, "This was by far the most beautiful and stately building in the city (Goa). Few cities in Europe could boast of possessing within their precincts such a magnificent building." Gamelli Careri, an Italian traveller, observed that this convent with its vast dormitories, numberless cells and spacious gardens looked beautiful with the finest trees found in India. The church precincts also had an extensive library which Dr Buchanan, who had stayed in this convent, has favourably compared with the library of the Cambridge University. While the construction of the vast nave was in progress, it collapsed twice. Undeterred, the third time, after the work was completed, the architect came and stood along with his only son below the same nave and ordered a huge canon to be fired from the church's close proximity to test its vibration bearing capacity. In case it collapsed the third time, the architect declared that he was ready to die along with his only son. The church, however, withstood the impact. But in 1931 and 1935, after years of neglect, various parts of the church fell down, one after the other.

Lost in thought about its magnificent past, I was standing before the desolate ruins of that church. The debris of the roof, the chapels, the altars and the front façade had also accumulated into huge heaps at various places. Rank vegetation and the South-West monsoon had played havoc on the church. It had become an Indian version of the Angkor Wat or Angkor Thom. No doubt, the dense vegetation and eerie surroundings provided the perfect backdrop for shooting the 1965 suspense thriller Hindi film Gumnam. The story is an adaptation of 'And There Were None' by the renowned novelist Agatha Christie. Christie, married to the equally well-known archaeologist Max Mallowan, had spent many years in excavation camps in the Biblical land. It was she who had famously said,"An archaeologist is the best husband a woman can have. The older she gets, the most interested he is in her." This pithy summation truly captures the entire personality of an archaeologist!

But looking at the ruins, I remarked to Dr SK Joshi, a veteran archaeologist, that "Even in its last gasp, the sight is awe-inspiring in grandeur and vibrant with life." While nodding to my remarks, he took me to one of the several heaps near the side of the main altar and said, "Here, we are expecting the holy relics of Queen Ketavan.". A storyteller of history and an accomplished guide, Dr

Joshy then narrated me about the visit of a delegation from Georgia in 1989, looking for the relics of their country's patron saint Queen Ketevan. That was well before Georgia attained independence and had no power in managing its own affairs. Although free from Soviet Russia in 1991, the fledgling state took a few years to steer clear of various vexatious issues.

A little research revealed that Queen Ketavan was the wife of David, the King of Kakheti in Georgia. In the tussle for the throne, she defeated her brother-in-law Constantine, secured the throne for her son Teimuraz and then acted as his regent. Sandwiched between Shia Persia and Sunni Ottoman, who were always at loggerheads with each other, Teimuraz and Ketavan had to maintain a delicate balance. In the quest to carve out an independent support base, Sha Abbas (1588–1629) tried to ensure the support of the Georgians, Armenians and Azerbaijanis by converting them to Islam and Shiaism. But Teimuraz and Ketavan, who were followers of the Georgian Orthodox Church, did not succumb to such pressure tactics. They weren't ready for any compromise when it came to religious matters and clung to their traditional faith.

In 1614 conditions assumed a frightening turn, and to avert an impending attack by Sha Abbas (1588–1629), Queen Ketavan offered herself and her two grandsons as hostages. She was kept as a prisoner in Shiraz for ten years. Then, intelligence reports were received from Kakheti about the rebellious intentions of Teimuraz at the covert support of the Ottomans. In a preemptive move, Sha Abbas forced Queen Ketavan, the hostage, to accept the Shia form of Islam. On refusal, she was tortured to death with hot pincers on 22 September 1624, in full view of the public. Among the public who had gathered to see the execution were two Augustinian Fathers—Ambrosio dos Anjos and Manul da Madie de Dues, who reached Shiraz in 1623. Although the Fathers were Roman Catholics and the Queen professed Georgian Orthodox faith, and there was no love lost between them, her painful death and martyrdom created a furore in the Christian world irrespective of the religious denominations.

The tragic death gave birth to some hagiographical literature. Teimuraz, an accomplished poet both in Persian and Georgian, wrote a pathos dripping poem about her martyrdom in 1625. The German author Andreas Gryphius wrote his classical tragedy of Catherina von Georgian (1653) and immortalized her memory. JeanChardin, the celebrated French traveller, had also written about her tragic death. The Scottish poet William Forsyth composed a poem based on the descriptions of Jean Chardin. Soon after this, Queen Ketavan was canonized as a martyr by Patriarch Zachariya of Georgia (1613–1630), and September 22 was instituted as her day of commemoration.

In an act of daredevil courage, her mortal remains were surreptitiously exhumed by Father Ambrosio and Father Manual in the dead of night and secretly kept in Isfahan till 1627. Father Ambrosio took a part of the relics to Goa for enshrining it at St. Augustin Church, while another part was taken by Father Manual to Georgia and presented to her son Teimuraz and buried at Alvaerdi monastery in Georgia. But during the transfer of the relics from Alaverdi monastery, in the process of saving it from an impending raid, the horse carrying it lost its balance and fell into the Argavi River in Georgia. Hence the only authentic remains of the relics are in India.

Ketavan seems to be one of the few martyrs in Christianity who transcended the barriers of all denominations. The fact that Ketavan was accepted by the Roman Catholic Church of Goa, even while Alexio de Menezes, the Archbishop of Goa and his successors were hell-bent on converting the St Thomas Christians of Malabar, and the terrible Inquisition was operating with full fury, in Goa, defies logic.

In which area in the St. Augustin Church could the relics of St Ketavan be interred? This was one of the main questions that had bothered the archaeologists working at St Augustin Church. The only vague clue was given to Dr AK Sharma, and Dr Joshy by the visiting delegation in 1989 was that it was somewhere below the second window of the altar of the main church. In 1991, after I had taken charge, we scoured the entire area of the main church for six years but with no success. Although the second window both on the Gospel side and Epistle Side were also excavated and many tombstones were exposed in the process, the relics of Ketavan could not be located. As we failed to locate it inside the Church, the last resort was to search for it outside the church below the second window. Fortunately, the excavation outside below the second window yielded several bones. However, it neither had tombstones nor were they proper burials. These were dump burials as if dead bodies were thrown into large pits. The only inference I could draw from the mass burial of soldiers was that it might belong to the soldiers of the Bijapur army whom Afonso de Albuquerque had killed while taking over the city on 25 November 1510. In the decisive war, 6000 soldiers of the Bijapur army had been killed in various parts of the city. Alternatively, it could also be the burials of the people afflicted by plague in the devastating pandemic of 1543, 60 years before the construction of St. Augustin church.

However, we miserably failed in our attempt to locate the relics after six years of work. Dr AK Sharma and Dr Joshy had put in another three years before me. I tried to console myself by arguing that not every excavation is expected to be the story of spectacular discoveries. But in the process, apart from the vast nave, the chapels of St William, St Thomas Villanova, St Joseph and St Monica on the Gospel side and the chapel of St Clare, Our Lady of Good Success, St John and St Anne on the Epistle side were excavated. Having lost all hope, I concluded that when the Church was abandoned, the relics of the queen might have been carried by the fleeing Fathers along with them as it was one of the most important relics. In one of my academic presentations at the University of Paris, I spoke about this failed attempt and later on got a small documentary made about it by Siddharth Kak of Surabhi fame. After my transfer to Patna in 1997, Dr JVP Rao and Dr GS Narasimhan, both seasoned archaeologists, continued the excavation up to 2003 with no success.

In 2003–2004, the excavation was further taken up by Dr Nizamuddin Tahir, Dr Abhijit Ambekar and Dr Rohini Ambekar.

Having lost all hope in the recovery of the relics in the main church, both inside and outside, they turned their attention to the monastery. The site was occasionally visited by Sid Mendiretta, a Portuguese student of Indian origin who could read old Portuguese. After one month of the excavation, the team chanced upon the tombstone Manuel de Sequira e Matos on the floor of the monastery. On his periodic visit, Mendiretta vaguely remembered having seen this name along with the name of Ketavan, in one of the 12 volumes of Silva Rego, who had compiled the names of all the tombstones of St Augustin. This information breathed a new momentum into the losing search of the last 14 years. Obviously, Dr Tahir, Mendiretta, Abhijit and their team could not sleep that night.

The next day Mendiretta, after consulting the Silva Rego Volumes at the St Xavier Institute, Porvorim, reached St. Augustin with a sketch of the site taken from the Documentacao para a Historia das Missoes do Padroda Fortuities do Oriente, Vol 12, p 90. The consultation confirmed the name of not only Manual Sequeira but also that Father Domingo Trindade was also buried in the chapter chapel along with Sequeira and Ketavan. It further added that Ketavan's remains were buried in a stone sarcophagus. Accordingly, the excavation exposed the second window on the Epistle Side, and the tombstone of Friar Domingo Trindade was also located in an upside down position. Either due to the impact of the fall of the heavy roof of the monastery or vandalism, all the tombs have been badly broken upturned and damaged. Slowly but steadily, they were inching towards their goal. Yet, the actual relics of Queen Ketavan was playing hide and seek.

After one year's (2004–2005) tremendous efforts and many missing heartbeats, Tahir and his team, could excavate part of the stone sarcophagus as described in Silva Rego's volumes and two bone fragments still stuck in the grave pit of the ever eluding queen. This was a great achievement, and Tahir and Abhijit could proudly look back to their work. The news of the discovery obviously made a sensation throughout Georgia as Queen Ketavan was their Patron Saint. Soon a high power delegation along with archaeologists and experts came to Goa in the year 2006 to verify the discovery and learn more about it.

Being the devil's advocate, Dr Tahir did not stop at that. Trained at the Scientific Laboratory in France, Tahir wanted his samples to be genetically characterized for DNA analysis in the Centre for Cellular and Molecular Biology (CCMB) Hyderabad. After seven years of hard work and a failed attempt in the period of 2006–2009 work, the team was finally able to extract 'mitochondrial DNA' in the second attempt spanning from 2009–2013 by two different sets of researchers. The Scientific team at CCMB, Hyderabad, consisted of Dr Lalji Singh, Dr Kumaraswamy Thangarajan, Dr Dipankar Singh and Dr Niraj Rai. The test conclusively proved that the sample group belonged to the Haplo group of Caucasians race to which Georgia belonged. As soon as Dr Tahir got the scientific confirmation from the CCMB lab at Hyderabad, he came to me in Hyderabad, where I was working for the Aga Khan Trust after I retired from the Archaeological Survey of India. We had a long chat about the archaeological discoveries and especially the long odyssey of the relics of St Ketavan.

I told him, as in the case of St Ketavan, India has always been an asylum for all those people who were persecuted and driven out of their countries like the Jews and the Zoroastrians. I then quoted from the well-known speech of Swami Vivekananda at Chicago, "I am proud to belong to a nation which has sheltered the persecuted and the refugees of all religions and all nations of the earth. I am proud to tell you that we have gathered in our bosom the purest remnants of Israelites, who came to Southen India and took refuge with us in the very year when their holy temple was shattered to pieces by Roman tyranny. I am proud to belong to the religion which has sheltered and is still fostering the remnant of the grand Zoroastrian nation." In conclusion, I said, "While all those communities came when they were alive, Queen Ketavan alone travelled to India in death."

Once there was a scientific attestation about the relic, a fervent request came from the Georgian Government to give them the relic on loan for an exhibition. Accordingly, after 400 years of vicissitudes of history, the Queen returned to Georgia in 2017 for six months to meet and bless the Georgians and receive their ovation. Indeed, the queen had come to India as a refugee but was now returning with all the trappings of a state guest. The day of the arrival of the relics of their patron saint after many twists and turns of history was celebrated by the entire country of Georgia with gusto, fervour and festivities. After six months of State visits and rejoicings in Georgia, the period of the exhibition was extended for another period of six months. After the end of one year, the Saint Queen returned to India, as agreed upon by both countries. No doubt, St Ketavan is the patron saint of Georgia with a prominent religious halo but with a permanent residential address in India. But the tragedy was that neither Dr Tahir, the guiding force of the discovery, nor Dr Abhijit Ambekar, the closest associate of Tahir in the long years of the excavation, was in the entourage selected by the Archaeological Survey of India to accompany the team to Georgia.

The Georgians were emotionally attached to the relics of St. Ketavan. There were earnest requests through diplomatic channels and otherwise for a permanent exhibition of the relics in Georgia. Finally, the Government of India, in its enormous wisdom, decided to accede to their fervent appeals and on 9th July 2021, part of the relic of St Queen Ketavan was ceremonially handed over by S Jaya Shankar, the External Affairs Minister, in an impressive ceremony, to a congregation of political and religious authorities of Georgia. Addressing the event, Shri Jaya Shankar said, "Today is a special day, not only for Georgia but also for India. I have the honour to hand over the holy relics of St Ketavan to the people of Georgia. I consider myself blessed that the purpose of my first visit to Georgia is such an auspicious one."

□

Bihar: In Search of Buddhist *Stupas* and Relics

"If I promote and post you to Bihar, are you ready to serve there? It is my state, and I want someone like you there." That was the last question, BP Singh, the Secretary, Culture, asked me before catching the flight from Bambolim Airport, Goa to Delhi. In those days, Bihar had acquired the dubious distinction of being a state where the rule of law had registered the lowest mark. It is a nightmare for an archaeologist, and that too for a 'Madrasi,' south Indians, posted there earlier, had the horrible tale of woes to narrate. "Yes, sir. That would be my proud privilege." I immediately replied.

For me, Bihar was the birthplace of Mahavir Jain and the *karmabhumi* of Mahatma Buddha. Kings like Bimbisara and Ajatashatru ruled from Rajgir. It was the land of Chandra Gupta Maurya and Ashoka the Great. It was also the land of Nalanda and Vikramshila universities. For years, it was the nerve centre of successive intellectual and scholastic impulses that swept through the country. Mithila was the Upanishidik land where, in the court of Janaka, the patron of Yajnavalkya, many philosophical scholars of Kuru and Panchala region had gathered "much as the intellectuals of Athens had gathered at the court of Macedonian princes." Vaishali was not only the birthplace of Mahavir Jain but also of the Republican and Democratic forms of Government. Around the same time, the Greeks were also experimenting with the nascent Republican form of Government.

My first challenge in Bihar was the conservation of ancient Pataliputra (Bulandi Bagh-Kumrahar), which was the second capital of India, where from Chandra Gupta Maurya and Ashoka had ruled. Kumrahar was also the capital of the Sunga and Gupta dynasties. According to Magasthenes, the Greek Ambassador from the court of Seleucus, who wrote Indica, the fortification walls of the city had 64 gates and 570 towers and surpassed in splendour the Persian cities of Susa and Ecbatana. The potentiality of the site (Bulandi Bagh) as the ancient Pataliputra was recognised by LA Waddell in 1895, who excavated its defence wall made of earth and timber, as described by Magasthenese. It was from here (Bulandi Bagh - Kumrahar) that Ashoka had sent a formidable army to conquer Kalinga and the gruesome massacres that followed changed the life philosophy of the King. It was also from here that Ashoka had sent emissaries to the Greek kings such as Antiochus-II of Syria, Ptolemy-II of Egypt, Antigonus of Macedonia, Magas of Cyrene and Alexander of Eorius. Being one of the crucibles of Indian civilisation, it provided the warp and woof of India's civilisational march.

The period from 800–300 BCE is termed as Axial Age by German Philosopher Karls Jasper (1883–1969) in his seminal book 'The origin and Goal of history.' It was during this period most of the religious and spiritual movements started in Eurasian countries, which influenced the mankind till today. This age produced men like Buddha and Mahavir Jain in India, Zarathustra in Persia, Laotse and Confucius in China, Isaiah and Nehemia in West Asia and Pythagoras, Socrates and other philosophers in Greece. The role played by Eastern India, consisting of Bihar and Uttar Pradesh, in this world movement of Axial history has been very little appreciated. If we look at the historical landscape of Bihar and Uttar Pradesh from the foot of Axial history, then the magnitude and importance of these states would multiply several times. All these factors played a key role in my liking the promotion and posting, although many of my well wishers had a different perception.

But when I joined the Patna Circle of the Archaeological Survey, Kumrahar the legendary capital of great dynasties which resisted the invading armies of the Greeks, the Sungas, the Kushans, the Huns and many others, have been reduced to a den of criminals, who would not allow even a compound wall to be constructed around the protected site. Whenever attempts were made to build the wall around the area, it was brought down on the night on the same day. Nobody wanted to fight with the criminals who had powerful patrons in state politics. Some of the students' politicians used to have their regular meetings at Kumrahar. In the present situation, nothing could be done without getting support from the media, the intellectuals, the students and a section of the politicians with a higher vision. With the help of Dr OP Pandey, I was able to rope in Shri Vinod Kumar Yadavendru, the MLA of RJD, the then ruling party. Several officers such as Dr Naseem Akhtar and Dr Umesh Chandra Diwedi from the Patna Museum, Dr Atul Sinha and Dr Atul Varma from the State Archaeology, Dr Jagadishwar Pandey, Dr CP Sinha, Dr Vijay Kumar Chaudhary from the KP Jayaswal Institute, and Dr Upendra Thakur from the Patna University extended their full support. In an overwhelming response to preserve their precious heritage, professors and students from Patna University joined for 'karseva' under the leadership of Prof RS Sharma and Prof BP Sinha. They were joined by the powerful media group who were quite active in those days in Patna. It sent a strong message to the criminals, and they immediately shifted their den from Kumrahar, never to return again. Some considered this show of strength by intellectuals to be a 'cultural revolution of Patna,' while others felt it as a cultural adjunct of the JP movement. As a precautionary measure, I had posted a posse of police personnel, on a payment basis, exclusively to stop the resumption of illegal and criminal activity in Kumrahar. The use of intellectuals, media persons, students and professors of the university for the conservation of the heritage of Patna paid rich dividends.

The next step was the conservation of the eighty-pillar hall, which was excavated by DB Spooner in 1912–14 and subsequently by AS Altekar in 1951–55. As this was wholly submerged under subsoil water, visitors were unable to see the magnificent eighty-pillar halls and imagine what a grand public audience hall might have once stood there. It was in the eighty-pillar hall that the proud kings like Chandra Gupta Maurya received vassals in royal splendour, coming from different parts of his extensive empire. A huge pillar even now stands as a solitary reminder of the pomp, panoply and pageantry of a bygone era. To showcase the eighty-pillar hall which was under subsoil water throughout the year, there were many suggestions from engineers and experts. While some favoured pumping out water, others suggested the construction of a cofferdam. Looking at a permanent solution to the perennial water logging problem in a low lying area, I suggested filling up the site and the construction of a replica of the eighty-pillar hall above the filled up portion, to enable visitors to visualise how the grand eighty-pillar hall might have looked.

I was also toying with the idea of installing replicas of few Ashokan pillars and Ashokan inscriptions, especially the inscription of Sanchi, which enabled James Princep to decipher the Brahmi script. A beginning was made by planting a herbal garden of medicinal plants near Arogya Vihar where Dhanvantari's Prayogshala (laboratory) was excavated. An interpretation hall explaining the rediscovery of Indian heritage from the time of William Jones, highlighting the unmatchable contributions of scholars such as Francis Hamilton Buchanan, Henry Taylor, James Princep, Markham Kittoo, Alexander Cunningham, Archibald Carlyle and others was also planned. A person visiting the site would be able to watch a small documentary about the story of the rediscovery of Indian history and would come out of the area with supreme satisfaction. Some of these plans, although in nebulous form could be crystallised due to the active cooperation of scholars such as Dr Dhani Babu, Dr Tashkant Albne, Dr DN Sinha, Dr KC Srivastava, Dr Bhagirathi Gartia and Dr Ashok Gupta.

Once the protective boundary wall was ready, the Regional Director of the CBI, UN Biswas, visited Kumrahar twice. Shri Biswas was the one who had led the investigation into the role of the then Chief Minister of Bihar, Lalu Prasad Yadav, in the fodder scam. He was deeply interested in the heritage of the country and wanted to see the place. But his security personnel had advised against it, as the neighbourhoods of Kumrahar was populated by Yadavs, the supporters of Lalu Prasad Yadav. "But now you have completed the compound wall, my security has no problem in permitting me to visit the place," he told me.

The next important work taken up was the conservation and preservation of the remains of Nalanda University. This sleepy little village shot into prominence when the local school (paathshala) gradually became a university attracting students from different parts of the world. Although the earlier date of the antiquity of the site was 5th century CE, the recent excavations have further pushed it back to the 3rd century BCE. In the adjacent village Jafer De, the excavation of Dr SC Saran, the antiquity of greater Nalanda, is dated to the 14th century BCE. Since the 6th century CE, the university has taught a variety of subjects such as medicine, fine arts, philosophy, languages, logic, astronomy and manuscript copying.

From the sixth century onwards, in the real sense, it was an international university with students from China, Korea, Central Asia, Afghanistan, Tibet, Nepal and South Asia. Chinese travellers such as Xuanzang (602–664 CE) and Yijing (635–713 CE) came to Nalanda to study and carry back as many authentic manuscripts as possible. While Xuanzang had taken 756 books to China from Nalanda Yijing carried along with him 400 books. Similarly hundreds of Far East Asian and South East Asian students might have taken thousands of books to their respective countries from Nalanda, the information source and diffusion centre of Eurasia. This added a new dimension to Northern and Southern Silk Route from a trade route to a new information highway. Slowly but, steadily it paved the way for the technology transfer of the ancient world. It was due to this international connection and importance that Balaputra Deva, the King of Sumatra in South Asia, donated five villages for the upkeep of the institution, especially the manuscript section. The Dharma Ganja section of the library had three important divisions known as Ratna Ganja, Ratnodhati and Ratna Sagara. The university taught a variety of subjects such as medicine, fine arts, philosophy, languages, logic, astronomy and manuscript copying.

The fact that Nalanda became an international university by the seventh century, /many hundred years before the establishment of the Bologna University (11th century), Paris University (12th century), Oxford (13th century) and Cambridge (13th century), brings into sharp relief the importance of it.

The university town of Nalanda was so imposing and attractive with its four-storied monasteries, nine-storied library and sky-piercing temples that those who came to its portals went back impressed by its imposing architecture. The Malad inscription says: "Nalanda has a row of *viharas* whose spires lick the clouds. It seems to have been built by the creator himself like a garland hanging up very high. Nalanda has temples that are brilliant with a network of rays from various jewels set in them and it is the pleasant abode of learnt and virtuous Sangha and resembles Sumeru, the charming residence of Vidhyadaras."

According to Xuanzang, the university used to have more than a hundred lectures every day with separate question and answer sessions at the end. Explaining about the quality of classes, he further says: "There were more than one thousand men in Nalanda who can explain more than twenty collections, five hundred men who can explain thirty collections and ten men including Xuanzang who can explain fifty collections and Shila Bhadra alone can explain all the collections."

The Nalanda teachers were so much respected outside India that Bodhi Dharma was deified and worshipped in China, Dipankara Atisa in Tibet and Dhyana Bhadra in Korea.

The sprawling university was destroyed in the 12th century by Bakhtiyar Khilji and burnt the magnificent library which provided 'Light to the entire Asia.' The fleeing monks escaped with some of the manuscripts to Bhutan, Nepal and Tibet. Subsequently, as the university was deserted and there was none to look after it, the remaining structures also fell and turned into desolate ruins. When bushes and trees grew over it, the public memory of Nalanda itself was forgotten. As a result, the first explorers like Francis Buchanan, when they saw the site in the wilderness, in 1811 and Martin in 1837–38, mistook it for the palace of some king, especially Bimbisara. Although Markham Kittoe inspected the site, narrowly missed its identification, as he preferred to call Giriyak outside Rajgir as Nalanda. Finally, it was Alexander Cunningham in 1861 who identified the site as Nalanda, based on Xuanzang's travelogue and two inscriptions found from the place, wherein the word Nalanda was mentioned. The seals of the university, recovered from the excavations explicitly saying the name 'Shri Mahavihara Nalandaya Arya Bhikshu Sangasya,' further confirmed it.

The Archaeological Survey of India started major conservation work under DB Spooner and JA Page. They gave more importance to underpinning, pointing and water tightening by using traditional materials such as lime and brick powder.

Although it was the biggest ever excavated international university, a person visiting the place never got such an impression, as the visitor's management plan was not proper, and the horticultural hedges and tree plantation were obstructing the majestic view at various places.

Hence, the first action was to remove all the visual obstructions from the front side so that the visitors could be exposed to a panoramic view of the sprawling university, creating a wow factor in them. For making this wow factor, creation of a visual corridor, a visitor's management plan, effort to excavate many buried structures and also to uplift certain sunken parts were envisaged. Wherever the monasteries suffered heavily due to brick robbing by the villagers, it had to be slightly uplifted by filling up the gap with special-sized bricks.

The acquisition of more land around the monument where buried structures are expected was decided after a thorough exploration of the place. To provide a heritage ambience, designed gateways drawn from Ashokan architectural elements, antique light poles, attractive cultural notice boards, etc. were planned.

Here, an interpretation centre and a documentary film was visualised with many thrilling anecdotes from the life of Xuanzang during his long journey from China to Nalanda and back, the manuscripts he had carried from India to China, the attack of Bakhtiyar Khilji, the burning of the library, the second attack and the escape of Dharmaswami along with his teacher Rahul Shri Bhadra, etc. It also included a section on how the early explorers had mistaken it for the palace of Bimbisara due to the sprawling buried structural remains and then the real identification of it as the location of the Nalanda University. (Please watch the documentary 'Nalanda-The Light of Asia'in You tube.

After watching this documentary, once a visitor goes to the monuments with a guide, the site would automatically turn into a vibrant hallowed ground with vigour and energy. They would realise that it is a thrilling experience to walk over the same piece of land on which Lord Buddha had sojourned, and Xuanzang had walked. Here one can walk along the trails of Sariputra and Maha Mugalyana, the most important disciples of Buddha, who had made sacred the place with their footprints. Sariputra's birth and death took place at 'Sarichak' in Nalanda. Such an experiential visit to any historical site, soaked in history, would be able to reawaken our dormant kundalini.

The most iconic structure of Nalanda is temple No 3, which various authorities consider to be the *Stupa* of Sariputra. From the lowest part up to the period of Harsha (3rd–7th centuries), it was a *stupa* with four corner towers and a solid central dome. In the Pala period (8th–12th centuries), the stupa was filled up, and a temple was constructed over it, using the stupa as the lower part and a *shikhera* superstructure added above it. This strange combination of *stupa* and *shikhera* remains an enigma even for the students of architecture unless laboriously explained.

After the excavation, as the structure was conserved to show various structural phases of different periods, mainly Gupta and Pala and sub-phases, the existing structure looks more like a European steeple than a Gupta period *stupa* or a Pala temple.

After indepth research work, Percy Brown, the renowned architect, had prepared an imaginary drawing of the Gupta period *stupa*. As part of an effort to explain the structure, I had got prepared a scale model of that drawing in fibreglass and installed it in the corner of temple No 3, so that a visitor could make a comparative study. It was appreciated by everyone as it explained the incongruous structure better. Since it was beneficial for the guides who used to guide international groups, they complimented me for the replica *stupa* of the Gupta period. Similarly, it was also appreciated by Dr Ravindra Pant, the then Director of Navanalanda Mahavihar. For the students of architecture, it was most helpful, as it explained various phases of Buddhist architecture. After my transfer from Patna, Kasturi Gupta Menon, the Director-General, visited the site. She could not understand why the replica was installed and immediately issued an order to remove it. Thus, the public lost an excellent opportunity to educate themselves about the Nalanda site.

In the neighbourhood of Nalanda, as part of the public outreach, I contacted Navanalanda University and monks of various monasteries for the upkeep of the Nalanda. They all participated with zeal as it offered them a direct connection with Lord Buddha, Xuanzang and the ancient university. I told them that by participating physically in the upkeep of the monuments, they were becoming shareholders and partners with the great Gupta kings, Harsha Vardhana and Yasho Varman, who patronised it. Blessed were those who could participate in the construction of Nalanda. But for the present generation, the best way to be a shareholder in it is by supporting it in its upkeep, so that it could be bequeathed to posterity. This message captivated their imagination, and many school children also joined in the conservation work. The opportunity was also used to administer an oath to the students that they would not disfigure monuments by scribbling and scratching on them. This oath was taken by the students in front of a replica of the Ashokan pillar, named Sanskriti Sthambha, which imparted solemnity to the programme.

Among the general public who took an interest in the heritage was Bhante Dr U Panyalankara of the Chinese Monastery, Ramchandra, an RSS activist; Ramvilas Paswan, a journalist and Tufail Khan Suri, a local teacher. When Tufail Ahmad Khan Suri located some Hindu and Buddhist idols at a place called Chandi Mau near Nalanda, he and Bhante Dr U Panyalankara informed me about it. I inspected and documented it and thought of moving them to Nalanda Museum to protect it from smugglers. But the local people opposed the idea of moving the idols to the Nalanda Museum and demanded the construction of a museum at Chandi Mau itself.

The ASI could not accede to their demand for setting up a new museum at such short notice. However, for the safekeeping of the antiquities that had been found, a village museum was built near the local Shiva temple, which was the safest location in the village. Thus, with the help and cooperation of ordinary people, we were able to build the first village museum. Bhante Panyalankara, a most remarkable man who was always on the side of the downtrodden local people provided the most generous financial assistance for this village museum. In the month of October 2021, I visited Chandimow as part of an invitation from NavaNalanda University. The villagers have maintained the village museum, and the Buddhological Trust has put up a plaque inside the temple premises, with my name and the name of Dr U Panyalankara prominently inscribed on it.

Rajgir, the first capital of India, was also the seat of King Bimbisara (544–492 BCE), his son Ajatashatru (492–460 BCE) and his grandson Udayin (460–444 BCE). Both Mahavira and Buddha were contemporaries of Bimbisara and Ajatashatru. After the death of Lord Buddha at Kushinagar, a part of his mortal remains were brought to Rajgir and enshrined in one of the *stupas*. In which part of Rajgir is this 'Relic Stupa of Buddha,' constructed by Ajatashatru located? The traditionally identified Relic *Stupa* at Rajgir, on excavation, could be dated to 4th century CE only. Had it been one of the earliest Relic *Stupas* associated with Buddha and built by Ajatashatru, it should have gone back to the 5th century BCE. As there was a gap of nine centuries between the two, archaeologists were looking for some other places as the buried Relic *Stupa* site.

But then came the news that Railway Minister Nitish Kumar wanted to lay down a railway track connecting Nalanda and Bodh Gaya. It was an excellent initiative to have a railway track connecting both these historic places as part of the Buddhist circuit. But that should not happen by destroying various Buddhist heritage sites, which we were frantically looking for. When I explained this vital point to some of the Railway officers who had come to meet me, they expressed that a realignment of the track would result in huge cost escalation. But did it mean that development should be at the cost of heritage? It is primarily because of the heritage people are coming to Rajgir.

Realising the gravity of the situation and fearing the destruction of the most valuable mound, I immediately informed about the impending danger to Dr Ravindra Singh Bisht, the Director of Excavation and with his permission started the rescue excavation. Within a week, a terraced Buddhist *stupa*, made of Mauryan brick, could be excavated for all to see. Once the *stupa* was exposed and published in the newspaper, the general public realised the importance of the site. A fragment of a relic casket in soft stone, like the early Buddhist relic caskets of Piprawa and Vaishali confirmed that it was the Relic *Stupa* (the body relics of Lord Buddha) built by King Ajatshatru. But this *stupa* was vandalised by treasure hunters who could not get anything except a green casket whose value they could not realise. Disappointed of the treasure, they left the broken casket at the site which was excavated by the ASI. This broken relic casket piece helped us to identify the relic stupa of Buddha at Rajgir, like the ornaments thrown by Sita Devi, during her abduction by Ravana that enabled Rama to trace Ravana's route map.

Thanks to the personal interest evinced by the then Railway Minister and the present Chief Minister Nitish Kumar, the Ministry diverted the route, and the ASI could save many sites associated with the Buddhist heritage. The Archaeologists who participated in the excavations were Dr Dani Babu, Dr Ambastha, Dr DN Sinha, Dr KC Srivastava, Dr Niraj Sinha, Dr DK Singh, Dr Jalaj Tiwari, Dr Baghirathi Gartia and Dr Shankar Sharma.

Vaishali being the birthplace of Lord Mahavir, and the *karmabhumi* of Lord Buddha, was a significant place from the archaeological and historical point of view. It was also the cradle of the republican form of government and democracy, rivalling Greece. The people of Vaishali used to elect their own king, and the ceremonial bath was given to the designated king with the waters of *Abhishek Pushkarni*.

It was Stephenson who recognised the archaeological potentiality of the site in 1835, and subsequently, Alexander Cunningham in 1861–62, identified it as Vaishali with the help of the description given by Faxian and Xuanzang. It was also well known as the capital of Licchavis and the meeting place of the second Buddhist council. Amrapali, the celebrated courtesan, had an Amra Vana here and once, she had invited Buddha to this garden and later on gifted it to him. As it was a centre of learning, scholars from far and wide used to come to Vaishali to participate in the discussions.

Many historical aspects of the life of the Buddha came to light during the course of excavations carried out in Vaishali by Dr Lalchand Singh. The Buddha's place of residence (Kutagarshala), the site where women were first admitted to the Buddhist Sangha (the first women's monastery), and the *stupa* that housed the Buddha's earthly remains were all excavated. Another major excavation was the Markat Hriday tank, which is so named because it is said to have been dug by *vanaras* (monkeys) for the Buddha to bathe in. Emperor Ashoka had the commemorative pillar erected here. Although my excavation of the site did not lead to any significant discoveries, I could substantially contribute to the conservation and development of the site.

During the process of excavation and conservation, some

criminal elements created obstructions and demanded a share of the funds earmarked for the project. This was nothing unusual in Bihar in those days. I brought this extortion demand to the notice of the Superintendent of the Police, who immediately rounded up the criminals. The assistant archaeologists Dr Ashok Gupta and Dr Manoj Dwivedi displayed extraordinary courage in filing a case and pursuing it. After the arrests, no criminal gang dared threaten the ASI work.

It was in the 'Chapal' Chaitya first and then in 'Kutagarshala' at Vaishali that Buddha announced his impending death, within three months. It was a shock for the people as they were very closely attached to him. On the borders of the Vaishali, a large number of people had gathered to accompany him against his wishes. When he reached Kesariya, he requested them to return and, as a mark gifted them his begging bowl. There the general public made a small mud *stupa*, which was converted into a brick *stupa* during the time of Emperor Ashoka. It was further enlarged into a terraced *stupa* during the period of the Guptas. King Harsha was the most important patron of it, and he further enlarged it.

As Buddhism was not a living religion after the attack of Bakhtiyar Khilji, there was none to look after it. A powerful earthquake in 1934 considerably damaged the structure and brought the domical part of the *stupa* crashing down. Over the years, it was covered with the earth of several centuries, and several trees had grown over it. It looked like a colossal mound. It was Colonel Mackenzie in 1814 who noticed it, and subsequently, Alexander Cunningham carried out some trial excavations.

When I reached Kesariya, 50 km from Vaishali for excavation, it was standing like a formidable mound over grown with a number of trees. A team under me, consisting of Dr KC Shrivastava, DN Sinha, Manoj Dwivedi, Baghirathi Gartia, Avinash, Rajneesh, and KP Singh, started the excavation, and within three years, half of the massive *stupa* of six terraces was excavated. It was this *stupa* that inspired the *Borobudur Stupa* in Indonesia, which is a world heritage monument. It has a circumference of 400 feet and a height of 104 feet. The recent excavation in 2020-21 by Dr Gautami Battacharya has exposed many fascinating facets of this huge *stupa*. The fact that it served as the model for the great Borobudur *stupa* in Java in the 7-8th centuries through maritime Silk Route further attest to the importance of Nalanda and various other Buddhist institutions, as the centres of information and technology transfer.

Vikramshila, another well-known university of Bihar, founded by the Pala King Dharma Pala (783–820) in the 9th century, was initially excavated by Dr BP Sinha for the Patna University. But the major part of the excavation was taken up by Dr BS Varma for the Archaeological Survey of India. Dr BP Sinha saw this as a huge mound. But after a protracted excavation that lasted over twenty-five years, these two archaeologists exposed a vast university complex with a great *stupa* at its centre.

The excavated complex is a quadrangle of 330 square metres on the plan with a massive Chaitya at the centre. The whole area is surrounded by cells with a running verandah measuring 3.10m. The cells, 208 in numbers, which also acted as a fortification wall, are quite spacious with a width of 4.15×4.15m. It had a unified plan with central Chaitya and monasteries surrounding it at equal distance. There are circular and rectangular cells at a distance of 21 to 23m. The massive double terraced chaitya occupying an area of 56×56m has an extant height of 16.25m.

While in Nalanda, Vaishali and Sarnath, there were individual or rectangular complexes in a linear pattern, Vikramshila has a centralised plan with monasteries all around the central Chaitya. The Sompura University in Bangladesh is almost a replica of it. Unlike Nalanda, it has 12 underground chambers either for undisturbed meditation or for keeping valuables from the eyes of invaders. It also had celebrated teachers like Naropa and Atisha Shrijnana, who made name and fame outside the country. Enamoured by the scholarship of Atisha, there were many failed attempts by the Tibetan king to smuggle out Atisha to Tibet. They came with gold bars to entice the great Guru, who did not evince any liking for it. But he was convinced of their sincerity. It was Atisha who introduced Lamaism in Tibet. Being a Tantric centre, Vajrayana form of Buddhism was taught and practised here.

When I proposed to visit the site for the first time in 1998, I had a lot of expectations about the upkeep of Vikramshila. But the day I reached the site, all expectations were dashed to the ground as it was in a deplorable condition. After the excavation of the site, since the baulks of the excavation were not yet removed, the area was providing an untidy and unpleasant look. Although the main *stupa* was in a tolerable condition, it had also developed cracks, and most of the monastic cells were strewn with fallen bricks. Owing to the neglect of the years, rank vegetation had grown on several parts of the complex.

In order to give a facelift to the site, both short and long programmes were envisaged. As part of the short-term programme, the removal of baulks and rank vegetation were given preference. The water tightening and pointing were taken up to stop any further damage to the site. The levelling-up of the ground in the quadrangular area was also given equal importance. Once the ground was levelled, and beautiful lawns were laid out, it imparted a lush green look to the entire site.

The excavation had yielded a rich crop of antiquities of Vajrayana Buddhism. Hence, a museum for showcasing the antiquities was planned and completed. Vikramshila was turned into a historical tourist site, complete with all facilities such as a museum, toilets and various other amenities.

All these were possible due to the relentless work of YP Thakur and LN Jha who had worked for the site round the clock for four years. Dr Ashok Kumar Pande and Dr DN Sinha played significant roles in the construction of the museum. Since both of them were museum experts, it attracted a large number of people from rural areas. This museum would not have been possible without the cooperation of Komal Anand, DG, ASI, Dr RC Agarwal, Dr Urmila Sant, Dr BP Saran and OP Pandey, who extended their wholehearted cooperation.

The man who was the happiest was Dr BS Verma, who told me: "Mr Muhammed, but for you, the site and the museum would not have been so beautiful and inviting. You know how to get the willing cooperation of the people." The refurbished site was inaugurated by Dr Verma, with a sense of satisfaction and fulfilment. I could not get Dr BP Sinha, as he was quite old and not well enough to stand the rigours of a long journey from Patna to Vikramshila. He, too, would have been as happy as Dr Verma. But when I showed him the photographs of the site and the museum building, with tears in his eyes, he blessed me and said: "It shows that a man can do a lot if he wants."

A few months back, I visited the site at the invitation of Syed Sha Hasan Mani, the Sajjad-i-Nashin of Khanka-i-Pir Damariya and the journalists of Vikramshila headed by Pawan Kumar Chaudhary. I was there along with Vikas Vaibhav, the DGP who, unlike other IPS officers, is a heritage activist and a prolific writer. There was Christal Pilz, a journalist from Germany, Mrs Geetha Badkaliya of Destination Heritage from Bangalore and Dr OP Pandey. Mrs Jayapadhak, the daughter of Rahul Sankrityayan was the most distinguished guest. The university scholars headed by Prof Rajeev Kumar Sinha, Shailendra Narain, Chandresh, Jyotish Chander, SS Parijat and BL Chaudhary were also there. We were also joined by Fr Verghese, Fr Albert and Fr Amlan from the nearby St. Joseph Christian missionary school. The binding force for such a diverse group was Syed Sha Hasan Mani, with a catholic and broad philosophy. If he was not there, such a diverse gathering from different walks of life at Vikramshila would not have been possible. We all visited Vikramshila along with many students from the schools. The students were happy to see the Vikramshila University site and came up with a lot of inquisitive questions. The site and the museum have been kept very well by the Archaeological Survey of India.

Sarnath in Uttar Pradesh, which was part of the Patna Circle, was another hotspot. The name Sarnath is derived from

Saranganath, the name of Lord Shiva. It is also the birthplace of the Jain Muni, Shreyansnath, the 11th Jain Tirthankara. It was one of the four important places (Chatur Mahasthan) where Lord Gautama Buddha preached and laid the actual foundation of the Buddhist religion after he had attained enlightenment at Bodh Gaya. From Bodh Gaya, he walked all the way to Sarnath for a discussion with his former disciples (Panchavargiya Bikshu), who had broken away from him.

Here there are three *stupas*, named Dhamekh, Dharmarajika and Chaukhandi which attract thousands of devotees from different parts of the world.

The site was earlier excavated by Alexander Cunningham (1835), Markham Kittoe (1851–52), C Home (1865), FO Oertal (1904–05), Sir John Marshal (1907), H Hargreaves (1914–15), Dayaram Sahni (1927–32) and Dr BR Mani and Dr Ajai Srivastav (2013–14). Dr Ajai Srivastav and I carried out trial excavations in 2001 near *Dhamekh Stupa* and *Chaukhandi Stupa*. The excavation at Chaukhandi yielded a Buddhist sculpture, whereas the trial excavation at the east of Dhamekh exposed some structural remains whose nature could not be determined. It is believed that Buddha met the Panchavargiya Bikshus at Chaukhandi, and then they moved to the *Dhamekh Stupa* site for the first sermon. It was here he spoke about the four noble truths and thus laid the foundation of the Buddhist religion.

Most Buddhist countries have constructed their *viharas* from a respectable distance from these *stupas*. When the ASI decided to introduce tickets to visitors and build a protective wall around the *stupa* complex, the Sri Lanka Mahabodhi Society, which is said to be closest to the BJP and VHP, raised a strange demand to provide a separate gateway from the Sri Lankan *vihara* to the *stupa* complex. It also demanded that group worship be allowed. As per the ASI rules, no such group worship is permitted there, as it was not under worship at the time of protection. Both these were strange demands from a foreign country. The ASI opposed these demands, as it was contrary to the rules applicable all over the country. Such a concession to one monastery could have set a wrong precedent for similar requests from other *viharas*. The Burmese Vihara also came with a similar demand, and the Ambassador personally came and met me to give them the required concessions. The Mahabodhi Society of Sri Lanka exerted much pressure through Shri Ashok Singhal of VHP and Minister of Culture, Dr Murli Manohar Joshi. But the local officers of the ASI, Dr ID Diwedi, Dr SK Sharma, and Dr Ajay Srivastava pointed out that such a demand was against the rules. As this stand was complicating the issue, Dr Murli Manohar Joshi assigned SB Mathur, Additional Director General of the ASI, the responsibility of inspecting the site and coming up with a positive solution.

In the meanwhile, at the request of the Sri Lankan Monastery, Shri Ashok Singhal arrived at Sarnath in person on 4 July 1999. This programme was led by a monk, Sumedh Thero, a Sri Lankan citizen and officer in charge of the Mahabodhi at Sarnath. He and the chief of the Mahabodhi Society of India, Revat Thero, from Calcutta, decided to take advantage of Shri Ashok Singhal's presence and gave a communal twist to this matter by saying that all the problems have cropped up as a Muslim was in charge of the Patna Circle of the ASI. The sharp barbs were exclusively aimed at me. Shri Ashok Singhal wanted the ASI officers responsible for closing the gateway to be punished severely. This news came out in the press also. On behalf of the District Administration, an Additional District Collector met us several times to find out a solution in favour of the Sri Lankan group. However, senior professors from Banaras Hindu University, such as Dr Vidula Jayaswal and others, gave a press statement in *Amar Ujala* on 6 July 1999 and upheld the point of view of the Archaeological Survey of India. To amicably solve the problem, Minister Dr Murli Manohar Joshi deputed Ajay Singh, National Chairman, Bal Bhawan, who was close to the Sangh Parivar and a skilled negotiator.

After protracted discussions, Bhante Sumedh Thero realised that he was not going to get any concessions, but he in bravado, stated that if he wanted, he could get the problem solved within two minutes from the Prime Minister's Office. Without batting an eyelid, we requested him to get the issue resolved from the Prime Minister's Office, as we would not be held responsible for the illegality. Ajay Singh kept a studied silence as he had by then understood that the ASI's stand was correct. No order from the higher-up came, which would have necessitated a change in our stand.

However, a few days later, the Mahabodhi Society succeeded in inviting the Deputy Prime Minister, Lal Krishna Advani, to Sarnath. The Deputy Prime Minister did not enter the monument compound. He merely looked at the closed doorway separating the Mahabodhi Society and the Sarnath Complex and commented that it was easier to go to Kashmir than to the monuments at Sarnath. He did not intervene in any way, nor did he issue any directives. We stood our ground firmly.

The report submitted by SB Mathur justified the stand of the ASI. Dr Murli Manohar Joshi, who initially had a soft corner for the Mahabodhi Society, changed his opinion and came round to the ASI's point of view. A decision different from the ASI's position could have set an unhealthy precedent as it would have resulted in similar demands from other communities for *puja*, *namaz* or prayer at the 'non-living monuments' all over the country. There would have been problems in Delhi, Agra's mosques, Goa's churches and various Buddhist sites like Ajanta and Ellora, etc., citing the Sarnath precedent. After the dust had settled on this controversy, Dr Murli Manohar Joshi told SB Mathur, "Your reports are so forceful that I had no way of overruling them." Dr Joshi officially withdrew his support for the Sri Lankan Mahabodhi Society.

Once the issue had subsided, I wrote a letter detailing the entire controversy to Ajay Singh, in which I also highlighted the decisive role played by him. Among other things, I wrote: "I was forced to bring this matter to your cognizance because Ashok Singhalji had jumped into the fray on behalf of Buddhist monks of Sri Lanka. If he had the nation's interest at heart, he should not have done so. The VHP's best interests are not the nation's best interests. The monk Sumedh had told him that a Muslim had enforced a ban on group prayer at the *Dhamekh Stupa*. It is natural that Singhalji would have been annoyed at this Muslim." (This is known from reliable sources). I further added: "I would like to record my strong opposition to this kind of remarks. I do not need certificates of secularism from the VHP or foreign nationals such as Sumedh." A copy of this letter was also sent to Ashok Singhal ji at the VHP head office in Delhi so that he could be aware of the difference between living and non living monuments.

When the Director-General of the ASI, Ajay Shankar, IAS, heard that I had also sent a copy of my letter to Shri Ashok Singhal, he was angry and reprimanded me for my indiscretion. He asked, "What was the need of sending a letter to Shri Singhal, when the Ministry had endorsed your position, and he had backed out?" When Bhante Sumedh failed in wresting any concessions, he instigated some local people to protest against the newly introduced ticket system in front of the Sarnath monument. The protesters assembled outside the gate and raised slogans against the ASI. Dr Ajay Shrivastava, who had enough experience in handling such protests in Sarnath, informed me not to stir out of my camp office, which was situated twenty-five meters away from the protesters, while he sat ten meters away from them, listening to all the speeches and threats hurled out by them.

Dr Shrivastava, an exceptionally courageous officer, who always maintained a good relationship with the local police and ordinary people, told the protesters that they were free to protest but should refrain from entering the monument compound. After shouting slogans for a while and making obligatory speeches, the protesters dispersed. I saluted Dr Ajay Shrivastava for his firm and yet delicate handling of this protest. In 2016, when I went to Varanasi to participate in a seminar in connection with the development of Benares, Sumedh Thero came and met me. He had now broken away from the Sri Lankan Mahabodhi Society and founded a new organisation of his own.

In another incident, some anti-social individuals planted idols of Hindu Gods and Goddesses in front of the Sarnath monument gate, a predominantly Buddhist site, to create social and religious tension. They were hoping to stir up trouble when I was visiting the site. The mischievous elements were hoping to gauge the ASI's response. Dr SK Sharma and Dr Ajay jointly uprooted the idols in my presence and sent them to police custody. Their timely and bold intervention nipped every attempt to foment trouble and ensured that the site was safe and has remained free to this day. In the present scenario, there would be few officers who would have the courage to resort to such timely action.

Kushi Nagar, where Lord Buddha passed away, had a similar dispute with the Burmese monastery headed by Bante Gyaneshwar. They had encroached and installed a donation box inside the *Nirvana Stupa*, and the ASI had filed a case against the monastery. Since it was far from Patna, and there were no attached offices to take care of the court cases, not much progress could be achieved. However, my successor Dr Urmila Sant vigorously pursued the case and partially succeeded. In all these cases, the biggest problem was the interference of some political leaders as supporters of religious denominations.

There is an inordinate delay in exploring, excavating and protecting important places mentioned in Indian historical traditions. An organised attempt should be made to identify such sites, acquire the land and fix the boundary so that it could be saved from encroachments. If urgent remedial measures are not taken to save whatever is not lost, that would also be encroached, and the precious pieces of history would be lost forever. The condition of places like Hastinapur, Ahichatra, Kampil and Mathura is even more pitiable. Even though some of these places are protected, the ownership of many of them are with the private parties. Some of these places are not even appropriately fenced, resulting in encroachments.

An initiative to reclaim such historical sites by removing the encroachments, freeing them from real estate lobbies and converting them to beautiful historical parks have been launched by Vineet Jain. With his Brij Historical Foundation, he has been able to transform some sites in Mathura, such as Nandgaon, Barsana, Govardhan, Gokul, etc., into new cultural centres. Only someone who knows the state of these places before, when encroachments overran them with filth and dirt, would be able to appreciate the magnitude of Shri Jain's efforts. Perhaps no one in India has done as much for the preservation of historical sites as Shri Jain. If there was an archaeologist with him, he would have been able to carry out archaeological rescue works at many of these places and document the innumerable antiquities from such sites. Mathura is very rich in terracotta, coins and sculptural antiquities. What is required in places such as Mathura, Ahichatra, Hastinapura, Kampil, etc., are that there should be a people's movement to educate the general public about the heritage of the site and collect all the terracottas, coins and other antiquities which comes out after every rain. Smugglers and antique collectors are active in all these places to dupe the unsuspecting villagers. Setting up some more museums in the sacred landscape of Mathura is worth exploring.

If excavated sites such as the Purana Qila, Fatehpur Sikri, Hampi, Champaner and Kumrahar are restored, their different historical layers strengthened, and replicas of the antiquities found in these layers properly showcased and explained, it will create curiosity to know more about the subject. Visitors must be able to view these historical layers from an appropriate distance. But as a prelude, it is necessary to identify these historical sites, protect them with boundaries to save them from future encroachments. Wherever necessary, the required acquisition of additional land should also be made as an essential component. Any delay in reclaiming the valuable antiquities of the place will result in irreparable loss.

□

Taj Heritage Corridor

Taj Mahal is often said to be a 'poem in stone' and a 'dream in marble.' For poet Rabindranath Tagore, it was an 'eternal tear on the cheek of time.' An architect treats it as the culmination of the architectural inheritance of the country. I have included this chapter to highlight the pitiable condition of historical monuments due to the avarice of political masters. It is possible to conserve and preserve the monuments without destroying their authenticity and integrity. However, what can be done with people who look at these monuments exclusively from a commercial angle, without caring for their heritage, cultural and artistic values? As an archaeological officer, I had to fight against these forces. One such major fight was while working in Agra as the Superintending Archaeologist. As per the rules, no construction is permitted within 500 metres of the Taj Mahal and 300 metres of the Agra Fort. However, some officials who were close to the then Chief Minister Mayawati conceived a plan to construct a business complex with more than 200 units between the Taj Mahal and the Agra Fort, in flagrant violation of the construction rules. As per law, they should have taken permission from the ASI for any construction within the prohibited and regulated area of these two world heritage monuments. As they were aware that the ASI would never allow them to construct such structures, they went ahead with the site's initial preparation by levelling the ground and constructing dwarf walls to make it a fait accompli. As an eyewash, the Uttar Pradesh Government called a meeting of officials of various departments, including the ASI, and promised to submit a Detailed Project Report (DPR) before starting the work. However, without submitting the DPR, they went ahead with the preliminary work of levelling the bank of River Yamuna between the Taj Mahal and Agra Fort and constructing the dwarf wall. Upon inspection of the site, I could see several tractors and other vehicles shifting and levelling sand. My persistent queries regarding who had ordered the illegal levelling and the construction did not yield any results. There were only labourers and drivers at the site, while the supervisors were conspicuous by their absence. It was evident that it was a planned ploy to evade any fixing of responsibility.

Had the project gone ahead, it would have destroyed the aesthetic, heritage and emotional value of the Taj Mahal. As a prisoner of his son, the grieving emperor Shah Jahan had breathed his last in the 'Musammam Burj tower' of the Agra Fort, gazing at the symbol of his undying love. And now, a shopping complex was going to obstruct and mar the lingering, melancholic and poignant memories of this place forever. I shuddered at the prospect of such a blatant and callous development. When my oral complaints elicited no official action, I wrote a letter to the Agra Commissioner, who called for an emergency meeting. The Commissioner severely reprimanded the Uttar Pradesh Pollution Control Division's officials, who were in charge of the Taj Corridor, for levelling the ground without prior permission from the ASI and other agencies.

After listening to the Commissioner's severe censure, the UP Pollution Control Board officer said in a lowered voice that all the works had been undertaken as per the instructions from Lucknow. He requested the Commissioner to speak with the Environment Secretary over the phone. The Commissioner immediately talked to the Environment Secretary, RK Sharma. On listening to the Environment Secretary's words, the Commissioner changed his tone and his objection. It was the Chief Minister Kumari

Mayawati's dream project, which had to be completed at any cost. Naturally, the state government officers had to maintain a studied silence. However, being from the Central Government, I registered my dissent note on behalf of the ASI. I also expressed my opposition to it, even in front of the Expert Committee, appointed by the Central Pollution Control Board (CPCB) to look into the case and insisted that my objection be recorded in the minutes. The committee comprised members from the School of Architecture and Planning, Delhi, HUDCO, the Ministry of Environment, the CPCB and the ASI. In this meeting, I submitted that no impact assessment had been made about changing the regime of the river Yamuna, altering its course and its impact on the foundation of the Taj Mahal. Apart from writing letters and raising objections, I also issued a press statement, which was prominently published by *The Times of India*

Immediately Jagmohan, the Union Minister for Tourism and Culture, intervened in the matter. He wrote to the Chief Minister against the project and personally inspected the site. The issue was also taken up in the Supreme Court. As both the Taj Mahal and the Agra Fort are World Heritage Monuments, the WHO representatives expressed their disapproval of the project. As a result, the illegal construction was stopped and four Secretaries were suspended including the Chief Secretary, the Principal Secretary and the Environment Secretary. Twice on the TV channel *Aaj Tak*, Chief Minister Mayawati indignantly asked why no action had been taken against the Archaeological Officer (me) in charge of the Taj Mahal.

On 18 September 2003, the Supreme Court directed the CBI to register an FIR against Kumari Mayawati and Naseemuddin Siddiqi, the Environment Minister. The action was also taken against the Union Environment Secretary and officials of the NPCC. Although I had tried my best to stop any construction, it was only when Jagmohan took up the issue and the Supreme Court cracked its whip that the illegal work was stopped. Not knowing how the Supreme Court would further react, I had mentally prepared myself to face any action.

There was a way to save me from impending action—by putting all the blame upon my subordinate officers, and some people even advised me to do that. But such a course of action ran contrary to my nature and convictions. In the meeting of the Expert Committee appointed by the CPCB, my suggestions were recorded in the official minutes. Quoting excerpts from it, I gave a detailed reply to the show-cause notice issued to me.

I would probably have been safe judging from the letters written, the inspections carried out and the objections raised in various meetings. But what about the conservation officers of the Taj Mahal and the Agra Fort, who did not report on the levelling of the bank of the river yamuna that was going on between the Taj Mahal and the Agra Fort? They did not do it as levelling the ground did not amount to construction. Moreover, such brazen and blatant violation between two World Heritage Monuments, when the Supreme Court-appointed Mahajan committee was monitoring every development regarding the Taj Mahal, was not expected from a state-level agency.

The ongoing violation was the combined product of greed and the temerity to flout the rules with impunity. However, the events had overtaken and affected the ASI officers also with lightning speed. To protect them from being blamed, I owned up the responsibility upon myself, stating that my subordinates had not reported the violation to me as I had instructed them that I would handle this issue. Further, I added in my reply: "If any action is to be taken on this score, it should be against me and not against them." On reading my reply, a senior official suggested that this course of action was potentially perilous. He advised: "If you are safe, you would be able to protect everyone else's career. Therefore, it would be advisable to include more people to share the blame." However, I was unwilling to do that. With my reply letter, I went to the ministry straight away. The Minister of Culture, Jagmohan, went through the letter and asked me: "Are you sure?"

"Yes, sir!" I replied. Some people were thirsting for my suspension. But Jagmohan was not convinced, and when the issue of not taking any action against me was raised in a meeting by DS Bagga, the Chief Secretary, Jagmohan defended me fully. Later on, the Taj Heritage issue brought an end to the BSP and BJP coalition, and the Mayawati government fell. When this news was being reported on television, I was sitting in the office of Jagmohan. On listening to the breaking news, he smiled at me meaningfully.

The ruling class often uses culture as a tool to serve its political ends. Very few politicians have a genuine interest in preserving our culture and protecting culturally significant places like Shri Jagmohan. The second most important quality about him was the efficiency with which he used to implement developmental decisions. He knew whom to speak to implement conservation and preservation and personally talked to the officer concerned without any intermediaries. This is an art and quality that many of the ministers are bereft of. For efficient implementation of government projects, the government should consign red-tapism to the Ganges with all the accompanying last rites.

Earlier, a large part of the Agra Gate, including the well-known Mina Bazaar where Shah Jahan had his first meeting with the thirteen-year-old Mumtaz Mahal, was in bad shape, but AK Gupta assisted by Shamsher Khan carried out some remarkable conservation work. Similarly, the neglected part of the upper side of the Delhi Gate was also conserved. A large part of the Agra Fort was under Army occupation. After a prolonged discussion with the Army officers posted at Agra Fort, the portion not used by them but under their possession was taken over and conserved. Generally, the Defence establishments do not forgo their claims, even if the structure is crumbling down, but at times, one is fortunate to come in contact with visionary officers. Social engineering with them may yield unexpected results. The 'civilian action' at Agra Fort Military area was such a silent operation carried out by the ASI.

Broad stone pathways, common to the Akbari style, were

laid out in places where muddy pathways were linking various parts of the fort. This provided a neat-and-clean look to the entire premises. In many parts of Machi Bhawan, Anguri Bagh and Moti Masjid, the carved and perforated screens and battlements had collapsed. AK Gupta brought expert artisans from Rajasthan to recreate the beautiful screens according to the Akbari and Shahjahani styles. This essential restoration breathed a new life into the monuments and changed the look of the fort.

After its conservation, the Ratan Singh ki Haveli inside the Fort where the Jat ruler lived was also showcased. Many prominent Agra travel and trade figures assembled at the *haveli* when it was thrown open to the public, marvelling at the transformation. The medieval water fountains were also revived by repairing the water system by harnessing modern technology and recreating a Mughal palace in its youthful bloom.

Some uncharitable words used by an Agra-based historian, Dr Ram Nath, against the Jat community and Chatrapati Shivaji were also erased from the official cultural notice boards of the ASI in Agra Fort. In a counter move, an Agra-based armchair-journalist Brij Khandelwal associated with that historian termed it as 'rewriting history.' But people at large ignored that journalist who had only nuisance value. The intelligentsia hailed my decision as a right step in the right direction. This healing process brought many organisations, groups and communities closer to the monuments. The Jaswant Singh's Chhatri and Jodhabhai's Chhatri were the two other monuments encroached upon by nearby housing colonies. All the encroachments were removed, and both of them were repaired and landscaped by the horticultural department.

Tapan Chakrabarti, a conservation officer, embarked on the wholesale conservation of all the monuments in the Sikandara Circle. Apart from the inlay work, the pointing and water tightening work taken up by him became the conservation hallmark. Once Raj Babbar, the Agra Member of Parliament, visited the *Idgah*, surrounded by several slums where the public would use any open space for toilets. He was ready to fund the construction of public restrooms from his MP fund. Naturally, he was disgusted to see open defecation. But when he saw the inner side of the *Idgah*, fully conserved and with a beautiful garden, was pleasantly surprised and asked me: "How do you maintain it so well amidst such bad surroundings?"

Munazzar Ali, another conservation officer, knew how to identify expert artisans who were loyal to the department. By deploying them at various places and extending all facilities to them at Fatehpur Sikri, he had also carried out conservation work on an unprecedented scale. His signature was visible at the western waterworks, the stable, the *hamam*, *dargah*, *Ibadat Khana*, *khushbu khana*, *cheeta khana* and many other structures of Fatehpur Sikri which were away from the public itinerary. He also took up the conservation of the tomb of Musa Khan, Tera Mori, Sikrawar Baoli and Gunga Mahal. Alarmed at the ongoing large-scale conservation of far-placed monuments by Munazzar, a historian sought the details of expenditure spent on them under the Right to Information Act. It was a shock to them to learn that all these monuments had been conserved on a shoestring budget.

Munazzar also refused to be dictated by some of the trade unions and as a result, I had to dismiss some of the union leaders like Geetham Singh and Mohammed Nazeer. This was a message for many union leaders who wanted to draw their salary without doing any work and by indulging in trade union activities. All the inquiries and cases were effectively managed by the security officer Captain Chandidas Mishra and Mrs Chitra Chaturvedi, the presenting officer. SK Sharma, a veteran conservator who had abundant practical knowledge, was the man who guided all these young conservation officers. It was he who took up the conservation of *sheesh mahal*, the hall of mirrors, for which Shah Jahan had brought concave glasses from Aleppo in Syria. MC Sharma, more than a conservator, was a management guru of crowds who stood in long queues in front of the monument. Since newspapers, guides and photographers were very active in the

Taj Mahal, managing such groups with heterogeneous interests was a Himalayan task, which MC Sharma carried out skillfully.

Earlier, it was a practice to let tourists go as far as the bedroom in Agra Fort in which Shah Jahan breathed his last while gazing at the Taj Mahal. Similarly, the public was allowed to enter the *Diwan-i-Khas*. Both these structures have *parchinkari* or pietra dura work in which delicate and intricate semi-precious stones are inlaid. Some tourists used to scratch or gouge out the precious stones. Nowhere in the world is the public allowed entry into the chambers of historically important personages. Even the bedroom of Jawaharlal Nehru at Anand Bhavan in Allahabad can be seen only from outside.

After a lengthy discussion, it was agreed that the tourists' entry into Shah Jahan's bedroom would be given restricted access so that they could only see the chamber from outside. Some close friends in Agra had already warned me about the serious repercussions of such an ill-advised action. However, I was of the view that what is best for the tourists is not necessarily the best for the monument and that protection of the monument is of greater priority. Therefore, a calculated risk was taken, and arrangements were made to view it from outside without physically entering or touching anything by erecting low chain-link fences.

Immediately, a hue and cry were raised. The people of Agra, the tourist industry and the guide associations were upset at my decision. It was quite natural for them to react because they had been used to entering Shah Jahan's bed-chamber from where the latter used to gaze at the Taj Mahal. Soon complaints were made against me to the ASI, and some of them met the Minister, Jagmohan himself. Alas, there were none to think of the interest of the monuments. Misleading banner headlines appeared in the *Indian Express* newspaper stating that the Agra Fort had been closed down. When Jagmohan asked me about the steps I had taken, I explained my side of the story in detail. I stopped short of saying, it was "My frozen turbulence." Soon the Bajrang Dal and the VHP jumped into the fray and added to the clamour, demanding

With Mrs. Indira Gandhi, former Prime Minister, during the Aligarh days

With Mr. Barack Obama, former American President, and Michelle Obama, the First lady

Mrs. & Mr. Obama with school children at Humayun's tomb, Delhi

Receiving the National Award, 2007-2008 from Shri Pranab Mukherjee

Receiving the Citizen's Journalist Award from
Shri Amitabh Bachchan and Shri Rajdeep Sardesai (CNN-IBN)

Receiving the National Tourism Award
2008-2009 from Shri P. Chidambaram

Receiving the SAARC Award from Shri Gulzar, eminent poet and film director, and Smt. Ajeet Caur, illustrious writer

Receiving the National Tourism Award 2009-2010 from Shri Mohammad Hamid Ansari

Receiving the National Tourism Award in 2010-2011 from Mrs. Meira Kumar and Mrs. Priyanka Chopra

Ayodhya excavation team under Prof. BB Lal (sitting fourth from the right in suit) KK Muhammed is sitting in the middle on the ground

Kesariya Stupa, Bihar, before excavation with a number of trees growing over the stupa

Kesariya Stupa, Bihar, after the excavation of six terraces

Kurdi Mahadev Temple, Goa, before transplantation

Kurdi Mahadev Temple, Goa, after transplantation to a distance of 18 km from its original place

Bateshwar Temple in dacoits infested Chambal valley, Madhya Pradesh, before reconstruction

Bateshwar Temple in Chambal valley, Madhya Pradesh, after the reconstruction of eighty temples

Ayodhya Excavation, richly decorated Sunga period terracota plaque speaks about the antiquity of the site.
Courtesy Meenakshi Jain

Ayodhya Excavation, Gupta period terracota indicates that the site was active in Gupta period.
Courtesy Meenakshi Jain

Ayodhya Excavation, Makara *pranali* used for letting out Abhishekha Jala from the temple is a conclusive evidence for the presence of a pre Baburi temple. *Courtesy Meenakshi Jain*

Ayodhya Excavation, an apsidal temple was excavated at the Ram Janmabhoomi site. *Courtesy Meenakshi Jain*

Ayodhya Excavation, stone pillars similar to this reused in the mosque suggest about the temple which pre-existed the Mosque. *Courtesy Meenakshi Jain*

Brick base prepared for the pillar base excavated during the Ayodhya Excavation. *Courtesy Meenakshi Jain*

A replica of Pashupati Shiva, Tala, in Chhattisgarh at Replica Museum, Delhi

action against me. After all, I was responsible for demolishing the illegally extended part of a temple near the Taj, and this was a golden opportunity to get me punished. Apart from these two, the Aligarh communist group was trying through one of the officers of the ASI for my transfer from Agra. Efforts of all these groups were responsible for my transfer from Agra to Raipur.

□

Chhattisgarh: Brush with the Naxals

As a result of the restricted entry introduced in Agra Fort, the demolition of the extended part of the temple and the covert attempt of Aligarh communists, I was transferred to a low-profile circle in Chhattisgarh. It was a virtual fall from the dizzy heights of the Taj Mahal to a Naxal-hit undeveloped region with few monuments.

The quotation of Jimmy Dean that "I can't change the direction of the wind, but I can adjust my sails always to reach my destination," lifted my spirit. There was neither an office nor a vehicle nor a residence to start with. With one lakh rupees taken as an advance from the Bhopal Circle, Dr Shivakant Bhajpai and I started our melancholic night journey to Raipur without reservation in the Chhattisgarh Express. With the help of Dr KK Chakravarthy, Add. Chief Secretary, we stayed in the University guest house for a week. When the order came to vacate the accommodation, we shifted to the small office of the conservation assistant, which served as both the office and residence. Dr Anil Tiwari, Dr Navaratna Kumar Patak, Dr Shivakanth Bajpai, and Dr Raj Kumar Patel were Archaeological officers and BB Sukhdev and Neeraj Tiwari, the conservation assistants, joined us. This young team was hard working and full of enthusiasm. Once Mr YP Takhur, Assistant Engineer, AK Mohanthy and T Dhanraj became part of the team, the conservation work was started. Young contractors like SK Baghel, Pankaj Jha and Sudheer Jha were ready to work round the clock. It was like family. Our small but effective army played a very decisive role in determining the contours of Chhattisgarh's heritage.

Chhattisgarh was a new state with no infrastructure. If that was to be seen as a disadvantage, it could be turned into an advantage in equal measure because a Central Government office is always warmly welcomed in the initial stages of State formation. The only thing is that one has to feel that the bottle is half full and make his presence felt. As Edward Gibbon said: "The winds and waves are always on the side of the ablest navigators."

Earlier, as the region was far away, no attention was paid to the monuments of Chattisgarh. After identifying the archaeological sites, the first thing to be done was to bring the land around it under the possession of the ASI. At that time, major part of the land in Chhattisgarh was no man's land and not clearly defined, which enabled the ASI to annex vast tracts of land for the monuments. The young team of archaeologists, namely Dr Anil Tiwari, NK Patak, SK Bajpai and Patel, gifted with a larger vision, took care to include all the nearby water bodies within the monument boundary. The land acquired by the ASI at that time with no payment or bare minimum amount if there was private land in between, is worth many hundred crores now. One cannot even think of acquiring an inch of land in some of these places as tourism has made substantial strides and land prices have sky-rocketed after the ASI developed all these areas.

In the beginning, most of the excavation works in Chhattisgarh was single-handedly carried by Dr AK Sharma. He faced many challenging situations courageously and carried out excavations at several places, especially in Sirpur. A man with a great passion for heritage, he worked as a one-man army. Had he not completed the excavations, we would not have been able to carry out the conservation work. Dr AK Sharma was awarded the Padma Shri in 2016–17 for his many valuable contributions to archaeology.

Usually, the ASI neither informs the public about the excavation work that it carries out nor advertises the site to bring in more tourists. In a refreshing departure from it, we prominently put up advertisements on the highways and airports to attract tourists. One catchy advertisement trumpeted: "Xuanzang came all the way from China 1400 years ago to see Sirpur. What are you doing?" This attractive and heady advertisement took Raipur by storm. The phrase was reported by several newspapers also. Soon enough, there was a steady stream of people wanting to see Sirpur.

Another hoarding showcased the Ganesha of Barsur, stating, "Unique is Chhattisgarh. Here in Barsur you have the third largest Ganesh in the world. What are you doing?" Still, a third hoarding proclaimed, "The earliest Vishnu image is in Malhar; go and salute it." In all these places, the distance from Raipur, Bilaspur and Jagdalpur was also given. All these things had already been in existence, but the ASI only advertised them and gave a new perspective and dimension to it by focusing on its "Unique Selling Propositions" (USP). This emphasis on its USP, often used by marketing strategists, was effectively used by a fledgling ASI office, which paid rich dividends. Archaeologist Dr SK Bajpai, a writer and poet, coined words with rhythm and melody. Even now, many in Chhattisgarh still remember those poetic billboards.

The young and ebullient 'foursome archaeologists' did not stop at that. They took a bus load of journalists with the help of the Press Information Bureau to all these places so that the journalists could see the transformation for themselves and write about it in their weekly columns. All the arrangements at the site were provided by Pankaj Jha, Sudheer Jha and SK Baghel. Thus, within a year, the ASI could establish a connection with the press and also with the general public. The state officers and the ministers began to recognise the ASI and its valuable contribution to the rich heritage of Chhattisgarh. We believed and practically demonstrated that 'heritage has the power to transform, educate and inspire people.' Earlier many political figures thought, and still many maintain, that heritage is a liability that should be dismantled at the earliest opportunity.

Shri Brij Mohan Agarwal, the Tourism Minister, was greatly impressed after being taken on an extensive guided tour. Such occasions were used to appraise the state administration about the difficulties faced and tourist facilities required at these places to make them attractive centres for tourists. Having realised the potential of the heritage sites and the enthusiasm of the archaeological team, the state administration extended all facilities. The rotating trans-lit board about the monuments at the arrival lounge of the airport was inaugurated by Shri Brij Mohan Agarwal. The ASI had created such an impression on him that he would call people from the ASI first, even if there was an array of officers from other departments waiting to meet him.

As a result of the wholescale conservation work that the ASI did in Sirpur, it has now become the most prominent tourist centre in Chhattisgarh. This has the potential to be in the tentative list of 'World Heritage Sites.' Dr Anil Tiwari, Shiva Kant Bajpai and NK Patak excavated the area near the Lakshman temple and brought out many unknown historical facts to enhance its claim to the world heritage list.

The Bastar region of Chhatisgarh consists of Kanker, Kondagaon, Jagdalpur, Dantewada, Sukma, Bijapur and Narayanpur. Most villages are depressing pictures of malnutrition, starvation deaths, no safe drinking water, illiteracy, and very few health facilities. Such a condition is very conducive for the growth of extremist organisations like Naxals. In 2006, *The Economist* noted that Dantewada had only a 30% literacy rate, making it the lowest in the country as it was one of the most insurgency prone areas. According to the police estimate in 2007, even though there were only 4500 hardcore Maoists in Bastar, 2,00,000 people (including women and children) were either members or sympathisers of the party. In Chhattisgarh, between January 2006 and June 2007, nearly 1 lakh people were displaced, and 529 people were killed. In March 2007, at Chintalnar in Dantewada, Naxals had killed 55 police officers. In 2003–04, Dantewada was one of the hotbeds of Naxal activity.

The dilapidated Shiva Temple of Samlur is at a distance of 11 km from Dantewada town. Earlier, the ASI could not pay any attention to the Samlur temple as it was deep in the forest, and no government officials would venture into it. We decided to take calculated risks by gradually carrying the work under Niraj

Tiwari, contractor Sudhir Jha and local social worker Jogi Pujari. Jogi used to do the networking with the locals and Naxals as he enjoyed political and social clout.

One day, when I reached Sampur along with my colleagues YP Thakur, Sukhdev, Niraj Tiwari, contractor SK Baghel, Sudhir Jha and Pankaj Jha, a group of Naxals surrounded us. They were simple ordinary forest folks with no barrels in their hands or intimidating looks. This time, Yogi was conspicuous by his absence. They engaged us in a discussion like local friends, asking us questions and noting down our address in Chhattisgarh and that of my native town Koduvally, Calicut. It was at that moment; I realised that there was something fishy about their dealings. The Naxals have a web of informants and networks all over the country. We now grew suspicious of them.

Once it was clear that they belonged to Naxal groups, I told them, "We have come to repair these dilapidated temples, perhaps after a gap of nearly many hundred years. The devotees who come to these temples are the ordinary local tribal folk. And so are the labourers engaged in the conservation of the work. If you stop us, we will have to abandon this restoration work, and the fund diverted elsewhere." I also added that our labour force had been recruited from among the local people, who were being paid the wages as per the schedule of rates prescribed by the government. There was no exploitation whatsoever. We neither make short payment nor indulge in any malpractices as far as the materials used for the conservation is concerned. I also told them that forest tribes were earning their livelihood very well because of the conservation work. After listening to us, the Naxals said that they were fully satisfied with both these aspects after enquiring about it thoroughly.

Once the discussion was over, they demanded a donation for running their organisation. I replied, "If you instruct, we will stop the work. If the demand is for a small amount, I can pay it, but if the demand is higher then, the conservation work would suffer." Their demand was only for a small amount of Rs. 10,000 in 2003–04. Arrangements were made for the payment through Sudhir Jha. In exchange for this money, they promised to alert us of the presence of rival Naxalite gangs from Andhra Pradesh. If any of them ventured close to us, we would have to suspend our work temporarily and resume it after the rival gangs moved away. With this understanding, our project made progress, and it was completed.

Although Chhattisgarh was a hotbed of Naxalite activity, our labour and tribal-friendly behaviour made it possible for us to work in all these places. We understood from our experience that even though the Naxals were dangerous, a little social engineering and a friendly attitude towards the downtrodden and deprived section could go a long way in managing them. The government allocates sizeable funds for the welfare of tribal areas; however, the funds often do not reach the intended destinations. Some corrupt officials and politically connected individuals embezzle the funds. Such depressing conditions gave rise to popular leaders such as Shankar Guha Niyogi, who founded the Chhattisgarh Mukti Morcha but was brutally assassinated in 1991. Dr Binayak Sen, the General Secretary of the People's Union for Civil Liberties, had been running 'Rupantar' (village clinics) in a number of villages. Their barefoot doctors served the poor people sincerely. But he was arrested and implicated in several cases. If government officials working in these areas demonstrate social commitment and sensitivity, the Naxalites can, to some extent, be controlled and brought to the mainstream. It is also necessary that the government selects suitable officers in such sensitive places. The help and support of people like Dr Binayak Sen, Prof Sai Baba, Salman Ravi, Malini Subramanyam and many others could be taken wherever possible. They enjoy greater credibility with the tribal people through their social network service. A closer look at the life and conditions of the Naxalites would reveal that the fault is not entirely with them, but also with the government and the society at large. However, their violent policies deserve to be condemned. If some of the committed members of RSS can work in such affected areas of Chhattisgarh, Andhra and Bihar that would pave the way for channelising the government fund to the right tribal groups.

On another occasion, I went to the Lafagarh temple (Chaiturgarh), situated at the height of 3,060 ft, accompanied by BB Sukhdev and contractor Baghel. The temple was in a dilapidated condition, and some parts had fallen down. The *shikhara* portion was about to collapse. In an appealing voice, the priest of the temple, Pandeji, asked me: "Sir, can you please do something?" I regretfully expressed my inability to help, as Chhattisgarh was a new circle and there was a dearth of experienced workers. All the expert workers with experience were in Bhopal and were already engaged in restoration works there. I was not confident that they would come at my request. With Chhattisgarh being a new circle, everything had to be started from scratch. I tried to explain this to Pandeji, who, with a deep sigh and anguish, expressed the hope: "Bhagavan will make way for everything." Even his lamentation contained rays of hope. After taking tea with Pandeji, we took leave of him.

That night Lord Shiva appeared in my dream and gently commanded: "Muhammed, my temple is falling down. Go and repair it." I expressed my inability as Raipur in Chhattisgarh is a new circle, and there are no expert workers for the risky work. The suitable workers were in Bhopal. Lord Shiva said: "That is my duty. I will do the needful for that."

I woke up in the middle of the night and then went back to sleep. The next morning, I had completely forgotten about it. But at 11:30 in the morning, I received a fax message transferring me to Bhopal circle with the additional charge of Chhattisgarh. I was immediately reminded of the dream that I had seen the previous night. I am not an atheist but do hold rational views. How did it happen to me who is more of a rational being? Certain things are inexplicable. Sometimes many strands of thoughts are intertwined, and one is baffled.

The famous twelfth-century Christian saint, St. Francis of Assisi, once had a similar dream, in which Christ appeared to him and said: "Francis, my temple is falling down. Go and repair it." I always quoted St. Francis because I have high regard for him. His life story is reminiscent of Gautama Buddha's life and teachings. I used to live in one part of the St. Francis church in Old Goa. Perhaps the influence of St. Francis manifested in the form of Lord Shiva in my unconscious mind. That way, I tried to rationalise my dream.

After joining Bhopal, the first thing I did was to instruct experts from Bhopal with a small personal contribution of Rs. 5000 to go and plan the conservation of the Lafagarh temple. This temple, which seemed perilously close to collapse, was repaired and beautified in the course of a year. Today, people climb the hill to get a *darshan* of Lord Shiva. Pandeyji also told me of a dream that he had seen the night before I arrived at Lafagarh to visit the temple. He had foreseen that a capable officer was going to come to repair the temple. He laughed and said that he could never have imagined that the afore-mentioned officer would be a Muslim. After the restoration work was completed, Pandeji used to phone me religiously every year on the day of Shivaratri. A few years back, when I received no call from Pandeji on the day of Shivaratri, I enquired from Sukhdev about Pandeji only to learn that he passed away a few months earlier. Thus as per the Government order, my next posting was in Bhopal.

□

Madhya Pradesh: As a Guest during the Mahashivratri Mahotsav

The Bhojshala temple, built by Raja Bhoj (1010–1054 CE), 30 km away from Bhopal, is also known as the Somnath temple of North India. Its majestic facade and cuboidal shape hold a unique attraction for inquisitive tourists. A number of stories have been woven around it over the ages, in which both myths and legends abound. Why was it left unfinished by one of the biggest builders of the 11th century is still an enigma! Although it enshrines one of the biggest *Shivalingas,* why wasn't there a *Nandi* in front of it as prescribed by the *Agamas*? Why was it designed like a *mandapa* with no *shikhara* to flaunt? Why was there neither an *antarala* nor *a Mukha mandapa* like any other Central Indian temple of the 11th century? It is also bereft of the intricate carvings as seen at the Khajuraho temple. Yet, it is awe-inspiring in grandeur and vibrant with life. The southern king, Raja Raja Chola 1 (985–1014 CE), built the Brihadishwara temple in Thanjavur, Tamil Nadu, roughly around the same time.

When I first saw this temple of Madhya Pradesh in a ruinous condition with fallen stones strewn around, still, the temple so overpowered me that I stood before it in silence and prayers. It was built on an imposing *jagathi,* measuring 115×82×13 ft. I noticed that the sanctum, 65 ft square, had been provided with a 33 ft-high entrance gate, which is unusual for any temple. The colour of the stone and the height in terms of a temple reminded me of the Buland Darwaza at Fatehpur Sikri (1572 CE), although the latter is three times bigger than the Bhojshala and centuries removed in time scale. It is conceived as a *pataleshwara*, going down partly into the ground for which steps have been provided. The Shivalinga, with a height of 22 ft, is second only to the Brihadishwara temple in South India. The four imposing pillars, each 40 feet high, take the superstructure's load, including the 28.5 ft long beams on the four corners. How could the engineers raise such massive pillars, weighing 30 tons each to 40 ft. height? Of course, behind the temple is a huge ramp that is 300 ft long and 40 ft high to roll and raise the stones with the help of elephants and manual labour. Such ramps were there in most of the ancient sites for raising the massive stones. But once the structure was completed, they used to level down the ramp. In this case, it was not dismantled as the temple was never completed.

It was raining heavily when I reached the spot. Water was pouring through its wide-open, broken, unfinished domical ceiling and all the four sides that were also open to the sky. Within minutes, the *garbha griha* (the sanctum sanctorum), where the tallest Shivalinga is enshrined, was filled with water. This had been happening for the last one thousand years and this waterlogging was affecting the foundation as there was no arrangement for the water to be drained out. On receiving information about my presence, Pawan Giri Goswami, the *mahant* of the temple, also arrived. He offered a special *puja* on my behalf as it was for the first time I was visiting the temple.

After the *puja*, we had an in-depth discussion on how to conserve the temple. Earlier, concerted efforts were made during the period of Dr BN Pandey, Dr RC Agarwal and Dr PK Mishra to conserve the structure by providing huge load-bearing pillars, but the project remained incomplete as one more 12-ton pillar was required. Although Dr Mishra had initiated the work of the domical ceiling, it was left halfway as it was feared that adding any more weight would bring the roof crashing down on the tallest Shivalinga, causing damage to it. It was one such calculation mistake and the consequent damage of the Shivalinga which had left the temple unfinished. A damaged Shivalinga, as per the *Agamas*, is never worshipped. But in this case, as nobody could replace such a giant Shivalinga, the devotees continued to worship it. As a remedial measure and to honour the *Agamas*, a small Shivalinga had been erected in front of the temple in a kiosk of the 19th century during the reign of the Nawabs of Bhopal.

After a thorough inspection, a comprehensive proposal for the conservation and environmental development of the site was conceived. It was decided that rainwater ingress should be stopped immediately by providing a ceiling and side cover to stop any further damage to the foundation. It had to be done without adding any extra weight. Providing a roof without adding weight and matching it with the red stone seemed an impossible task. But the ASI carried out this task by providing a fibre-glass ceiling with all the intricate carvings that a visitor would never be able to detect that the roof was made of fibreglass. It perfectly matched with the remaining part of the dome. The covering of the four sides was completed with the red stone itself as it added no excess weight. Similarly, the four external corners of the temple were repaired with red sandstone so that water would not seep inside the temple through the broken walls.

The biggest challenge was to provide a load-bearing pillar of 12 tonnes. After six month's work, the pillar was prepared, but now the question was: how to hoist them to the temple gate across the wide platform? None of the crane experts was ready as the boom of the cranes was not long enough to reach the temple entrance without damaging the platform.

NK Bharadwaj, the Assistant Archaeological Engineer, got the riskiest task of hoisting and joining the 12-ton pillar at the gate with the help of chain pulleys. He was ably assisted by Ravi Mittal and his expert team of workers from Agra. Although both Bhardwaj and Mittal were fully confident of completing the work without any damage to the main structure, we were full of tension and anxiety. A slight slip could bring the stone crashing down.

But both Bhardwaj and Mittal were known for executing such challenging works in Agra Fort, Fatehpur Sikri and Tajmahal.

While the pillar was being raised inch by inch, the temple priest performed the *aarti* (evening *puja* at sunset) with the chanting of hymns and lighting of lamps. The synchronised raising of the stone to the accompaniment of the *aarti* was not planned earlier but quite an accidental one. Bhojpur's *aarti* against the setting sun and lighting of the lamps a few kilometres away in Mandideep has always created ripples in my mind. The environment is simply magical. The hymns and the chiming of bells can easily pull anybody out of emotional turmoil. The notes of the hymns can calm the nerves and soothe the agitation of the mind. It was on such a divine, magical and musical note that the most challenging task at Bhojpur was brought to a successful finishing point.

No conservation is complete without environmental development. Wherever I had taken up conservation, environmental development had been part and parcel of it. In this case, there were no funds for landscaping and garden work. If the gardening and environmental development had to be postponed for the next year, one is unsure whether it would ever be completed. In Government service, one can be transferred at any moment. In an attempt to complete the gardening work, I sought the help of the Panchayat and the *mahant*, Pawan Giri. They provided the soil free of cost as it was necessary for laying out the garden. The horticulture division of the ASI, under Dr Harbeer Singh, laid out a beautiful garden, which greatly enhanced the aesthetic value of the temple's surroundings. Within one year, we were able to complete the entire structural work and environmental development around the temple. The temple *mahant* and the general public have always acknowledged my contribution to the site. The *mahant* used to say: "What Muhammed Saheb has done for Bhojpur, nobody could do so far." In all the Mahashivratri programmes, I have been one of the distinguished guests as long as I was posted in Madhya Pradesh.

In March 2020, I visited Bhojpur after a gap of 12 years at the invitation of the Madhya Pradesh Tourism Department and *The Times of India* for the 'Times Passion' programme. Along with me were many journalists and blog writers from different parts of the country. When the public saw me, all of them came forward and greeted me in acknowledgement of my contribution to the temple as if they were meeting one of their long-lost family members. It was a pleasant surprise for the journalist fraternity.

Once, it so happened that a disgruntled officer of the ASI, with a journalist's help, tried to create problems in Sanchi, a World Heritage monument, by planting a story that the *stupa* had developed cracks and was profusely leaking. As Sanchi was a Buddhist monument, he succeeded in instigating a Buddhist member of the Madhya Pradesh Minority Commission also. But we took every challenge in our stride as an opportunity to emerge on top. Since I believed in the adage 'a crisis is too precious to be wasted, on the day the Member of the Commission was visiting the site, I took a busload of journalists from Bhopal to Sanchi to explain what conservation programmes had been initiated and what we proposed to do further.

It included the total conservation of the monument along with a garden all around. It also envisaged a herbal garden by having plants and trees, as mentioned in ancient Buddhist literature. As a tourist facility, an excellent set of toilets and refreshment counters were set up. The toilet interiors were designed with photographs of different styles of hair decoration as taken from ancient sculptures of the Mauryan period onwards. This was a new learning experience for many tourists.

As part of the conservation work, SK Verma, under the supervision of DS Sood and NK Bharadwaj, took up appropriate conservation work by using lime, *surkhi*, *urad ki dal*, *bael* fruit juice (wood apple) and jaggery. After much research work, Dr RK Chaturvedi, a reputed chemical conservationist, carried out the chemical cleaning and waterproofing task. The chemical cleaning removed all the fungus that had grown over the structure and was slowly eating into its core. After the chemical cleaning, Dr Chaturvedi also treated the delicate works with preservatives to reduce the effect of the sun and rain on the monument.

Once the physical and chemical conservation work was completed, the garden expert Umesh Sharma undertook the horticultural operation. While the horticultural process was in progress, it was stopped by few archaeologists on the ground that the lawns were not matching with the period of Ashoka. It was explained that such lawns had been provided in all the monuments worldwide to control dust pollution and create a pleasant microclimate. It took six months of continuous persuasion to get the required permission to continue the horticultural activities. After the permission, a beautiful, charming and slopy garden was laid out around the Stupa, which is a spiritual and visual treat for the tourists. On the one side of it, a small aviary with pigeons and ducks was provided, integrating the site with the Buddhist philosophy of peaceful coexistence of all creations. At the same time, the aviary makes it lively and chirpy. Now, it is the rendezvous of children coming from different parts of the country.

Once completed, the beautiful garden ascending like a musical note with its ups and downs and light and shade makes Sanchi one of the most beautiful sites in the county. A few tour operators, who had come from Delhi, compared this garden to the Mughal Gardens at Rashtrapati Bhawan. Thus the concerted efforts by officers of three branches of the ASI—the circle, the horticulture and the chemical—were able to showcase Sanchi as one of the most coveted destinations. The contribution of the Madhya Pradesh Tourism Department to Sanchi is noteworthy as it constructed a connecting concrete road from the railway station to the *stupa*.

In the foothills of Sanchi, the MPTDC has laid out a theme park based on the life of Buddha. There, in co-operation with the Forest Department, I was toying with the idea of developing a 'valley of flowers' through social forestry. But as a government servant, time was running out in my hourglass. From the elevated *stupa* site, the valley down below with its sprawling agricultural fields, orchards and lush green landscape provides a spectacular view. A light and sound programme introduced by MPTDC has added colour to the nightlife of tourists staying in Sanchi.

Impressed by the site's transformation, Ashwini Lohani, the Managing Director of the Madhya Pradesh Tourism Department and Veena Raman, one of the Directors, told me to apply for the National Tourism Award. The selection committee had no problem in selecting Sanchi for the National Tourism Award (2005–06) as it richly deserved it.

This incident serves as an example of how to deal with challenges posed by vested interests and how to turn them into opportunities for the development of monuments in the country. We should not allow obstacles to stop us. If we run against a wall, as Michael Jordan said: "Figure out how to climb it, go through it, or work around it."

DS Sood, Superintending Archaeological Engineer, was responsible for repairing and restoring several monuments in Madhya Pradesh. An unassuming but highly technical officer, he was the man behind many challenging conservation works in Madhya Pradesh. He has also rendered meritorious service in Angkor Wat and earned laurels for the country. At Angkor Wat, he had to prove his metal amidst several international competitors, mostly from Europe and the Far East. On account of his ability, even after retirement, he is still working at Angkor Wat in various capacities.

Officers of Madhya Pradesh, such as Pankaj Sharan, Mardan Singh, AK Soni, Bhagvanta, Vijay Sharma, Ashok Kumar, Rahul Tiwari, Subhash Kumar, Milind Angetkar, and others made excellent contributions to the conservation and beautification of monuments. Dr Manuel Joseph, Dr Dileep Khamari and Dr Hashmi, being researchers, provided valuable guidance in all the projects.

DK Richariya is a dedicated officer who conserved the

monuments at Mandu, under Dr SS Gupta's supervision. He carried out most of the restoration of the structures on a large scale, without waiting for inspections, sanctions and funds. Sites such as Jahaz Mahal, Munju Talab, Ashrafi Mahal, Tomb Hushangshah, Baz Bahadur's palace, Rupmati pavilion and many other monuments were conserved with minimum funds. I had given them standing instructions that if a monument was in a critical condition, the more knowledgeable conservation officer should take immediate action without waiting for the budgetary allocations. A stitch in time will save nine.

Richarya took steps to stop unauthorised tourist guides and issued notices against illegal constructions within 100 meters of the protected sites. In retaliation, vested interests tried to implicate him in false cases. A case was also filed against him in the Scheduled Castes and Tribes Commission to pressure the ASI to take action against Richarya in an offence that he had not committed. The Commission summoned C Babu Rajeev, IAS, the Director-General of the ASI, to explain the conduct of an employee whom he did not know personally at all.

Being Richariya's officer-in-charge, I, and the Director Administration Shri Agarwal, accompanied Babu Rajeev for the hearing. Richarya had been accused of harassing and abusing a member of a Scheduled Tribe. I defended Richariya by saying that he was not an ordinary officer but a man of high virtues and moral character. I further said that being a member of the Ram Chandra Mission, he did not discriminate against anybody on the basis of caste or creed. I fully defended him as I respected him for his qualities.

Babu Rajeev submitted before the Commission that he did not know the officer in question, nor was it possible for him to keep track of every sub-circle officer. It is an all India organisation with employees from different parts of the country. He also said clearly that if they had an issue with any officer, the said officer should have been summoned and not the Director-General. If this had been an administrative and policy matter with larger implications, summoning him (Babu Rajeev) might have been justified. However, this was a trivial personal matter, and they should not have summoned him for such a non-issue. After a forceful fifteen-minute-long presentation, Babu Rajeev left the chamber without seeking the Commission's permission. I stayed before the Commission and explained the matter at length. The case was laid to rest, never to be raised again. This case amply illustrates how honest and upright officers are harassed by Commissions and Tribunals in the name of Scheduled Caste people and tribes, minority commissions, etc. Sometimes such forums are misused by vested interest with impunity.

Rahul Tiwari, working under the direction of Dr OD Shukla, was another excellent archaeological engineer who did commendable work at Khajurao. Over a period of time, some of the temples had developed water leakage problems. This had affected major temples like Kandariya, Lakshmana, Vishwanatha, etc. Water tightening of these temples was given the top priority along with the restoration of the *shikhara* of Adinath and Parshwanath.

The major thrust was given for the land acquisition around western and eastern groups of temples. For the comprehensive development of Khajurao and knitting together, both the groups into one single harmonious whole, more than a hundred acres of land in-between the two groups were acquired under the supervision of Dr OD Shukla and Rahul Tiwari. As Khajurao had organic growth, many patches of the land were in the hands of private parties. Getting them evicted from such traditional landowners was a gigantic task. Along with it two huge water bodies—Shiva Sagar lake and Khajur Sagar lake—under the State Department were also acquired by the ASI for smooth future planning.

In the meanwhile, some powerful business group based in Delhi, with the help of some locals, attempted to encroach upon a corner of this acquired land. Both Shukla and Tiwari not only resisted it but constructed a complete boundary wall in a night operation. There was even an attempt by some police officials, who tried to arm-twist the Archaeology officials on behalf of the business group. Countering this move by the police, OD Shukla told them: "If you think we are wrong, why don't you arrest us for trespassing?" This bold move brought the policemen to their knees. Later on, the case went into the local court and the judgement was in favour of the Archaeological Survey of India. With the vast tract of land under the ASI, Khajurao is now poised for a quantum jump and lateral expansion. Indian Oil Foundation has come forward for transforming Khajurao into one of the best archaeological places on the Asian continent.

All the cases involving monuments in Madhya Pradesh used to be handled by Dr Rekha Radha Vallabi. These cases were quite successful in the competent hands of advocates such as Jaswant Singh Rathore, KN Pethiya, RD Jain and Inosh George. All these learned advocates took a personal interest in the cases and took them to their logical ends. In some of the cases, like the demolition of the Bade Baba's Jain temple by its own devotees, we had to sit with KN Pethiya, the whole night to prepare the case. Advocate Inosh George, young and dynamic, often fought departmental matters like activists and brought them to successful completions. As good luck would have it, he is now serving on the green tribunal of Madhya Pradesh.

Two political figures who demonstrated excellent sensitivity and extended full co-operation in cultural issues were Yashodhara Raje Scindia and Jyotiraditya Scindia. Both of them were deeply concerned about the heritage sites and their environment. I was always very careful with projects in their constituencies (Shivapuri and Guna) and posted the best officers. Moreover, I used to make periodic visits to their constituencies to monitor the progress of the conservation. In the case of Bateshwar temple mining, Yashodhara Raje Scindia stood solidly behind the ASI and wrote to the authorities concerned against rampant mining. The entire credit for Shivpuri Museum and the conservation of monuments in the area go to Yashodhara Scindia. Once in a joint meeting of officials, one member raised some unnecessary objections. Raje told him that we had convened a meeting of the positive thinking officials to solve a problem. If it was not solved in this meeting, it would remain as an ever-festering thumb. Did we want to solve the problems or just keep them boiling? For some officers with a negative bent of mind, such meetings were the management classes of Harvard University.

Jyotiraditya Scindia was very clear and well-read on all heritage issues. He used to speak to me directly regarding the conservation and museum works. Once a Joint Secretary was aghast when he handled one of the letters written by me to Jyotiraditya Scindia and asked me, “Isn’t it against the protocol?” I informed him that the Minister spoke to me over the phone, giving instructions and my letters were the action taken reports in terms of specific instructions by the Minister. That was another Harvard Business class for that secretary who was careful about protocol but not about the ground results.

Twice, Jyotiraditya Scindia surprised us with his unconventional behaviour. He came to the ASI office at Janpath for a meeting regarding the development of Chanderi. Being a Central Minister, the usual protocol was to call the meeting at the Minister’s chamber. Although by that time, I was transferred from MP, he had instructed that I should be there in both the meetings. My presence was insisted even though he knew that I did not share his views on the introduction of an aerial ropeway in Gwalior fort. While he was opposed to it, I was in favour of it, for it saved all the Jain statues from the effects of vehicular pollution. India needs such efficient and unconventional Minsters to inspire faith in the younger generation.

For long, the visible face of the Archaeological Survey of India in Chanderi had been Dr GN Srivastava. Living away from civilisation, in Singpur Mahal, which was infested by robbers, he assiduously built up both the old and the new museums. No officer was ready to be posted there as it was a dangerous place, but Dr Srivastava, ably assisted by his wife Seema Srivastava, took up the challenge and completed the museum mission. He also acquired a lot of land for the ASI and carried out explorations in the adjoining areas. Owing to their untiring work, the entire landscape of Chanderi was transformed within a short span of four years. But this was possible because of the extraordinary political support extended by both the royal family members. Shivapuri and Chanderi developments are role models for political leaders of other regions to emulate.

Most of the ASI's work in Chanderi, the constituency of Jyotiraditya Scindia, and in Shivpuri, Yashodhara Raje Scindia's constituency, was the responsibility of a young engineer, Milan Angetkar, who is a very active field worker. In a short span of four years, Milan carried out conservation of temples located in the interior villages of Mahua, Amrol, Terahi, Kadwaha, etc., where even working space was not available.

In all these places, working space had to be created by managing the village folks, who had encroached upon the protected land in various ways. Management skills and interpersonal skills are the most important qualities one should be endowed with. My own name and religion was a problem when issues with temples cropped up, but once they realised that I was sincere and passionate in my profession, the simple village folks turned into temple warriors and extended full support that often a Brahmin could not have mustered. To resolve complicated issues in religious monuments in the Indian context, one has to transcend the gravitational forces of religion, caste and creed, which pull us down in opposite directions.

The office of the Superintending Archaeologist should provide full support to field officers to deal with such situations. Often the field officers would have to walk an extra mile in complicated situations. Officers under me had complete faith in me, and they knew that even if they committed a mistake unknowingly in the best interest of the monument, I would be there to stand behind them solidly. This implicit trust and faith gave them the courage to walk that extra mile. Extraordinary works happen when the subordinates are ready to walk those extra miles with full confidence in their senior officers.

Ashwini Lohani, the then Managing Director of Madhya Pradesh Tourism, was a most innovative and positive extraordinary officer I had the privilege to work with. Earlier, he served as the Managing Director of Indian Tourism Development Corporation, a central government enterprise. Later, he also served with distinction as the Chairman of All India Railways and even Air India.

Every State Tourism Department is allocated a sizeable sum of money by the Central Government. Since ninety per cent of tourism is dependent on heritage sites, they are expected to spend a major part of their funds on the preservation of the environment of the monuments. As archaeological rules are stringent, some such well-meaning projects have often resulted in unsavoury discord between the two departments. Few of the constructions were stopped half way for want of clearance by the ASI, resulting in wastage of government funds.

With little understanding and a positive mind, if the same rules are reinterpreted and grey areas are looked into, keeping in mind the interest of the monuments and the tourists, every source of friction could be turned into a connecting bridges between the two organisations. This is exactly what we did in Madhya Pradesh during the period of Ashwini Lohani. While the ASI was starved of funds, the Tourism Department enjoyed excess funds, unable to utilise the money usefully. If certain components of the tourism departments are taken as infrastructural facilities, which are essential in a monument, such as washrooms, lightings, designed antique benches, cafeteria and landscaping, it would be a great relief for the ASI.

This change of mindset and broader interpretation of rules of the ASI paid rich dividends by enhancing visitors experience in the monuments. This happy cooperation led to a great improvement in all monuments in Madhya Pradesh, and the number of tourists visiting began to show a marked increase compared to the years before. Shri Lohani also upgraded all the hotels in various parts of the state, which led to an increase in the occupancy of the MPTDC hotels. Known as a 'turnaround specialist,' he scripted a changed perspective and perception for MP Tourism from a loss-making organisation to a highly profitable one.

A positive interpretation of the rules and their implementation should be done at the circle level by the Superintending Archaeologist, who is aware of the practical problems, without referring it to higher authorities in Delhi. Once this problem goes to Delhi, the decision would be taken on a note put up by a lower/upper division clerk who does not know anything about the practical difficulties at the circle level. If the file is handled by a Director who is aware of the problems at the circle level and modifies the opinion of the LDC/UDC that would solve much of the problems. But if it is handled by people with a negative bent of mind, all further development of the circle would be stopped. While taking independent decisions, the Superintending Archaeologist should be discreet, moderate and logical without tripping up on the red line.

The fight put up by Dr BM Pandey at Agra against the undue intervention of Dr Ammar Rizvi, a Minister from Lucknow with the help of District administration at Agra, constitutes a brilliant chapter, with regards to the iconic monuments like Tajmahal and Fatehpur Sikri. Dr Pandey refused to toe the line of the Lucknow Minister and the District administration, despite pressures from the state capital. No doubt, the District administration resorted to many arm-twisting methods. The issue finally went to the then Prime Minister, Mrs Indhira Gandhi, who was very sensitive to such matters, issued a clear cut direction to all the state governments, not to misuse and hold any functions in the nationally protected monuments of the country. Officers like BM Pandey were trail blazers who left behind an inspiring legacy for the future officers of the ASI. Many of the veteran Archaeologists have in the past used their administrative acumen and financial powers effectively, keeping the larger interest of the ASI and the country.

Often, their vision, homegrown tactics and management of the press and the public are not handed over to the next generation. The ASI should conduct in-service courses to upgrade its own officers' managerial skills in the management of the monuments, the media, acquisition of the land, and marketing strategy. That would provide their natural talent with professional sharpness and refinement. The Institute of Archaeology should be a launchpad for preparing its officers as the best heritage managers. This book is partly a humble attempt to disseminate that homegrown practical experience to the coming generation of site managers.

□

Chambal Dacoits and Bateshwar Temples

While sitting and discussing with Dr Achutanandan Jha and Dr AK Pandey, my classmates and now colleagues in the Gwalior division of the Archaeological Survey of India, I asked them about the most challenging conservation work in the region. KM Saxena and Shashikant Rathore, the conservation officers of Gwalior, also joined us in our discussion. They were unanimous in pointing out Bateshwar in Morena district as the most challenging site, where a large number of fallen temples lay in several massive heaps, overgrown with vegetation. The Gujjar Pratihara dynasty (8–11th century) built these temples, who initially ruled from Ujjain and then shifted their capital to Kannauj. The kings of the dynasty played a most significant role in resisting the incursions of the Arabs by inflicting a crushing defeat on the army of Junaid and Tamin, the Arab army officials. The Gwalior inscription recorded that King Nagabhata "crushed the large army of the powerful *mlechcha* king." The defeat was so devastating that Sulaiman ul-Tajir (851 CE), an Arab traveller, writes: "A place of refuge, to which the Muslims might flee, was not to be found."

The credit for stopping the invasion of Muslims for 300 years, who had conquered Sindh in 712 CE, goes to the Gujjar Pratihara dynasty. Although many able kings ruled, Nagabhata 11 (805–833), Mihir Bhoja (836–886) and his successor Mahendrapala (890–910) were the most powerful kings. During Mahendrapala's reign, his kingdom extended from the Himalayas to the Narmada River and was bigger than the Gupta kingdom. Sulaiman further writes: "The ruler of the Gujjars maintains numerous forces, and no other Indian prince has such a well armed a cavalry. He is unfriendly to the Arabs; still, he acknowledges that the King of Arabs is the greatest ruler. Among the princes of India, there is no greater foe of the Islamic faith than he is. He has got riches, and his camels and horses are numerous." The role played by the Gujjars in keeping the country free from Arab invasion has not been adequately appreciated, and it requires a reappraisal.

However, the infighting among the Gujjar Pratiharas (central India), the Rashtrakutas (Maharashtra and south India) and the Palas (eastern India) weakened all of them. This situation encouraged their feudatories, notably the Parmars of Malwa, the Chandelas of Bundelkhand, the Kalachuris of Mahakoshal, the Tomars of Haryana and the Chahamanas of Shakambhari. The Gujjar Pratihara king, Rajyapala was defeated by Mahmud of Ghazni in 1018 CE. Although his son Trilochanpala and Jaspala continued for some time up to 1036 CE, the kingdom remained a pale shadow of its former glory.

The biggest challenge at Bateshwar was its location at the heart of the Chambal valley in Morena district, where nothing could be done without the express permission of the various dacoit gangs, who were constantly on the move. In the closing months of 2004, there were three groups, comprising notably of Nirbhay Singh Gujjar (UP and MP) Ram Babu Gadariya (Shivpuri-Datiya) and Jagjivan Parihar (Morena). In the Chambal valley, Gujjars and Gadariyas were traditional enemies. Of them, the most important group in and around Bateshwar was the Gujjar group. Hence, clear permission was required from them before undertaking any conservation work at the site. Now the question that arose was how to seek permission from them and who would act as the intermediaries?

Friendly journalists told me about Vijai Raman, then, the Additional Director-General of Police in Bhopal, famous for shooting dead the legendary dacoit, Pan Singh Tomar, on 1 October

1981, in an encounter which lasted 14 hours. Pan Singh took to the ravines after retirement from the military service and winning many sports medals. I had read about Vijai Raman in a book titled *Answered by Flutes,* written by Dom Moraes. Raman also played a crucial role in the surrender of the female dacoit Phoolan Devi in 1983, who had earlier killed 20 Thakurs at Behmai. It was Raman who also supervised the team responsible for killing Gazi Baba of the Jaish-e-Muhammad, the Pakistani terrorist who masterminded the bombing of the Parliament House on 13 December 2001. At that time, he was the Inspector General of Border Security Force in the Kashmir range. Vijai Raman was one of the founder members of the SPG, responsible for providing security to the Prime Minister of India. He was also one of the first persons to alert Arjun Singh, the then Madhya Pradesh Chief Minister, about the Bhopal gas tragedy.

Could he prove helpful to me in securing the permission of the dacoits in carrying out the conservation of Bateshwar temples? I wondered! This thought kept on rankling in my mind, but with a positive ring. But how do I approach him? That was the big question and that too, with a strange request. Was there any connection between a police officer and a temple conservationist?

Then, at a Madhya Pradesh Tourism Department programme, I happened to meet Veena Raman, one of the Directors of Madhya Pradesh State Tourism Department Corporation (MPSTDC). The cordial and dynamic officer impressed me. In India, archaeology and tourism are like conjoined twins; together, they can perform wonders, but archaeology finds it difficult to move along with tourism due to its many rules and restrictions. In a refreshing departure, I started identifying common grounds and many tourism officials appreciated this. During the tea break, I enquired from Veena Raman, with a little bit of hesitation, whether she was related to Vijai Raman. "Why not? Vijai is my husband," she shot back with her characteristic smile. For me, a new world was gradually beginning to unfold. Then, things began to move at an amazing speed.

The next day, Veena Raman fixed up my appointment with

Vijai Raman. I narrated my apprehensions and worries regarding the smuggling of antiques and the need to conserve Bateshwar temples. He gave me many valuable tips about how to deal with them. He also explained the different stages in a dacoit's life, ranging from revenge, accumulation of wealth and ultimately death or surrender. He added disarmingly: "Hindi films often lionise and romanticise them, but it is not like that. They are constantly on the move and do not stay in one place. Sometimes, they cannot even sleep properly."

The second man to deal with was Lachu Singh, a surrendered dacoit from Malkhan Singh's group. After undergoing punishment, Lachu Singh was rehabilitated in Bhopal, in one of the government offices. I invited him to my office in Bhopal and discussed the work I proposed to carry out in the Chambal area. He was kind enough to extend his full support. I introduced him to the two union leaders Bhaskar Verma and Saleem Beg, and with Lachu Singh's help, they set up a co-operative society in the ASI office, which now lends money up to Rs. two lakhs to needy employees. Wherever I was posted, I used to take personal interest in setting up co-operative societies for ASI employees so that the employees could take loans from the departmental society without being fleeced by private money lenders.

Apart from them, some of the employees, daily-wage labourers, notably Ram Gopal, Jaswant Singh Gujjar, Ratan Singh Gujjar and Manghu Gujjar, who had a close connection with the Gujjar group, also helped in ensuring the support of the dacoits in all possible ways. These four were the real field workers who managed everything on a daily basis at the ground level. There was nothing to be feared, they assured me.

In the initial stage of the discussion, the first question asked by the *dacoits* was, "What is the need to rebuild destroyed temples, and what interest could a Muslim possibly have in temple construction?" They were told about me that as an officer, I held a sterling record of reconstructing innumerable temples in different parts of the country.

It took me four months to dispel their doubts and obtain the necessary permission. Finally, we reached Bateshwar by jeep. Dr Achyutanand Jha, the officer of the Gwalior Range, was the leader of the team, which led us to our destination. Our team members—Dr SS Gupta, Dr AK Pandey, KM Saxena, Shashi Kant Rathore, and I followed him. When we reached the site, an eerie silence gripped the air. An uneasy calm prevailed! Naturally, we suffered from intense tension and trepidation.

Then we started exploring the area comprising massive heaps of stones that had been strewn all over. Like the Biblical Joshua, the patriarch of the Israelites, I had the first glims of the 'promised land.' Apart from the thousands of boulders of varying sizes, there were pillars, pilasters, friezes, grooved discs, entablatures, *amalkas, kalashas,* etc., all lying around in upside-down positions. It appeared as if the entire temple town had been razed to the ground in a powerful earthquake, without sparing anyone to narrate even the details of a horror-stricken story. A few temples stood like silent sentinels as if holding out its head to speak about their glorious past. The whole site stood as described by Julia ward Howe "It stands like a broken eggshell of civilization which time has hatched and devoured."

At a higher level stood a Vishnu temple in a very precarious state. As the external layer of stone had fallen away, the temple seemed to be dragging on with its melancholic existence. A mild tremor could bring it down any moment. On its doorway, the *dashavatara* (ten incarnations) story of Vishnu is carved.

Two hundred meters away stood the Bateshwar Mahadev temples, badly battered and bruised but still keeping its head above death and destruction. A kind soul had installed a Shivalinga inside it. Folding my hand in reverence and respect, I murmured: "*Shashvatam Shivam Achutham*" (only Shiva is everlasting). In between the Shiva and Vishnu temples, amidst the ruins and destruction, stood a sculpture of Hanuman painted in saffron colour, and trampling on Rati and Kamadev. The dacoits, before undertaking any daring operation, offered *puja* here with full devotion. Jaswant Singh Gujjar explained with a meaningful smirk that he too had participated in many such *pujas*. But now, he is a different man.

The way the ruins lay in their last sleep was the most captivating sight for a photographer. The music of the sprawling ruins was alluring and at the same time, awe-inspiring. The desolate ruins stirred the emotional depths of my soul. Similarly, for a journalist and a poet, this would be an unparalleled site, as he has only to write an essay or compose a poem. But for an archaeologist who is given the task of its restoration and reconstruction, it signifies a Himalayan task. Never before in India had an archaeologist been called up on to shoulder such a task of conservation and engineering feat. But, before taking up the conservation, one should listen to the story of the fallen stones of the temples. Here one is reminded of the verses of Nida Fazli:

"Sun ne ki Muhlet mile to aawz hai patharon mein
Ujdi hui bastiyon me aabadiyan bolti hain
Koi nahin bolta jab tanhaiyan bolti hain
Deewar–o-dar se utar ke parchaiyan bolti hain"

"Provided you have time, these fallen stones can narrate their story to you; the dead and gone generations from the deserted habitations can tell you their story. If no one speaks, the silence can communicate with you. Having come down from the walls and doors, the shadow can talk to you."

In the inner recesses of my mind, there emerged several pictures of the conserved and reconstructed temple complex. As said, here I was expected to speak to every stone and ask where it belonged to, when the original temple stood with all its glory. As an archaeologist, I had to sift and sieve through thousands of pieces, repeating the same question to piece together the scattered fragments with steel rods and binding pastes into the 9-11th century temples, as per the temple construction treaties of the time. When all the massive jigsaw puzzles were put together, a magnificent composition was expected to emerge out from the womb of the earth. I tried to imagine it, and spectacular visions of the future floated before my eyes

In the 14th century, a massive earthquake devastated the Delhi-Gwalior region, and the same must have brought down the Bateshwar temple groups. In *Futuhat-i-Firoz Shahi,* Sultan Firoz Shah Tughlaq (1351–1388) says that he repaired the Qutub Minar when lightning struck it. It was not simply lightning but an earthquake accompanied by lightning. That earthquake must have dealt a severe death blow to this temple group also. It was not the vandalism of the invading Muslim army. They mostly break idols, deface and chop off limbs.

As Bateshwar was far from the main trade route and devoid of patrons, the site was forgotten and sank into oblivion. Gradually, wind-laden earth was deposited, and trees took roots over it. Some roots of the trees have split the temples into multiple fragments. In our long years of service at the Archaeological Survey of India, none of us had ever seen a site in such a ruinous and deplorable condition. When Alexander Cunningham had seen it in 1882, he wrote: "...a confused assemblage of more than 100 temples, large and small, but mostly small, to the south-east of Padavali."

In Bateshwar, Alexander Cunningham had spoken about 100 temples, but despite our best efforts for one continuous year, we could locate only 40 temples and these too hidden within all kinds of dense vegetation growth. It was only after we began to clear the forest of trees and plants that we could see some semblance of the temples emerge. Even after removing trees, the actual counting of temples was not possible at many places as several heaps of stones lay strewn all around. Looking at the photo of the fallen debris before conservation, the widely-travelled English photojournalist Kevin Standage termed it an 'astonishing archaeological site' and 'India's largest jigsaw puzzle.'

In a place like Jageshwar in Uttaranchal, where one of the Jyotirlingas is enshrined, a complex of only 125 temples stands. There also, I had the privilege of taking up some conservation work in the year 2002–2003, but that conservation work was not so challenging. In the same way, at Aihole, the Bangalore Circle of the ASI had taken up similar conservation of 120 temples. In Bateshwar, after a complete survey, the remains of 200 temples could be located, each rivalling the shrines at both Jageshwar and Aihole.

After the initial survey, the question that worried us was about where to start the conservation work? Usually, we are supposed to begin from the entrance gate of the temple complex, but in an area where stones lay in several heaps, it was impossible to determine where the entrance gate had once stood. As we stood discussing and meditating over several spots to start with, we saw an innocuous 'pillar base' jutting out in the surroundings.

That was enough for an archaeologist to stir his spirit. My sixth sense started to wake up. The 'pillar shaft' lay quite close to the pillar base. Not far from it, the 'abacus' and the *'phalaka'* were also visible. These are the parts of the gateway we were looking for. The archaeological instinct in me murmured. But still, there are some more missing links. The debate was raging within my mind.

Nobody dared to steal anything from here due to the presence of the dacoits. It was indeed a great blessing in disguise! We were as excited as Christopher Columbus must have been on losing his way in the uncharted ocean but suddenly sighting birds above, which was enough indication of land being close by. It was of immense relief to us, but it made us raise one more question: "How could we have an entrance gate with only one pillar?"

The other pillar, which was essential for an entrance gate, was not visible anywhere. However, before searching for it, we decided to piece together the visible parts of the first pillar of the gateway. That was accomplished by inserting steel rods within broken parts and applying matching stone powder within the affected parts.

Then, by using the archaeological instinct, the adjacent area where we apprehended the other pillar to be buried was excavated. It also yielded all the architectural members of the other pillar. Every archaeologist is endowed with a 'third eye' and a penetrative mind.

In this case also, after a careful study, the pillar base was joined to the pillar and other architectural members by inserting strong steel rods and strengthening it with Araldite, like an expert knee surgeon. It was an entrance gate of perfect beauty and absolute finish. Only the beam that spanned the pillars was still missing. That might have been removed before the dacoits made their presence.

The four temples adjacent to it stood precariously with sagging foundations, heralding its imminent collapse. After carrying out basic documentation of them, they were dismantled, stone by stone and laid bare on the ground as per the elevation of the temples. This is the native and homegrown method for dismantling and reconstruction. Strong foundations were laid out, and then all the four temples were re-erected, one by one, in their original shape and form.

Look, the miracle has happened! The pillars that had fallen, broken and in many pieces, now stood with renewed vigour and energy. All the four dismantled and reconstructed temples now throbbed with life. When completed, a marvellous transformation took place, eliciting unstinted appreciation from the dacoits.

Another temple stood, of which the external layer and upper portion had fallen down. The *amalka* lay upside down and broken up into a few pieces. Inside the *garbha griha,* there was no idol to be found. Could it be a Shiva temple or a Vishnu temple? In the absence of an idol, it was difficult to corroborate anything. While trying to find an answer, I saw an innocuous slot on the front floor of the temple. This slot was rectangular in shape. That provided the answer. The rectangular slot denoted the *Nandisthan,* which meant that it was a Shiva temple. Like a devoted humble supplicant, I recited the vedic hymn '*Shiv shadakshar strotram:*

'Vahanam Vrishabho yasya
Vasuki kanthaBhooshanam,
Vame Shakti dharam devam vakaraya namo namah.'

(Salutations to Shiva who rides a bull, wearing the snake Vasuki round his neck like an ornament and supporting Goddess Shakti on his left.)

After reciting the mantra, while taking the circumambulation (*pradakshina)* of the temple, I happened to glance at the slope below. There, I saw a small and beautiful Nandi, looking at me with longing eyes, as if he had been waiting for me for the last one thousand years. This was nothing short of a spiritual union. We ceremonially lifted the bull, cleaned and reinstalled it in the slot where it sat looking perfect and a little proud. Thus, the dethroned Shivavahana has been restored to its original place. What else does he want?

In another case, a giant tree had strangulated the temple *shikhara* like an octopus with several branches. Its roots had pierced the temple through its ribs, splintering it into several fragments. The temple was in such a pitiable condition that it could not even gasp for its last breath. Again, it was a romantic sight for a photographer with the caption, 'A picture is worth a thousand words. But here, my mission was to save the temple first. There were methods tc keep the temple and the tree intact, but that would have been temporary life-saving ventilator support for a few months or years.

After weighing all the pros and cons, it was decided to cut down the tree. As per the *Agamas*, one cannot cut down a tree without taking permission from the tree and also from the birds roosting over it and insects nesting on it. We followed all the rules as enjoined in the scriptures and recited:

'Namaste vrksha pujeyam vidhivat sampragruhyatam
Yaaniha bhutaani vasanti taani
balim grhitvac vidhivat prayuktam
Anyarta vasam parikalpayantu
kshamantu taaryadya naostu tebhya'

(Oh tree, salutation to you! This worship offered by me in accordance with the scriptural rules may kindly be accepted by you. May all those beings that dwell in the tree accept the offerings made according to the scriptural rules and migrate to another tree to reside. May they pardon us now! We bow to them!)

After reciting the mantra, when the tree was cut down, the entire temple came crashing to the ground like a pack of cards. Then, it was reconstructed with meticulous care and precision. Fresh, clean and unspoiled by time, it now looked like a freshly minted temple. Its *shikhara*, with its intricate carvings, looked like a gem of rare workmanship.

The conservation work progressed very well without any hindrance. One day, while I was on the way to inspect the work at Doda Math, an isolated temple from the group, I noticed a man sitting and smoking. Although he was outside the temple, I asked him: "Are you not ashamed to smoke in the temple premises?"

He looked at me contemptuously and did not respond at all. By that time, Ram Gopal and Jaswant Gujjar, who were in touch with the dacoits, came forward, caught hold of my hand and stopped me from any further misadventure, instructing me, "Sir, don't say anything to him."

Although the smoker's face was partially covered, I could faintly recollect that I had seen his interview on *Aaj Tak* Hindi news channel. In that interview, he had expressed his desire to surrender to the police in Uttar Pradesh, in the presence of Mulayam Singh Yadav, the then Chief Minister of Uttar Pradesh. In this interview, he had flaunted his high political connections, which had brought him under severe media glare. On knowing his identity, I immediately apologised and profusely thanked him for saving all the gods and goddesses from the hands of antique smugglers. I also told him that 'God had deputed him to Bateshwar with a mission.' Later on, I termed that moment of my meeting as 'JAB WE MET.'

Now his curiosity was aroused. He wanted to know the secret of the mission. It was then explained to him that all these temples were built by a powerful dynasty known as Gujjar Pratihara, and he being Nirbhay Singh Gujjar, belonged to that illustrious caste and dynasty of the Gujjars. God has deputed him to the ancient temple town of Bateshwar with the mission of protecting the temples and gods and goddesses of his own Gujjar ancestors. The realisation that he was a descendant of a powerful dynasty who had built beautiful temples helped us in our mission of conservation of the temples. "*Mera jadu Chalgaya*" (My magic has hit) I told myself. Here, for the first time in his life, he was blown off his feet! Not by the bullet of the police. But, by the impact of the realization that he belonged to the Gujjar pratihara dynasty that once ruled the country. As I knew that all the dacoits are Devi worshippers, I recited some mantras from Devi Mahtmyam:

"Mahishasura Nirna shavi daatree varade nama

Ruupam dehi jayam dehi Yasho dehi Dwisho jahi"

The chants from Devi Mahathmyam had a sobering effect. The atmosphere was turning spiritual.

With 205 criminal cases of murder, dacoity, kidnapping etc., registered against him in Uttar Pradesh and Madhya Pradesh, he started running a parallel government in many villages. But now, time and technology are changing. How long could he hold on and continue to spread a reign of terror in the Chambal forests?

Mulayam Singh Yadav and Babu Lal Gaur, the respective Chief Ministers of Uttar Pradesh and Madhya Pradesh, in a joint meeting on 9 October 2005, had declared zero-tolerance against criminal activities. As a follow-up action, a Special Task Force (STF) was constituted by both states. It appeared that although ready to surrender, he wanted to exit in a blaze of glory. He made high-sounding demands for surrender; the government could not agree to meet them.

As a result of the coordinated efforts of the Task Force, different groups were eliminated, one after the other. Hotly pursued by the combined action of the STF, he was made to run from pillar to post. Although Nirbhay Singh Gujjar initially had 40 persons in his gang, many of them had been shot dead, and his foster son, Shyam Jatav surrendered to the police.

On 9 November 2005, Akhil Kumar, Commandant and Rajesh Diwedi, Deputy SP of the STF, on receiving an intelligence report, went to the Cheetapur ravines under Ajitmal police station of Etawa, equipped with night vision devices. At the time of operation, Nirbhay Singh Gujjar had five of his gang members with him. The operation, which started at 8.30 p.m., lasted for one-and-a-half hours in the dark night. Both Akhil Kumar and Rajesh Diwedi had a close shave with death but managed to kill all the gangsters before 10 pm. With the death of Nirbhay Singh Gujjar, the Chambal waters and ravines were gradually losing their frightening look.

As long as Gujjar and other groups operated in the area, the mining mafia was afraid of coming to Bateshwar. But once they found out that the entire gang had been eliminated, the powerful mining lobby started rampant mining, savagely plundering the precious preserves of the environment and seriously damaging the painstakingly conserved temples. The thunderous blasts of mining ripped through the body of the conserved temples, causing cracks in them.

Letters to various state authorities did not yield any tangible results. As I suspected the involvement of a Madhya Pradesh minister, Lakshmi Kant Sharma, I wrote him a demi-official letter and personally met him and expressed my grave concern. He plainly told me that he had not received my letter. I sent him a second letter and sought his intervention as he was the Minister for Culture and Mining. Later on, Shri Sharma was imprisoned in the infamous Vyapam case. Despite all these efforts, mining continued in full swing, causing damage to the temples. I was desperate to find out a way to stop the mining.

Nothing was working, and all the doors seemed to be closed. I was completely disillusioned. Then I could see a ray of hope filtering through from the other side of the tunnel. I resolved to write a letter to KS Sudarshanji, the then Sarsanghchalak of the Rashtriya Swayamsevak Sangh (RSS). Had I discussed the proposed letter with my close colleagues, Dr SS Gupta and Dr AK Pandey, they would have stopped me from this misadventure. Sometimes you have to act according to the dictates of your conscience.

Without informing them, I went to my office on 14 October 2007, which was a Sunday and requested Vijai Agarwal and LK Shukla to join me in the office. I told them that rampant mining was in progress at Bateshwar and that it was endangering the conserved temples, and as a last resort, I have decided to write a letter to Sudarshanji. Both Vijai Agarwal and LK Shukla were shocked. The letter had to be in Hindi, using the appropriate words to reflect the grim situation at the site. From their faces, it was clear that they were not in favour of my action. They discussed with me the pros and cons of such a letter. On seeing me hell-bent on my mission, they reluctantly relented.

After one hour, they came with the first draft. I edited it by using slightly stronger language by comparing the mining at Bateshwar with the demolition of temples at the time of Muhammed Ghazni and Aurangzeb. That was the punch line of the letter. When the second draft was ready, I had an unexpected visitor. He was Nitin Deve, a journalist working for *Nai Duniya*. He could discern that we were grappling with some serious issue.

I discussed the mining problem at Bateshwar with him and pointed out that some influential people were involved in it. Then I also revealed my programme to counter it by bringing it to the attention of Sudarshanji. For a moment, he was rendered speechless. A strange solution to an unusual problem! He also had his reservations about the path I was going to adopt and gently cautioned me. He was now sure that I had decided to send it. While leaving my room, he told me: "Once you send the letter, please inform me so that I can file a report. But I am not in favour of it."

What a crisis is for an archaeologist happens to be a scoop for a journalist! Since he was a young journalist in *Nai Duniya*, he immediately flashed the news, and it was printed in all the editions of *Nai Duniya*. I wanted to give some time to the RSS to act, but in this case, things had overtaken me, and I had no control over the situation.

The next day the news that KK Muhammed, a Muslim officer, had written a letter to the RSS against the ruling BJP government in Madhya Pradesh for the protection of temples came as a rude shock to the state government. It also gave the journalists of all hues and colours enough fodder to fire a few shots. To make it sensational, the story had all the ingredients, such as the Chambal ravines, dacoits, temples, mining, the RSS, BJP and a Muslim!

Immediately, the state government took remedial measures as they were rattled and had to defend themselves. All the newspapers and channels immediately picked the news up. Kumar Shakti Shekhar, who was working with *NDTV*, on learning that mining was still going on, surreptitiously went out in the dead of night to the site where mining activity was going on. The District Administration pleaded with him not to venture into

Chambal, the forbidden land, at such an unearthly hour and even warned him that he was stepping into a region where even his shadow would refuse to accompany him at night. But he, like a war reporter on the firing line, feverishly shot every detail of the covert mining operation. In the illegal mining area, the most feared weapon is the journalist's camera. Its cutting edge is sharper than the AK-47 rifle of the police.

Following in his footsteps, journalists like Manoj Sharma of *CNN-IBN* wove an entire story around dacoits of Chambal, highlighting the rampant mining and the fragile heritage of the site. Manoj Sharma even took an interview with Lakshmi Kant Sharma, the Minister of Culture and Mining, who had told me that he had not received my letter. Showing my letter to the viewers, Manoj said that this was the copy of the letter written by Mr Muhammed, but the minister had claimed that he had not received it.

The fearless reporting by Vijay Manohar Tiwari, Jayashri Pingle and Anil Pateria of *Dainik Bhaskar* Sarvani Sarkar (*Hindustan Times*), Dhanashyam Saxena (*Raj Express*), Rishi Kant Saxena (*Dainik Jagran*), Atmadeep (*Jansatta*), Deepak Tiwari (*The Week*) and other journalists and channels highlighted the grave situation at Bateshwar.

On 22 October 2007, the District Magistrate and the Superintendent of Police rushed to Bateshwar along with a large contingent of police officers. The mining lobby was equally very well-armed. This resulted in an exchange of fire between the police and the mining mafia. Both the District Magistrate, Akash Tripathy and the Superintendent of Police, Dr Hari Singh Yadav, being experienced officers, did not give in. Dr Hari Singh Yadav had the formidable reputation of wiping out the entire Jagjeevan Parihar dacoit gang in the month of March 2007 in Gadhiya village near Morena. Firing on such a group was nothing short of inviting death. Rajesh Mishra, SDOP, had a providential escape.

Although a case of murder under IPC 307 was registered, the police could not arrest anybody who had fired on them. Two cranes and two tractors, which were operating on behalf of the mining group worth Rs 70 lakhs were seized. As a follow-up action, all the arms licenses in the area were cancelled. Sharat Sarvate was called from Indore to drill 40 to 70 ft deep holes at regular intervals in the mines, which were blasted to desist the mining group from further mining. On the same day, Ambika Soni, the Central Minister for Tourism and Culture, wrote to Shivaraj Singh Chauhan, the Chief Minister of Madhya Pradesh, requesting him to extend full support to the ASI, as law and order fell under the state government. Ambika Soni also had a telephonic discussion with Shivraj Singh Chauhan. She also referred to the report of Kumar Shakti Shekhar, on *NDTV*. By that time, the state government had taken appropriate action to stop mining in Chambal. But the Chief Minister was upset at the turn of events. In a statement to the Press, he openly questioned my way of functioning and speaking to the media. In his reply, dated 31 October 2007 to Ambika Soni, the Chief Minister explained, in brief, that the action initiated by his government to stop the illegal mining included the cancellation of the mining licenses. But the last part of the letter that "I am leaving the issue of the propriety of some correspondence that the Superintending Archaeologist had indulged in and also his conduct of addressing the press, for your kind judgement" sounded my suspension bell in no uncertain terms. It was a letter from a Chief Minister to a Central Cabinet Minister against a Central Government officer. A copy of this letter was given to me by one of the many friendly journalists of Bhopal.

On receiving it, some of the officials in the Ministry of Culture, Delhi began to flip through the pages of Central Government Conduct Rules to pinpoint under what rules the accused officer could be suspended from government service. My cup of sorrow was now full to the brim; my future sealed and head on the block. Dark clouds hovered over the sky.

My *shikwa aur shikayat* (complaint) to Lord Shiva was: "Is this the reward you shower on your devotee who walked into the forbidden land and reconstructed your abode?" Now, it looked as only a miracle could save me from the inevitable. There was no other way for me but to recite the *Mahamrtyunjai Mantra.*

"Tryambakam yajaamahe
Sugandhim pushtivardhanam
Uruvarukamiva bandhanan
Mrityor mukshiya maamritat."

(We worship the three-eyed Lord Shiva, who nourishes and spreads the fragrance in our lives. May he free us from the shackles of sorrow, change and death effortlessly, like the fall of ripe brinjal from its stem.)

By now, Narayana Swami, the Congress observer for MP and Subash Yadav, the MP Congress leader, had approached the Governor, Balram Jakhar, in my support. They also spoke to Ambika Soni. I did not know either of them. A few journalists, who had visited Bateshwar and seen the remarkable transformation, met Ambika Soni to plead on my behalf. I did not know them either.

Then I received a call from an unknown number, asking me not to worry and assured full support. The conversation was brief and short. He was none other than Yashovardhan Azad, IPS officer, the IB in charge of Madhya Pradesh. He was speaking from Delhi. Some powerful authority might have called him for a factual report.

Later on, he became Secretary (Security) in the Cabinet Secretariat. I had a chance meeting with him once, but the IB keeps a full record of the Central Government officers. I felt as if Lord Shiva had deputed them as *ashtadikpalas (eight guardians of cardinal directions) to* save his devotee.

Rays of hope started filtering in, but the picture was not very clear. It was hazy. Two days earlier, I had an unsavoury exchange with a Secretary in the State Secretariat. In the morning, Anshu Vaish, IAS, the Director-General Archaeological Survey of India, telephoned me to know the condition of conservation and mining at Bateshwar. Mrs Vaish, a very efficient officer from Madhya Pradesh cadre, was under much tension due to some of her former colleagues' pressure in the state and the impending action. My own office was abuzz with a possible suspension order. Mentally, I was now prepared to face the action and discussed it with my officers.

There were hushed discussions in many corners, and a gloomy atmosphere prevailed throughout the day. Sensing the proposed action, many journalist friends visited me, but I requested them not to publish anything to avoid further precipitation of the situation.

Around 6:30 pm, Anshu Vaish again telephoned to inform me that the worst was over and no action was being contemplated. Sometimes Shiva acts in strange ways! Like a typical Malayali, I said: "*Krishna*...*Guruvayurappa*...It is your *Leela*! You manifest in manifold ways." Also, I recalled the words of assurance given by Yashovardhan Azad.

After this 'tryst with destiny,' the temple restoration progressed very well. The conservation team, headed by KM Saxena, Shashi Kant Rathore, and a few research scholars from Gwalior University, such as Om Prakash Narwariya, Sundar Lal Arya and Hukam Chand Arya, continued with their conservation work. They worked hard with local labourers. In order to prepare new pillars and brackets, we also employed some very expert craftsmen from Chanderi. With the combined action of diverse groups, a temple town rose out of its own ashes and debris like the proverbial Phoenix.

At one end of the site, heaps of stones lay in four terraces; only the steps were visible, and the temples to which they led had collapsed beyond recognition. We carefully studied the fragments accumulated near each step and concluded that fragments of 20 temples lay on the ground. The strategy and the process were chalked out. Within one-and-a-half years, 29 temples were reconstructed from their own fallen debris and restored to their pristine glory. The sight of the eighty reconstructed temples, rising up from their own tombs, was a heavenly and spiritual experience. Each stone that had gone into the construction was finely chiselled, cut and polished like a sparkling piece, and then they were crafted one over the other to make each temple a brilliant work of art. The sweet melody of the temple architecture and the cadenced grace of its carvings combined in making it into an enchanting musical note.

The lush green garden, laid out by the horticulture wing of the

ASI, headed by Dr Harbeer Singh added charm and beauty to the sprawling premises. It now looked so beautiful and ethereal that with a little bit of imagination, one could experience the cosmic dance of Lord Shiva casting his magical spell over the universe. How accurate was Kevin Strange when he penned his feelings during one of his visits to the site: "I don't think I have ever visited a temple site anywhere in the world where there are so many temples packed relatively in a small area...with the blend of chaos and conservation, you would be forgiven for thinking that the temples are currently being freshly built and the workers have just clocked off for lunch...." He further added: "Here is an example of what an amazing thing can happen with the right cast of characters in the play and the mutual desire (and resources) to make a real difference."

In 2008, I was transferred to Delhi due to the ensuing Commonwealth Games at Delhi in 2010. My mission was to prepare Delhi monuments with all amenities for tourists from different parts of the world. Even in those busy days also, I visited Bateshwar and gave necessary instructions to the employees and workers as I was passionately attached to my temples. My successor, Dr Venkatesaiha, carried out the work with much enthusiasm and enhanced energy. During his short tenure of one year, he restored ten temples.

From 2011 onwards, mining again started with renewed energy. The business of the mining mafia, which had come to a grinding halt, began again. The white stone from the area was in good demand in European countries. Huge blocks were cut and loaded into waiting tractors to be sent to the factories. Every third day, 70 containers of blocks were dispatched from Malanpur industrial area. As it had political support from all the parties, it was difficult for the officers to raise their voices.

A young IPS officer, Narendra Kumar mustered the courage to stop it. He had joined the IPS in 2009 and posted at Morena in 2012. Daring and dynamic, he started taking action against the mining mafia. A policeman in uniform but a poet at heart, he was deeply influenced by the early revolutionary fervour of freedom fighters like Shaheed Bhagat Singh, as evident from some of the poems, he recited at the Mussoorie training centre and uploaded on YouTube. He recited it with such fire and force as if a streak of Sardar Bhagat Singh's undying patriotism ran within his veins

On 8 March 2012, on the day of the Holi festival, after breakfast, when he left the house along with four constables, he did not sense anything unusual. He knew that the mining mafia was using such holidays to transport illegally mined sand and stone. When he sighted a tractor with illegally mined stones, he asked the driver to stop. Instead of stopping, the driver sped fast but was hotly pursued by Narendra Kumar. Although he could jump into the vehicle, the driver kicked him in his stomach, causing him to fall from the running tractor. The loaded tractor ran over his athletic body. Thus, a brave young officer was crushed under the wheels of the truck laden with the illegally mined stones by the mafia.

Narendra Kumar became one of the martyrs who lost his life for saving the environment in Morena. His wife, Madhu Rani Tiwatia, an IAS officer posted in Gwalior, was on maternity leave at the time of Kumar's death. Sad and distraught in this hour of trial, she displayed remarkable composure. The tragic killing caused political turmoil in Madhya Pradesh. Anna Hazare, the renowned social activist, declared from Jantar Mantar that nothing short of a CBI enquiry would be acceptable.

I did not know Narendra Kumar personally as he was posted in Morena in 2012. When the news of the martyrdom trickled in, I was in Calicut, my home town, on holiday. On the same day, KM Saxena and Shashikant Rathore telephoned and informed me about the martyrdom of this brave heart. I was shocked. Our team members felt that we would have met the same fate much earlier, but fate wanted it otherwise.

Free from dacoits and the mining mafia, a large number of people now visit Bateshwar. Rakesh Rustham organises travel and tour programmes for tourists from various parts of the country. He began by organising tours for former IAS and IPS officers who were earlier posted in the Chambal area. A group of artists and writers soon followed. Rakesh also arranged a tour for womens hockey players from Holland, who had won the Olympic Games in 2012. Presently, several college students visit the place from various parts of the country. The Minister for Tourism and Culture, Prahlad Patel (2019–2021) inspected the site, and all were looking at him with hope and expectations. But, nothing happened apart from the usual enquiries and assurances and posting of some photos on Facebook. Shri Suresh Soni, the RSS leader, had also visited the site and then had a webinar discussion with me. Eager to follow it up, he had one more meeting with Dr PK Mishra, the Regional Director and Dr Piyush Bhat, the Superintending Archaeologist. But as usual, it is painfully noted that during the entire BJP period of seven years, not a single temple has been reconstructed at Bateshwer. It is indeed a grave reflection on the stated philosophy and the work efficiency of the BJP government under reference. In this hour of total inertia and lack of vision, it is quite natural to recall the verses of the late Atal Bihai Vajapayee ji.

"Ahuti baki Yagya Adhura
Apnon ko Vignon ne ghera
Anthim jay ka Vajra Banane
Nav Dadeechi haddiyan galayen
Ao fir se Dhiya jalaen"
The oblation is incomplete,
The yagya ritual is only half done
To prepare the sword for the final battle
O, new Dadeechi, melt and forge the bones in the sharper crucible.
Come, let us lighten the new lamps."

Although I had retired from the Archaeological Survey of India in 2012, the poor performance of the ASI had started bothering many of us. There was no hope of any temple reconstruction at Bateshwar. During the Congress period, eighty temples were reconstructed. Since then, it was standing at a grinding halt. In some of the meetings which were exclusively attended by RSS, Pragya Pravah, Samskar Bharathi and BJP, I took up the issue and criticised their policy towards culture and archaeology. There was no positive response except from Shri Suresh Soni.

Then, unexpectedly one day, I received a phone call from Mrs Sudha Narayan Murthy of Infosys Foundation. Besides being one of the co-founders of Infosys, Madam is a business person, an eminent author of many books, and a philanthropist, all rolled into one. That gave me a ray of hope that Lord Shiva is listening to my prayers. Mrs Murthy had many questions about the conservation work of Bateshwar temples and wanted to see the place. We visited Bateshwar in the month of February 2019, just before the Corona brought the entire world to a standstill. Not only Bateshwar but many other monuments around Gwalior and Jhansi for four days.

The resurrected and reconstructed temples from the heaps of fallen stones, in the lap of nature, surrounded by manicured lawn, was a visual treat for the visiting party. As Mrs Murthy is an expert in art, architecture and iconography, our visit to various monuments were very good interactive sessions for all of us. We rarely get such scholarly visitors. When we showed them the photographs of the fallen condition of each temple, but now, proudly standing with a new life breathed into it, they could realize the enormity of the task that has gone into each temple. The awful presence of the dacoits, the fight with the mining mafia and the letters written to various authorities all have added fire and colour to Bateshwar. They were engrossed in the action drama of the resurrection of each temple as we moved, narrating the story from one to the other. After completing our first round, we came to the platform in front of the lower mut (temple residence) to have a total view of the site. This panoramic view offered them an opportunity to relish and savour the lyrical and musical shades embedded in the temple carvings.

This was the platform (Chabutara) where the dacoits used to congregate and plan. Sitting on the same platform, we had a simple village lunch. Then came the question we all wanted to hear. “If the Infosys wanted to support the temple reconstruction, which part would you like to assign to us?”- Madam asked.

“It is the Vishnu temple which is precariously standing, and we should take up its immediate reconstruction”- without losing any time, I answered. The estimate was prepared, and Infosys remitted the first instalment of the financial assistance amounting to around three crores and eighty-six lakhs through National Culture Fund (NCF). Let us hope with the help of Infosys, the second leg of the reconstruction of Bateshwar would be a reality.

Why did I take so much interest in the reconstruction and conservation of Hindu and Buddhist monuments? Even after my retirement, the interest has not abated. Of course, it was part of my passion and commitment to archaeology and heritage. What else could be the driving force behind this unadulterated passion? It was a realisation that my Muslim ancestors had wantonly destroyed a number of Hindu temples and Buddhist viharas, and I have been provided with an opportunity to sincerely repent for the past sins of my ancestors in a constructive way. This inner remorse and repentance were an all-consuming motivating force behind the extraordinary work of some conservation work at Nalanda, Vikramshila, Sanchi, Amarkantak, Bateshwar, Bhojpur and many other sites. A Bible proverb says, "Many are called, but few are chosen." Since I was one of the few chosen persons by God, that doubled up my responsibility. That way, my life in Archaeology is an unabashed and sincere apology for the past sins of my ancestors. There are many Muslims who silently suffer from this guilty feeling.

In 1998 I met Dr Ishri Arshad, a well-known doctor of Bihar Sharif who used to do free treatment and service at Nava Nalanda University. I enquired from him the reason for doing free service at Nalanda, in a Central Government Institution. He said my ancestors had destroyed this University and many other ancient institutions, and it is my duty to repent for it through free service for the students studying at Nalanda. I told him that it is the same force that is driving me also in my conservation attempts. He warmly embraced me and said that there are a number of Muslims who share our views. But it does not find resonance in the main media. Dr Faizal, the son of Dr Arshad still keeps the tradition shown by his illustrious father and serves the Nava Nalanda University. Tufail Ahammed Khan Suri is another such passionate explorer and protector of Hindu and Buddhist heritage in different parts of Bihar. Tufail Khan Suri spent a lot of his personal wealth for such explorations, and even at this advanced age, also keeps the interest alive. Yasin Pathan, a devote Muslim Pathan, is another Muslim who spearheaded the movement of the protection of 34 terracota temples for the last 42 years in Pathra village of Midnapur district in West Bengal. When Yasin took up the mission of protection in 1971, he was opposed by both Hindus and Muslims. Due to the continuos efforts of Yasin, it is now a centrally protected monument of the Archaeological Survey of India since 2003. After the destruction of Babri Masjid, Yasin was in hiding to save him from Muslims, who did not look kindly to Yasin who protected Hindu temples. With failing health and two heart blocks, Yasin is still fighting for the seventy farmers whose land the Archaeological Survey of India had acquired for protecting the temples. Who knows that Dr Ishri Arshad's, Tufail Suri's and Yasin Pathan's ancestors were in the army of Bakthiyar khilji and were personally instrumental in destroying temples and Viharas or not? If so, what a surprising turn history is now taking!

In 2019, I sent a proposal to the Madhya Pradesh Tourism Development Corporation to set up a 'Dacoit Museum' at Bateshwar after the model of Robinhood Museum in England and Robbers Museum in Spain.

The Chambal region comprises parts of Uttar Pradesh, Madhya Pradesh and Rajasthan with hotspots at Bhind, Morena and Gwalior (in MP) and Eta, Etawa, Mainpuri, Auraiya and Jalaun (in UP). The landmass of Chambal is unique as it is covered in a maze of mezzanine ravines, some of them with a depth of 80ft, in which the legendary dacoits of Chambal not only roamed but also ruled. They evoked both fear and respect, and their writ ran in the entire Chambal terror-land.

The dacoits and their daredevil exploits are now a part of the folklore and 'intangible heritage.' It has gone down into the 'generational memory' of Indians. The constant feud and the general insecurity has forced everyone to keep both licensed and unlicensed arms. As per an earlier report, Bhind, one of the districts of Madhya Pradesh had 29,800 licensed guns, while

Morena boasted 27,626, mostly 12-bore or 315-bore rifles. Illegal arms are much more than one could ever guess.

In the bazaars of these districts, at one point in time, it was a common sight to see ordinary persons pedalling their cycles with guns hanging from their shoulders. Some of the dreaded dacoits, whose names bring awe and fear are Man Singh, Sultana Daku, Putli Bai, Mohar Singh, Pan Singh Tomar, Chavi Ram, Kalu Yadav, Malkhan Singh, Madhav Singh, Phoolan Devi, Nirbhay Singh Gujjar, Seema Parihar, Ram Babu Gadariya, Daya Ram Gadariya and Hafizullah. Malkhan Singh used letterheads and titles such as 'King of Dacoits' to extract money from the relatives of the kidnapped. Both the jagged topography of the land and the spine-chilling accounts of the dacoits could be sold out as 'unique selling propositions of the site.' Both these are 'fear factors,' which no other site in India can replicate and hence have become the USP of Chambal alone.

The surrender of the Chambal dacoits started in 1960 when Acharya Vinoba Bhave and Subha Rao took the initiative at the request of Tehsildar Singh, son of dacoit Man Singh. In the initial stage, only 20 dacoits had surrendered; the second spell of surrender was due to the efforts of Jay Prakash Narayan, the socialist leader. While the negotiations for the surrender by dacoits in 1971 was going on, Mrs Gandhi made it clear that the terms would be acceptable to her if Mohar Singh headed the surrender party. MP Chief Minister Arjun Singh arranged many such surrender events, the most important being that of Phoolan Devi in 1983. After spending 11 years in prison, she contested the election from Mirzapur in Uttar Pradesh and was twice elected as a member of the state legislature.

Several Bollywood films have been made on the life of dacoits. Although the film *Mother India* set the tone in 1957, films such as *Ganga Jamuna* (1961), *Mujhe Jeene Do* (1963), *Khote Sikke* (1973), *Mera Gaon Mera Desh* (1971), *Kache Dhage* (1973), *Sholay* (1995) and *Bandit Queen* (1994) soon followed suit. *Pan Singh Tomar*, *Sholay* and *Bandit Queen* became iconic films, running for many weeks in theatres. Hollywood alone has produced more than 26 films. All these films have made the dacoits much larger than life. Prancing down on horses from the ravines or chasing a running train in the valley are some of their highlights.

There are hundreds of arms, rifles and AK-47s used by various groups, and each one of them has a story of its own. More than 26 films have popularised the Chambal land, but outsiders rarely know how fierce the terrain actually looks! If the Tourism Department of Madhya Pradesh comes forward to set up a museum at a convenient place in Bateshwar, the place has the potential to attract several tourists. Its proximity to Agra and Gwalior will make it a successful initiative.

Since this is a land of transformation (from dacoits to obedient citizens), feminine energy zone (Mitaoli) and the place of 'Rural Tourism,' it would be proper to train the surrendered dacoits and educated girls from the villages to run the tourist facilities, such as the security arrangements, watch-and-ward duty in the monuments, running of the cafeteria, etc. Both the surrendered dacoits and the village folks should be partners and beneficiaries of the new tourist destinations. The presence of the surrendered dacoits can still be used as an attraction for foreigners and Indians, who would love to have lunch or tea with transformed dacoits.

Along with this, the village's up-gradation should also be taken up by providing toilets in all the houses, widening the roads, and initiating improvements in education and sanitation. A yoga, massage and meditation centre would match with the character of the Chausath Yogini temple. Since it was a centre of temples, training may be imparted in classical dance. Subsidies may be considered for encouraging the villagers to switch to organic farming and horticultural activities.

In India, 68.84 per cent of the population lives in 6,38,000 villages. Rural tourism can regenerate and revitalise the economy of the villages in the emerging world of post-Covid. Since the philosophy embedded and transformation envisioned in rural tourism at Chambal is of significantly higher denomination, let a beginning be made by the Madhya Pradesh Tourism Development

Corporation and the Archaeological Survey of India. Let me repeat once more, "The real voyage of discovery consists not in seeking new landscapes, but in having new eyes and vision." Marcel Proust. Let this third eye lead our political leadership in understanding, projecting and marketing our heritage.

□

Amarkantak: On the Footsteps of Adi Shankara

My service in Madhya Pradesh provided me ample opportunities to restore several temple groups. One such group was located at Amarkantak, the original source of the river Narmada. It flows mainly through Madhya Pradesh, Maharashtra and Gujarat. Being the source of the Narmada and the lifeline of all the three states, the public regards it as the holiest river of Central India. Naturally, it was home to many ruined temples dating back from the 8th to the 11th centuries. Sometimes, such places become havens for anti-social elements. Although it was a site protected by the ASI, its ownership was still in private hands right from the beginning. This meant that ASI did not have full authority over it, and as such, it was not possible to evict the encroachments and restore the temples. Several huts and cowsheds dotted the site, and cows could be seen freely roaming around and dirtying the area. The huts were occupied by all kinds of drug addicts dressed in *sanyasi* clothes. To add to its woes, the local Panchayat used it as a dumping ground and installed a big dumping bin also. The situation was such that no action could be taken despite all the pressure that the ASI could put on the government. We appealed to a number of officials, but no one helped. The attempt to acquire the ownership of the land miserably failed as the ASI officials in Delhi did not comprehend the importance of land acquisition around protected monuments in its scheme of developments. Protection of a monument without ownership is a perennial source of friction and a festering wound.

Dr RC Agarwal, the former Superintending Archaeologist, had unsuccessfully tried to acquire the land from 1990 onwards and solve the problem. Following his example, after a gap of fifteen years, I too did my best to convince my officers in Delhi to acquire the land. As usual, nobody paid any heed to my fervent appeals either. It was only a question of 10 lakh rupees, which the ASI could easily spare. But in government services, it is often a negative note written by a lower/upper division clerk, which decides the fate of many projects, unless a higher officer overrules it. But, the higher officer should be endowed with that kind of farsightedness and vision.

When there was no positive action, I wrote one more letter to the Director-General in desperation and stated: "If Lord Shiva who is enshrined in Amarkantak is not able to protect himself what poor Muhammed could do?" I thought that my passionate appeal would mellow the heart of some government servants. But that did not happen. It did not elicit any favourable action. On the contrary, after reading the letter, the officials in Delhi appreciated the sharp barbs shot against them but did nothing to solve the problem. This revealed our typical mindset.

The repeated failure of the mission convinced me of the necessity of changing the track. There is no point in smashing the head against the wall. If plan 'A' did not work, the alphabet has twenty-five more letters. The plan had to be changed, but never the goal. This time I approached UK Verma, Chairman, Narmada Valley Authority (NVDA), and shared my concerns about the appalling condition of the Amarkantak temples and the land acquisition issue, which was at the root of all these problems. Now, he alone would be able to save the temple group from the present pitiable condition. Since NVDA is there because of the Narmada River, its source is equally important for NVDA and the ASI. Having said this, I further explained that the ASI had completed transplantation of the Chaubees Avatar temple on behalf of the NVDA for which the estimated cost was Rs 25 lakhs, out of which the NVDA had paid only Rs 15 lakhs rupee to the ASI. Rs 10 lakhs were still due from the NVDA for the transplantation of the temple.

My submission was that instead of paying the ten lakh rupees to the ASI, it would be appreciated if the same amount is paid to the Collector of Amarkantak for the acquisition of the temple land for the ASI. Usually, nobody would have agreed to such unusual requests unless the officer was very positive. But he discussed it with the Minister concerned, got the land acquired through the Collector, and handed it over to the ASI. What the ASI had not done for the last 15 years was done by him within a few months. The difference was in the attitudinal change and the perspective with which one looked at it. Later on, he told me, "Muhammed, if you were not so passionate about Amarkantak, I too would not have gone to that extent." "A positive attitude gives you power over your circumstances, instead of your circumstances having power over you" Joyce Meyer.

Once the land was acquired, notices were issued to all the encroachers to vacate the area. As expected, when they refused, SK Singh, a very competent conservation officer, removed all the encroachments, including the *gaushalas,* within a day. He carried out the work without even informing me. When he came back and showed me the photographs and the videos of the encroachment removal, I was pleasantly surprised to see the demolition of several houses and cowsheds, which was a very sensitive issue, especially when the state head of the ASI is a Muslim. The encroachers put up a cloth banner stating, 'Nobody is listening to the wailings of the holy cows,' but the public did not pay any attention to it as SK Singh, Advocate Anil Singh and contractors KP Pyasi and SS Parihar had managed everything smoothly at the ground level. SK Singh and his team would not have resorted to such a bold action unless they had implicit faith in me. Left to me, I would have taken some more time to remove encroachments and that too only after deploying enough police force to maintain the law and order situation.

The *ashram* of Shankar Acharya of Dwarkapeeth, the spiritual head of Dwarka and Haridwar, lay close to it. A legal case was in progress between the *ashram* and the ASI as the *ashram* had carried out illegal construction within hundred meters of the monument. Alarmed at the demolition, the *ashram* authorities approached Smt Ambika Soni, the Minister for Tourism and Culture. It was widely perceived that the Dwarkapeeth Shankar Acharya was close to the Congress party, and the Minister would be won over. Some people tried to depict me as a chronic troublemaker, as I had earlier, attempted to stop the activities of the mining mafia at Bateshwar. While the BJP was violating the rules at Bateshwar, in Amarkantak, a religious group considered closer to Congress was on the wrong side of the law. Soon complaints went to Ambika Soni against the ASI and its demolition activities.

Anshu Vaish, the Director-General, ASI, was called by the minister to discuss the encroachment removal and demolition. As I happened to be in Delhi, the Director-General took me for the discussion but asked me to wait outside the Minister's chamber until permission was taken from her. On my entry, the Minister found it hard to believe that I was the man who was fighting both with the BJP and the Congress in Madhya Pradesh. Madam asked me: "Are you, Mr KK Muhammed?"

"Yes, Madam!" I replied.

"Why are you creating troubles for the followers of the Shankar Acharya?" Madam asked.

In my defence, I laid before her three photos of the site—the first showed the area before the conservation of temples encroached by several slums, cowsheds and littered with municipal waste. The second photo showed the same area after the removal of all the encroachments. The third photo showcased the temples in their full glory after the conservation and the development of a lush green landscape. The site with beautiful red laterite pathways and heritage furniture stood in stark contrast with the earlier two photographs. I added that in addition to it, we had also conserved the historic *pushkarni,* where Adi Shankara bathed to its pristine glory. The Minister looked at the last photos admiringly and murmured: "Unbelievable transformation! No one could have imagined such a change!"

I clarified further: "Although the ASI protected the site, it did not have ownership rights over the property. How, then, could you remove the encroachers, especially those who wear religious ochre robes?" I also explained that we had been requesting the senior officers of the ASI to grant permission for the acquisition of the holy land for years. When there was no positive response, we adopted a different stratagem. Without spending even a rupee from the budget allocated to the ASI, the transformation was brought about through the intervention of the Narmada Development Board, especially with the help of UK Verma. (Incidentally, it may be pointed out that later on, Shri Verma worked under Ambika Soni as the Secretary, Information and Broadcasting).

When I said this, the Secretary got up from his chair and told me: "Now you come and occupy this central seat."

I further added: "Adi Shankara had hallowed this land by meditating and performing puja in the 9th century. But for the last many years, this place was being used as a slum, a dumping ground for garbage and a haven for drug peddlers. Now, this is neat and clean and has become a proper abode of Shankara with its sanctity and spirituality restored.

After listening to what I had said and being convinced, the Minister made only one request that I should not demolish the structure of the *ashrama*, which they had already constructed. I assured her that it would not be demolished unless there was a court directive. On emerging from the Minister's room, I noticed a representative of the Dwarakapeeth Shankar Acharya sitting in the reception room.

That night I received a phone call from an unknown number. It was from the lawyer who was representing Shankar Acharya's case in the court. He congratulated me for beautifully conserving the site after removing all the encroachments and undesirable elements. I requested his help and cooperation in retaining the spirituality and pristine purity of the site. He assured me that although both of us were on different sides of the fence, this was an area where we could work together.

One day, His Holiness the Shankar Acharya himself visited

Bhopal. He stayed in the house of the owner of a popular newspaper published locally. A manager of His Holiness, who was not aware of the latest development at Amarkantak, wanted an article to be published against the ASI in the context of Amarkantak. He was probably not aware of my discussion with the Minister, Ambika Soni. As per the instructions of the editor, the assistant editor Sharmaji met me and asked for the details about the removal of the encroachments and anti-social elements. In reply, I showed him the same photos I had shown to Ambika Soni, which was enough to convince even a diehard opponent. And then, I spoke to him about the spiritual aspect of the site. This was one of India's holiest places as it has been associated with the life of Adi Shankara. Who would have liked such a place to be under the control of drug peddlers? Shankara was born at Kaladi in Kerala. Being a Keralite and a heritage lover, I had an emotional attachment with Adi Shankara and his *ashrams*. The next day, he published a very objective and logical article on this in his newspaper so that none would be offended.

The real heroes in the story of Amarkantak are SK Singh, Adv. Anil Singh, KP Pyasi and SS Parihar. If they had not followed up on the encroachment removal, Amarkantak would not have scripted a success story. Their efforts were amply rewarded when the site was selected as the best-maintained monument by the Ministry of Madhya Pradesh Tourism. My successor, Dr Nizamuddin Tahir received the award and added to the value of the site by setting up a beautiful museum. As a commander, you can only choose the goal and strategy to motivate your soldiers because the battle has to be fought by them.

□

Kashi, the Eternal City of Salvation

In 1997, I visited Benares (Kashi) as an archaeological officer of the area, which included Bihar, Jharkhand and parts of Uttar Pradesh. Before that, I had gone there twice on a two-day casual visit. As I got down from the train, I noticed a huge crowd waiting to get on the train. The platform was densely packed with people of all hues and colours. They were all devotees who had come from distant parts of the country for taking a ceremonial bath at the Ganges, which they believed would wash off their sins. After the bath, *puja* at Kashi Vishwanath temple is considered the holiest part of a pilgrim's itinerary. At Dasashwmedha Ghat, there was the hustle and bustle of vegetable sellers, pilgrims and tourists. In the middle of this hustle, cows could be seen roaming here and there unconcerned by the multitude. On the steps of the *Ghats*, one could see several mendicants with sacred marks on their foreheads. Smoke billowed out at the Harish Chand and Manikarnika Ghats, where the dead are cremated. It is believed that those who are cremated at Benares, especially at Manikarnika Ghat, go straight to *Vaikuntha* (heaven). As there is a rush of people who wants to reach *Vaikuntha*, the funeral fires never are extinguished here.

The history of Kashi dates back to 1800 BCE when history was fresh and time stood still. The excavations conducted by Prof Vidula Jaiswal at Aktha and Ramnagar has pushed back the chronology to 1800 BCE. Located on the confluence of Rivers

Varuna and Assi, it soon developed as a religious, cultural and trade centre. This is the city of Shiva and Ganga and the city of death and salvation. As the origin of the town is attributed to Shiva, music and dance runs in the city's veins. It is also the city of many Jataka stories associated with the previous births of Buddha. A widely popular proverb exhorts people to escape from *raand* (widows), *saand* (male cows), *sannyasis* (mendicants) and *seedis* (steps). But, in Benares, it is impossible to escape any of these things. The narrow lanes, the widows, the cows, the mendicants, and the innumerable steps impart the city its unique colour and flavour. Here, legends and logic combine to make the city one of the oldest living cities, which is a paradox of many opposites.

Among the seven holy cities that people visit before death to achieve *moksha* (salvation)—Puri, Ayodhya, Mathura, Haridwar, Ujjain, Dwarka and Benares—the last name is undoubtedly the most important. Here is enshrined one of the 12 *Jyotirlingams* of the country. It is equally important to Buddhists and Jains as it is to the Hindus. It is the birthplace of Suparshwanath, Chandraprabhu, Shreyanshnath and Parshwnath, the 7th, 8th, 11th and 23rd Tirthankaras. Buddha, after enlightenment, made his first sermon at Sarnath, in the vicinity of Benares.

The evening *aarti* with thousands of lamps flickering to the accompaniment of temple bells and the chanting of Vedic hymns is simply a mind-blowing sight, seen nowhere in the world. When the *aarti* is seen from the middle of the Ganges with the boat slowly gliding over its waters, it creates ripples in the mind, and one feels spiritually elevated. In the morning, in the tranquillity of the hour, the *Surya Namaskar,* yoga and other ritualistic practices by hundreds will take one back to the ancient period providing greater spiritual bliss. Yellow-robed *sannyasis* with matted hair and the heads of half-shaven priests imparts the impression that one is on a different planet.

All through the visit, I was constantly reminded of the comment of Mark Twain, the American writer, who said: "India is the cradle of the human race, the birthplace of the human speech, the mother of history, the grandmother of legend. Benares is older than history, older than traditions, older even than legend and looks twice as old as all of them put together. No museum I had ever visited provided such an encompassing sense of history, as wandering the dusty warrens of the ancient city."

After my five-days visit to Benares, I was convinced that Benares deserved a place in the list of UNESCO's World Heritage cities. It was on the steps of the Ganges that the celebrated encounter of Adi Shankara took place with Chandala, the outcaste. Instead of getting out of the way from the path of Shankara, Chandala raised some profound philosophical questions. Shankara was much impressed by his questions that he accepted him as his guru and composed *Maneesha Panchakam*, which sums up Shankara's philosophy and *Aham Brhmasmi*.

Ramananda, though born in Prayag, made Benares his *karma bhoomi*. He was equally influenced by Vishishta Advaita of Ramanuja and Nath Sampradaya, one of the Shaivite ascetic groups. Kabir, the *bhakti* saint, was born in a weaver's hut and grew up in the Kabir Chauraha. Although serving as a bridge between Hinduism and Islam, he often questioned and sometimes mocked the ritualistic beliefs of both the Hindus and the Muslims.

Moko kahan dhunde se bande
Main to tere pas mein
Na teerath mein, na moorat mein
Na ekant niwas mein
Na mandir mein na masjid mein
Na Kabe Kailash mein.

Guru Nanak (1469–1539) paid a visit to the city in 1507 and held discussions with the pundits of Kashi Vishwanath. Sant Ravidas was also born and grew up in the city. Tulsidas wrote his *Ramcharitmanas* sitting partly on the banks of the Saryu River at Ayodhya, and the final finishing touches were made on the *ghats* of the Ganga. When Tulsidas had a vision of Hanuman at Benares, he preferred to spend his last days at Assi Ghat.

Pundit Jagannath, a Telegu Brahmin of the 17th century,

composed his magnum opus *Ganga Lahiri*, sitting on the banks of the river and waiting for his final call by the Ganga, which honoured him with a watery grave (*jal samadhi*). Guru Har Gobind and Guru Teg Bahadur came to the city in search of spiritual purity and tranquility. Dara Shikoh also spent a part of his time discussing with Hindu scholars while writing *Majmu-ul-Bahrain* (Mingling of Two Oceans) and translating the *Upanishads* into Persian.

The credit for reclaiming Kashi and restoring Kashi Vishwanath in 1780, against all odds, goes to none other than Ahilyabai Holkar. By reclaiming the Hindu spiritual landscape and undertaking conservation of ancient temples in various parts of the country, right from Badrinath, the Queen demonstrated a vision that no other king or queen had displayed in Indian history. It is to be noted that her efforts came much before the establishment of the Archaeological Survey of India in 1861. Unfortunately, her contribution to the field of conservation has been largely ignored by modern India. It is high time the Government of India came forward to acknowledge her valuable contribution and institute a conservation award in her name in a befitting manner. Later on, in 1839, Maharaja Ranjit Singh covered the spires of the temple with gold.

Sri Ramakrishna Paramahamsa, Swami Vivekananda and Swami Dayanand Saraswati also came to Benares for spiritual enlightenment. Acknowledging the spiritual eminence of the city, almost all the local kings constructed huge mansions on the *ghats* for royal members and the common man from different parts of their respective states. In short, Benares is a mini India with all its diversities and contradictions and the metropolitan city of India's spiritual journey. The more I studied about the city; the more my conviction grew that it should be the first city to be nominated in the list of World Heritage Cities from India.

All over the world, some 250 cities have been granted the title of Organisation of World Heritage Cities (OWHC). Founded in 1993 at Fez, Morocco, it has grown into a strong organisation of 250 cities with a population of more than 130 million. Although

Ahmedabad, Jaipur and Vellore are included in the list of World Heritage Cities, it is unfortunate that Kashi, the mother of all cities, has not found a place in it. From India, Kashi fully deserves to be included in this list. Two cities from Sri Lanka and three from Nepal have made it to this list. However, Kashi is historically more significant than any of them. What is needed is a positive outlook and a long-term vision.

Similarly, there is not even a single museum dedicated to Lord Shiva in this holy city so dear to Lord Shiva and the River Ganga. In this crowded city, it is admittedly difficult to build new edifices or even to acquire land for that purpose. In 2001, I had suggested to RVV Ayyar, the then Secretary of Culture that the Man Mahal, which is already under the ASI's supervision, be converted into a museum for Shiva and Ganga. Professors from Benares Hindu University and the Tibetan Institute supported me in the initial discussion with the Secretary. Unfortunately, although Ayyar was positive, I was transferred from Patna Circle to Agra before I could get written permission from him. With about 15,000 tourists visiting the city daily, the museum would have been an excellent educational ground and a befitting tribute to Shiva and the Ganga. I planned to have replicas of the Shiva sculptures from all over the country.

Everything seemed perfect. The location of Man Mahal on Dasashwamedh Ghat is the best as it is visited by all. The structure of Man Mahal, a protected monument by the Archaeological Survey of India, is there to house the museum. A few encroachers on the lower side had to be evacuated by rehabilitating them in alternative places. Not much investment was required. Having a Shiva Museum in Shiva Nagari on the banks of River Ganga with a guided tour would have been a great experiential experience for a tourist. He would have gone back from the city, fully informed on the city's lores and legends.

At a seminar on the development of Benares, now called Varanasi, in 2014, I again made the same suggestion. It was organised by the Managing Editor of the popular Hindi newspaper,

Dainik Jagran, Mahendra Gupta, and I was one of the few people to be invited from outside Varanasi.

My speech during the first session made it clear that "If we succeed in getting this most ancient city, a place in the list of World Heritage Cities, it will be an important milestone." The audience greeted it with thunderous applause. When I said that Varanasi was the very heart of Aryavarta and corroborated my statement with the help of some Sanskrit *shlokas*, the audience endorsed it heartily. Finally, when I proposed the idea of a Shiva-Ganga Museum, the audience gave another applause.

At lunch, Mahendra Mohan Gupta told me that the idea of promoting Varanasi as a World Heritage City and setting up a Shiva Museum would be placed before the President of the BJP, Amit Shah. When the latter came to attend the second session, Mahendra Mohan Gupta placed the suggestion before him. Shah's response was positive, but for some reason, the matter did not proceed further.

Of course, the World Heritage proposal for a city like Benares has some practical problems as is clear from the latter-day Kashi Vishwanath corridor and subsequent demolitions. However, setting-up up a Shiva-Ganga Museum posed no problems whatsoever. A simple order from the Director-General of the ASI to the Superintending Archaeologist would have been enough. We hope the Prime Minister Shri Narendra Modi would take steps to turn his own constituency Varanasi into a World Heritage City and establish a museum in honour of Lord Shiva and the holy Ganga at Man Mahal.

In 2017, I revisited Benares at the invitation of the Benares Hindu University to participate in a seminar. In the evening, I went to Man Mahal to see if any progress had been made in setting up a Shiva Museum. I was totally disappointed. There was no effort to set up a museum there.

Later on, I came to know that in 2019, a 3D museum, the first of its kind in eastern Uttar Pradesh to showcase the Kashi *ghats* and other items of heritage value, like music and dance, had been set up there. The virtual tour extending 90 minutes starts with a short film introducing the city in its various cultural layers. It also highlights the true meaning of different rituals, the story of Shiva, the Ganga, Ram Lila and finally, a virtual dip in the Ganga created by sensor-controlled sprays. Although a museum for Shiva and the Ganga could not be set up, this virtual museum effectively compensates for the drawback and the same was inaugurated by the Prime Minister Shri Narendra Modi.

□

Delhi: Commonwealth Games, 2010, and Showcasing India

In the year 2008, I was transferred to Delhi while conservation work was in full spate at various monuments in Madhya Pradesh. Transfer to Delhi was based on my excellent performance in Bhopal. Delhi was frantically preparing for the Commonwealth Games in 2010. Works, related to the monuments had to be planned and executed as per the schedule and much before the commencement of the Games. Face-lifting of the 45 monuments which the sportsmen and the tourists were expected to visit was a highly challenging and most crucial task to be accomplished. Along with it, public conveniences and other facilities had to be upgraded. Development of the landscape and illumination was the third important aspect where the ASI had to concentrate.

Using the funds allocated, the ASI had managed to transform all the 45 monuments and provide them with tourist facilities. Along with this, vast land stretches on both sides of Siri Fort, Qila Rai Pithora, Jahanpanah and Red Fort walls were reclaimed and converted into beautiful gardens. This remarkable achievement and transformation was an unplanned extraordinary bonus. In the long run, it is this bonus that is more lasting and enduring than the main conservation work itself. But unfortunately, neither the performance audit nor the investigative journalists have appreciated this outstanding and unsurpassable work of the ASI. The reclamation of land is often preceded by the removal of encroachments and subsequent arguments and fights with influential groups. Around Vijai Mandal, several encroachments and illegal shops and houses had to be dismantled. During this operation, while I was engaged in a heated exchange with the opposition lawyer, the officer at the police station played a crucial role in favour of the ASI. Earlier, this lawyer had manhandled two of the ASI officers. Captain Chandidas Mishra, Security Officer of the ASI, pursued this case very diligently on our behalf. Generally, the Superintending Archaeologist doesn't go personally to the site during the demolition because he would be the target of all encroachers. But in most of the cases, I was present at the site to take quick decisions and change strategy if required. Moreover, the entire Delhi Circle office was also stationed in Vijai Mandal to support ASI's encroachment removal drive. General Norman Schwarzkopf was right when he said, "it does not take a hero to order men into battle, but, it takes a hero to be one of those men who goes into the battle."

In two parts of the sprawling Siri Fort (at Panchsheel Park and Mahmudi Masjid) and Qila Rai Pithora (Jahanpanah wall and Saidul Ajaib), much of the fort walls had disappeared due to stone robbing by the building mafia. As per historical records, the stones of the Siri Fort wall were also used by Sher Shah Suri while constructing the Purana Qila. At several places, only the foundations were visible, and these were much below the ground level. Hence, the fort wall had to be raised from the foundation to a height of one to two meters above ground level. Following the removal of encroachments and conservation of the walls, the boundary fixation and landscaping were taken up by the horticultural wing to secure and define the area. In the Saidul-Ajaib area, vast stretches of land running up to the Qutub Minar was expected to be reclaimed, but only half of the task could be accomplished as we ran short of funds. Similarly, the entire Lalkot and Tughlakabad areas, where the first and the third capital cities were established, have their walls and gates still lying in shambles.

In Lalkot, the city of Anangpal Tomar (1051–1081 CE) and Prithvi Raj Chauhan (1178–1192 CE), many of the city gates like the Ranjit gate are still lying there with broken architectural members. If the gates and walls are reconstructed, and the inner area excavated, it would resuscitate the brave Rajput history of the early period. Such a structurally rejuvenated and environmentally developed area would work as the cultural hub for the people of Mahrauli.

The land and fortification wall of Lalkot had some ownership issues with the DDA. I tried my level best to sort it out in one of the meetings convened by then Lt. Governor Tejendra Khanna. But the case could not be pursued as we were left with no funds to start the work. Thankfully, now, the Ministry of Culture and the National Monument Authority under Shri Tarun Vijay has already organised a seminar with the active assistance of Dr BR Mani, the former Director-General of the National Museum. Dr Mani had earlier excavated the site continuously for years and brought out many hidden facts of history. In a place like Lalkot, the vast stretches of land which has not been excavated need to be explored, excavated and conserved. If conserved and showcased properly, it has the potential to attract tourists to the early part of the Rajput and Sultanate period.

As soon as the encroachments were removed and the ASI properly fenced the area on the western side of Red Fort, the Municipal Corporation of Delhi also laid claim over the land. Earlier, there were many petty shops and bus ticket booths in the area, making it an eyesore in front of the Red Fort, which is a World Heritage Monument. As long as these petty shops were present, the MCD did not make any claim over the land, but once the ASI removed the encroachments, the MCD not only laid a claim over it but also sent officials to remove the ASI's newly-erected boundary wall. Here, Milan Angetkar, the Red Fort in charge of the ASI and the rest of the staff members managed to stop the demolition drive by the MCD for the time being. Later on, this dispute was amicably settled on mediation by KN Srivastava, the former Director-General of ASI, as it was a fight between two government departments, and the land is under the ASI till today.

The eviction of low-income families was carried out with a

heavy heart. Ajai Kumar, the Conservation Assistant, carried out the task with remarkable diplomacy and firmness. Soon after the demolition, without losing time, the conservation work was started by different ASI officials such as KK Razdan, Shri Kishan, Bahadurchand and Milan Angetkar, depending upon the area. It was possible to carry out removals and reclamations due to the Commonwealth Games when most of the departments were ready to help one another.

But the most important helpful factor was the Supreme Court-monitoring committee comprising KG Rao, Bhure Lal and Major General SP Jhingon set up on 24 March 2006. The intervention of this committee played a crucial role in helping the ASI remove the encroachments that had come up in and around many of the Archaeological monuments.

Although technically under the ASI, some of the land near Humayun's Tomb, particularly the Chota Batasha and the Bada Batasha, had been in the control of some powerful lobbies who enjoyed political protection. The credit for helping the ASI to win its legal battle and remove the encroachments from over 12 acres of land in the heart of Delhi goes to the Aga Khan Trust. In removing the encroachments, major roles were played by Vasant Swarnakar, AK Pande, Capt. Chandidas Mishra, Capt. Ashri, Satbir Singh, Deepak Bharadwaj, SS Rana, RK Jhingan, Ajay Singh and the Contractor Himanshu Sharma. In the case of Humayun's Tomb, the ASI advocate, Jayant Tripathi, stationed himself at the site till the last moment. When the encroachments were being removed and structures demolished, the staff of the ASI and the AKTC stood behind me till the last encroachment was removed.

In two sensitive operations, namely the Imam's house of the Qudasia Masjid and an extension made to the *dargah* behind Firozeshah Kotla, the demolition was completed before protestors could gather at the sites. In both cases, police officers had to be posted at the sites to control the unruly mob.

Under the initiative of the Aga Khan Trust, more than 25 houses built over and in the immediate neighbourhoods of the Nizamuddin Dargah, which were endangering the monument, were demolished, and the displaced persons were rehabilitated at alternative sites by the Trust. Had the ASI been left to its own devices, it would not have been able to remove such critical encroachments on such a large scale unless someone like Jagmohan had been on the driving seat.

In Tuglakabad and Adilabad, vast fortification walls and bastions were reconstructed for the first time after Asiad 82. Soon after the reconstruction, beautiful gardens were laid out in all these places by the Horticulture Department under Dr Harbeer Singh supported by NK Aheer, Naresh Chand, RK Kaul, MK Bhatt and SC Agarwal. While the gardens defined the boundaries, the pathways enabled morning walkers, who appeared on the scene as the newly-reclaimed land patrons. NK Aheer and Naresh Chand surprised me by developing a beautiful garden on the top of Adilabad Fort, and this was an impossible task with no water source around. As it was a rocky area, it was not conducive for horticultural operations.

Altogether, 40 acres of land in Delhi proper, was thus added to the property of the ASI within four years. It was the personal devotion and dedication of officials from both the ASI Circle and the Horticulture Department that enabled fulfilment of this impossible task. The ASI staff members are the unsung heroes who helped this silent reclamation and transformation without much noise. If we had funds to the tune of Rs 25 lakhs, apart from reconstructing the rest of the Qila Rai Pithora wall, another eight acres of land from Sayidul Ajaib to the Qutub Minar would have been added to the ASI property.

It was the happy conjunction of the Commonwealth Games and the Supreme Court-monitoring committee that provided the much-needed congenial background for removing many such encroachments. How true is Paulo Coelho when he said, "When you have the right goal and passion for it, the whole world conspires in helping you to achieve it." Reclamation of the land was one such achievement. Had we missed the Commonwealth opportunity, we would perhaps never have got another one to free the monuments from such encroachments.

While the ASI spent 20 crore rupees from the Special Repairs Fund for Commonwealth in two years (2008–2010, ten crore rupees for each year), what it achieved was not only conservation of major monuments but also the reclamation and acquisition of 40 acres of land. Incredible it may sound, nevertheless, it is true! In terms of the land value of the prime property in Delhi, the cost of this 40 acres of land is astronomical. Bliss was in those days to be part of that conservation and reclamation movement of the ASI.

Being the national capital, Delhi attracts hundreds of visitors from India and abroad every day. In the Golden Triangle comprising Delhi, Agra and Jaipur, there are numerous historical sites for them to see, including the Red Fort, Humayun's tomb, Qutub Minar, Taj Mahal (at Agra), Agra Fort, Fatehpur Sikri, and many other places. They are all either Sultanate or Mughal monuments. In Jaipur, even if we call them Rajput monuments, architecturally, they are all Mughal monuments with arches and domes. What impression would a foreigner formulate about India by seeing only the Islamic monuments in the Golden Triangle? India is full of Islamic heritage and nothing more than that.

To understand India's rich Hindu, Buddhist and Jain heritage, one has to visit the historical monuments of other states or see the masterpieces of Indian art created by ancient kings in different parts of the country. Various dynasties, right from the Mauryas have left the imprint of their powerful personality by constructing historical structures and masterpieces of Indian art and sculpture. A visitor coming to Delhi does not get an opportunity to see the temples of its many provinces and their sculptures. A foreign visitor who comes only to Delhi does not get the chance to see the Ajanta, Ellora, Elephanta caves, Mahabalipuram, Brihadishwara, Hampi, etc. He also returns without being able to appreciate the Didargunj Yakshi of Patna, the preaching Buddha of Sarnath, the Trimurti of Elephanta, the Ugra Narasimha of Hampi, etc. He does not have an opportunity to feel the rich and diverse strands of the magnificent Indian cultural tradition.

For a proper projection of the ancient Indian civilisation, a 'replica museum' was envisaged in Delhi to be set up near the Siri

Fort Auditorium, a prominent cultural centre. It was proposed to house the replicas of the masterpieces of Indian art from various states of the country. Since I had served in different parts of India had a fairly good idea of selecting the best from each state. An excellent research team consisting of Dr Sunita Tiwatiya, Dr Shamun Ahmed, Dr Bipin Negi, Dr Alka Negi, Dr Anil Dagar, Dr Deepti Trivedi, Dr Manoj Kumar and Dr Jyothi Bhargav under Dr Vasant Kumar Swarnakar collected the rest of the details. The question that arose was where to house this proposed museum?

All the ASI museums in Delhi are period museums. In Red Fort, there are three museums, namely the Mumtaz Mahal Museum, the War Memorial Museum and the Freedom Struggle Museum. They deal specifically with a particular and relevant period only. The proposed replica museum did not fit into the scheme of any such existing museums, as it would be from various states, stretching from the 3rd century BCE to 12th century CE.

While searching for a site to house such a museum, I happened to meet Padma Shri Ajeet Kaur, the renowned social activist and her daughter Arpana Caur, a well-known painter. Ajeet Kaur runs the Foundation of SAARC Writers and Literature (FOSWAL), which unites writers and literary figures from eight countries. The international body has recognised Mrs Kaur's outstanding services by elevating the FOSWAL to the only SAARC apex body's status.

Madam Kaur told me about a DDA officers' club for which she had fought a legal battle to get it transferred to the ASI. In this case, the public interest litigation was filed by VP Singh, the former Prime Minister and the entire payment for the advocate and other expenditures was incurred by Ajeet Kaur. Both Ajeet Kaur and Arpana Caur used to visit the site to ensure that no encroachments occurred at the site.

In this effort, they were effectively supported by an ASI employee, Prem Singh, who stood guard of the site day and night. Arpana says that if Prem Singh had not displayed so much vigilance, the land would indeed have been captured by some influential people. Within a few days, the prime land of three acres, within the heart of the city was taken over, and a temporary children's museum was inaugurated as per the directives of Ambika Soni, the Minister of Tourism and Culture. Mrs Soni herself inaugurated it and hailed the museum as a new cultural hotspot for the children.

Apart from other social activities, the mother-and-daughter team ran a school for underprivileged children in their homes, which inspired me to run such schools in the monuments. Their life and struggle reminded me of what John Maxwell said: "A difficult time can be more readily endured if we retain the conviction that our existence holds a purpose—a cause to pursue, a person to love and a goal to achieve."

As this museum had to be inaugurated at a very short notice, the items displayed were only a few excavated potteries from the area, photographs of the World Heritage Monuments and an excellent exhibition on how the general public is misusing our heritage. This exhibition shows how the rich heritage is being vandalised and destroyed by groups, individuals and youngsters. In stark contrast, it also displayed a section where students are shown taking the initiative to conserve monuments through the 'Adopt A Heritage' move. The brain behind this exhibition was Dr Manavi Seth of the National Museum under VS Madan, the then Director-General of the National Museum.

Sensing it as the right opportunity, I brought a group of Fine Arts students of Patna College, who had earlier worked with me in Bihar. They surprised us by making exact replicas of the sculptures in fibreglass just by eye copying from the photographs of the antiquities. Usually, reproduction is made by preparing a mould of the original one, but here the students under Rajender, the ASI artist, were making exact life-size replicas with the help of photographs supplied to them. None of them had seen the original pieces, yet they made them from the photographs with remarkable accuracy and perfection. This museum is another tribute to another set of unsung heroes of the ASI.

While the work was in progress, Arpana Caur happened to visit our replica workshop in Purana Qila. Herself a renowned artist, Arpana was highly impressed on seeing the replicas at various stages of their making. Briefed about this development, Ajeet Kaur wrote to Ambika Soni about the replicas being prepared at the ASI workshop and requested her to get it completed at the earliest.

As there was no special fund for it, it was decided that savings from the funds of annual maintenance of the monuments for the museum would be used for this. Some objections and fears were raised, but the work progressed ahead. Some others advised me against undertaking this venture without fully thinking about its consequences. While each piece was costing three lakh rupees in the bazaar, our cost was only one lakh. There are many ways to complete projects at a bare minimum cost.

Since we expected encroachment of the land from the backside from a powerful lobby, these replicas of Gods and Goddesses were strategically displayed in several lawn corners to stop any encroachments from that side. It also thwarted another attempt by some elements of the DDA to recapture a part of this land, as was reported in a newspaper. In the initial stages, these sculptures served as our *ashtadikpalas (protectors of eight corners)* to protect the site. Jim Rohn was right when he said: "If you don't design your own life plan, chances are that you will fall into someone else's plan." Here the ASI designed its plan and executed it with determination. In a partial modification, in this case, it was Ajeet Kaur and Arpana Caur who prepared the design for the ASI, and we executed it.

The most important replica was the sculpture of Pasupathi Shiva from a temple at Chhattisgarh. This was brought to light by the renowned archaeologist-cum-administrator, Dr KK Chakravarty. Despite its name, many scholars think it to be a Pashupati Shiva, a concept wherein Shiva is considered to be the lord of the entire animal kingdom and, hence, a composite being. In this hybrid form, Shiva's turban is made of the snake Vasuki and the ears of peacocks. Other body parts, like eyes, moustache, chin, and arms, are made out of frog, fish, crab, and crocodiles. He has genitals in the form of a moving tortoise and legs are those of an elephant. Nine human faces on his body represent the nine planets. Of all the Shiva images conceived and executed so far, this is a very unique piece, and one cannot find another sculpture like this in any other part of the world.

In addition to this sculpture, there are beautiful replicas of the sculptures from Mathura, Sarnath, Patna, Ajanta, Ellora, Elephanta, Mahabalipuram, Tanjore, Hampi, etc. It would take at least a few weeks for an average Indian to visit all these places, but a visit to the replica museum would provide him with an opportunity to see them all under one umbrella. The cultural noticeboards attached with it are sufficient enough to give a better idea of each object. The museum also houses sculptures of Ashoka, Akbar and Shah Jahan. While the Ashoka model comes from Karnataka, Akbar's and Shah Jahan's sculptures are based on Mughal paintings.

It was suspected in 2010 to be the brainchild of the BJP by some pro-communist bureaucrats. I replied that it had nothing to do with BJP or Congress, and for me, it was an Indian idea. After the completion, I spoke to Smt Sheila Dikshit, the Chief Minister of Delhi, and a student of history, who appreciated it and also agreed to inaugurate it. However, the same pro-communist lobby stopped me from the formal inauguration but, on my insistence, agreed to throw it open to the public without a formal inauguration.

When the BJP came to power, it was believed that the party would give proper place to heritage and archaeology as the 'glorious civilisation' has always been one of the vociferous slogans of the party. It was also expected that there would be some kind souls in the party, RSS, Sanskar Bharati or its intellectual wing (Pragya pravah) who would realise the importance of a project like a 'replica museum' in a city like Delhi. But that proved to be another magnificent delusion. Ever since the BJP came to power, it has had no time for such simple projects. The party leadership, which speaks volumes about the 'glorious civilisation' of the country, does not understand the value of such museums. But, if there is ever a rumour that some miscreants have damaged an idol of the replica museum, BJP would be the first to send its fringe organisation members to call for a Delhi *bandh*. Unfortunately, BJP has no heritage intellectuals like Dr SP Gupta, the former Director-

General of Allahabad Museum, who understood the value of the country's real culture. If Dr Gupta were alive today, he would have been the biggest critique of the present ASI policy of the BJP government. I still remember clearly when he was informed of a wrong course that the MP Government proposed to follow regarding State Archaeology of Madhya Pradesh; he spoke to me, decisively intervened and got it stopped. Alas! Now there is no such insider to feel the anguish and agony of the ASI. Recently, I came to know that this Museum has been closed down by the ASI with a board out side that renovation work of Museum is in progress.

Presently, the Delhi replica museum houses thirty-five replicas. My original programme was to display 200 select reproductions from South Asia and Far East Asia. If completed, this Asian Museum would have been one of the best cultural centres in Delhi. Many retired archaeologists of the ASI, such as Dr BM Pandey, Padma Shri RS Bisht, Dr RC Agarwal, and Dr BR Mani, were delighted to see the growth of the museum. The descriptions of the replicas were all written under the supervision of Dr BM Pandey.

Although it has not attracted the attention of the Indian Government, the replica museum has fired the imagination of a few NRI intellectuals and industrialists such as Dr Srinivasa Rao, based in New York, and Architect Srinivasa Murthy, etc. They are seriously toying with the idea of establishing a similar museum in America. An idea can travel very fast as it recognizes no boundaries. “No weapon can destroy it. No power can conquer it except the power of another idea,” said John Roy. On the occasion of the 75th year of the Independence day of India (Azadi ka Amrit mahotsav) such a replica museum of masterpieces from all over the country and also from other Asian countries would have been the best gift for the nation.

In Japan, Otsuka Pharmaceuticals established such a replica museum in 1998 on the occasion of the 75th celebration of its anniversary. It houses over a thousand full-size ceramic replicas of significant works of art, including those of the Sistine Chapel, Villa of Mysteries, Guernica, etc., in porcelain. Here a robot named Mr Art acts as a guide. This museum's beauty is that while the original pieces are susceptible to degeneration, the replica is impervious to ageing as the porcelain pieces have been fired over 1200°C. In the case of Ajanta, Bagh etc., we should seriously consider transferring all such valuable art pieces into porcelain.

The Bagh paintings have been partly transferred to a nearby museum under the direct supervision of Dr NK Samadhiya of the Chemical wing of the Archaeological Survey of India. In 2007, I had thrown open this museum to the public while working in Bhopal. There are some more paintings in the Bagh caves. Instead of allowing them to die a slow death in the dingy cells of the caves, the ASI should take measures to strip them from the caves and transfer them to the museum. The museum also should be upgraded and air-conditioned to prolong the life of these rare paintings. As a long-term measure, it is also necessary to preserve all these perishable paintings by transferring them into porcelain.

As a part of showcasing Delhi for the Commonwealth Games in 2010, the ITDC had proposed introducing a 'light-and-sound show' at the Purana Qila, on a trial basis. Usually, the script for such a show is submitted to the Superintending Archaeologist of the Delhi Circle, who after closely scrutinising it, recommends it to the Director-General, who then appoints a committee of specialists from the ASI to study and discuss all aspects of the show. Every point is discussed minutely so that when the show is opened to the public, there is no room for any historical controversy. Indian history has always been a matter of debate, not only between historians but also between political parties. Once an argument raises its head, it spreads like wildfire in society and creates immense ill feelings. The ASI is cautious about nipping any possible controversy in the bud itself. However, the 2008 Purana Qila 'Light and Sound' show's script was not sent to the ASI for reasons best known to the ITDC.

When I was invited to see the first show, I found it technically superior to the show at Red Fort. However, I was shocked that the Indraprastha, which the Pandavas had founded as their capital, and where the light-and-sound show was being organised, did not find any mention in the script. Along with Tilpat, Bagpat, Sonepat and Panipat, Indraprastha was one of the five villages given to the Pandava's under a treaty. In addition to Rajput sources, the name Indraprastha is mentioned in the *Taj-ul-Ma'asir*, written by Hasan Nizami, and the *Tarikh-e-Firoz Shahi* by Isami.

Earlier, Prof BB Lal had excavated Purana Qila and found a few PGW pottery pieces from the explorations. Later on, Dr BR Mani further explored the area between Purana Qila and Humayun's Tomb and discovered painted grey ware, which is popularly known as 'Mahabharata pottery.' Before Independence, revenue records of the area mention an inhabited village called Indrapath.

The omission of a reference to Indraprastha and that too in a historical show presented at the very site was shocking! If a group of historians deliberately tried to conceal the historical truth, the ASI is not prepared to be a tool in their hands-on account of their ulterior motive. Immediately, I took up this matter with the ITDC person concerned, Mr Kumar, who was in charge of the sound-and-light show. I was told that it was a trial show and that inputs from the ASI and other scholars would be incorporated in the final show before being presented to the public.

At the next screening, Dr Gautam Sen Gupta, Director-General, ASI, and Dr BR Mani, Joint Director-General, were also present. After the screening, Dr Sen Gupta walked out immediately, as he was disgusted with the contents. The next day, Dr BR Mani submitted a note to the Director-General listing the script's various shortcomings. As a result of the objection from the ASI, the script was modified, and the Mahabharata part was inserted into it. However, the new insertions were not made properly.

In fact, the script should have started with the Mahabharata as PGW was located at the lowest level in the area between Purana Qila and Humayun's tomb. However, instead of presenting the simple and clear facts, as per the chronological order, the Mahabharata story was now included in the show with the Dinpanah, the sixth city of Humayun and Sher Shah Suri. As a result of this incongruous patchwork, the impact and the flow of the story was lost. Since the new insertion was in a very incoherent and improper way, one was rudely jolted out, and the story's organic flow was lost. Naturally, the show failed to attract the discerning public of Delhi interested in art and heritage. Compared to it, the Red Fort show many decades earlier was still doing a roaring business.

The scriptwriter of the show was Najaf Haider of Jawaharlal Nehru University, a favourite disciple of Dr Irfan Habib of Aligarh Muslim University. I knew him from my days at Aligarh when he was in the History Department. When I was posted in Agra, he had come to see me twice. On one occasion, he was accompanied by his wife, and she even invited me for delivering a lecture at the General Education Centre of the AMU, where she was working. However, I could not oblige as I had some other engagements. On another occasion, he had come accompanied by Madhuri Gupta, editor of *Perspective* to meet me. Madhuri Gupta had expressed an interest in my article on the Buddhist *stupa* at Kesariya, which I had excavated when I was posted in Bihar. Madhuri told me that the story of the excavation of this Buddhist *stupa* would be a matter of interest for overseas readers as her journal was published in several foreign languages and had many international subscribers. The article was published with many good photographs taken by the ASI. In 2015, I learned that the police had arrested her on the charge of having leaked sensitive documents to Pakistan.

Dr Najaf could not forgive me for being one of the persons responsible for amending his script and incorporating the Mahabharata part. He was always on the lookout for a way to belittle me. He got his chance when Prof Mahalakshmi of the Historical Study Centre at JNU invited me to deliver a lecture on the Conservation of Bateshwar temples in Chambal Valley. On the day of the lecture, I was informed by someone in the JNU that the lecture had been cancelled. When I enquired about the reason from an old acquaintance, Prof Ranvir Chakravarty, he explained that the lecture had to be cancelled for want of a free classroom. Further inquiries revealed that the lecture was cancelled at the insistence of Dr Najaf Haider, who alleged that I was a BJP man and my lecture would lead to violence on the campus. Later on, Prof

Mahalakshmi was very apologetic and added that her husband felt immense remorse for it since he was responsible for the original invitation. She further said that she was not strong enough in the department to overrule Dr Haider.

In a meeting at the ASI, where Dr KP Poonacha, Dr BR Mani and Janwich Sharma were present, I suggested the setting up of an Interpretation Centre at Purana Qila, where a film about the Eureka moments of the archaeological discoveries in India could be screened. Here, the turning points of Indian History, such as how did the Indian civilisation, which was earlier dated to 600 BCE, could be pushed back to 2600 BCE based on the excavation at Harappa and Mohenjo-Daro be explained. How did John Marshal feel when he came to know through his research that the Mesopotamian and Harappan cultures were not only contemporary but also had trade relations with each other? How did a few inscriptions from Sanchi enable James Princep to decipher the Brahmi script? How did Alexander Cunningham and Markham Kittoe identify Kaushambi, Sankisa, Pataliputra, Rajgir, and Nalanda as the same historical sites mentioned in the travelogues of Faxian and Xuanzang? How did Prof BB Lal correlate the flood mentioned in *Vayu Purana* with the flood layers excavated at Hastinapura? What inner thoughts were going on in the minds of Dr MC Joshy and Dr BN Pande when they deciphered the Ashokan inscription at Srinivasapuri in Delhi? How excited were the Dholavira team under Dr Ravindra Singh Bisht when they discovered the longest Harappan inscription, the water tank and the pillars from the excavation? One more such spectacular discovery was recently made at Sinauli by Dr Sanjai Manjul and Aravind Manjul by excavating the long eluding chariots of ancient India. Apart from the resounding discovery, the meticulous care and precision with which the Sinauli team exposed the decayed wood and metal wheels is a testimony to the excavation craft of the ASI team.

If these thrilling and defining moments of Indian history and the little clues that finally led to the Eureka moments are told in a storytelling way in a documentary film, it would not only enlighten the public at large but also trigger the imagination of youngsters. If these are not told attractively, the world would be as poor as such Eureka moments had never happened in Indian history. How many research scholars of Indian history in various universities are aware of these Eureka moments of Indian history?

This journey would be enjoyable and exciting, as it would give a tourist an experiential experience of an excavated site. Such a walk through historical layers of a dim and distant past is sure to change a tourist's perception about archaeology and ancient civilisation, as it is a life-enriching journey through the corridors of time. With the help of modern technology, digital cultural heritage (DCH), 3D graphic technology, augmented reality system (ARS) and computer simulations, etc., it would take them back to a time when life was lived on a grand and glittering scale. Since the tour leader is a scholar and a trained communicator, he would be able to take a tourist to the lanes and bylanes of an enchanted journey to make it an intellectually intoxicating experience.

As part of it, I also proposed the idea of re-excavating the trenches, earlier excavated by Prof BB Lal at Purana Qila, firm up a longitudinal section, place the replicas of the antiquities, which Lal had excavated, in the respective layers with an appropriate transparent air-conditioned roof over it, to enable the general public to know how an archaeologist excavates, segregates different dynastic layers and makes discoveries. This should also have the provisions for the inquisitive tourist to enable him to go down to the lowest part of the excavated trenches by an escalator and study closely and feel the antiquities. This should also show how samples for carbon, potassium-argon, thermoluminescence (TL), optically stimulated luminescence (OSL) datings and various other experiments are collected. How techniques of GPR survey, remote sensing, lithic analysis, archaeometallurgy, palaeobotany, palynology and zooarchaeology are used in an archaeological excavation. This would be part of an attempt to demystify archaeology.

When I laid out these plans as a concept, the Conservation Director Janhwij Sharma was very much excited. The Director-

General KN Srivastava was receptive to new and out-of-the-box ideas. I had already discussed my plans with Prof BB Lal, and he was appreciative of the idea and welcomed it wholeheartedly. We decided to re-excavate where BB Lal had excavated along with few more places and showcase them properly.

The plan was that the visitor would be taken to the actual archaeological excavation site after familiarising him with the documentary about the archaeology and history of the site and the Eureka moments in the interpretation centre. At the actual site, the tourist could go through the Mughal, the Sultanate, the Rajput, the Harsha, the Gupta, the Kushana, the Sunga, the Maurya, the NBP and the PGW periods.

In Purana Qila, the ASI has large areas both within and outside the fort. There are several cells for housing the infrastructure. During my period, many such cells had been restored, reconstructed and put to fair use. A very good museum could be established on the protohistory of India, i.e. Harappa, OCP, PGW and NBP and the various periods of Indian history. The Central Antiquity Section in Purana Qila has such a wealth of antiquities that several museums can be opened in different parts of the country. Similarly, there is another hidden wealth of antiquities in several *malkhanas* of different states rotting or idly lying. All this archaeological wealth can be documented and exhibited in museums under public-private partnerships. What is required is a vision, a few ignited minds and dynamic leadership.

After all the officers orally approved this, I submitted a formal request for the mandatory permission to excavate the site, which was placed in front of the Central Advisory Committee for Archaeology, authorised with the task of granting permission for excavations all over the country. But unfortunately of the committee members was Dr Shireen Moosvi, a close colleague of Dr Irfan Habib. The moment she saw my name listed as the Director of the Purana Qila excavation, she vehemently objected to it, saying that since Prof Lal had already excavated the site, there was no reason for a second excavation. Dr BR Mani tried to impress upon her that it was with a grand vision of showcasing the heritage land that the excavation was being proposed. But Dr Moosvi was adamant that the site should not be excavated at all. If the excavation itself is prevented, there would certainly be no question of an underground Interpretation Centre. Thus, the credit of ensuring that visitors never get a chance to take a guided underground tour of the historical layers of history at Purana Qila goes to Dr Moosvi. "You can never win an argument with a negative person and a conditioned mind. They only hear what suits them and listen only to respond in a negative tune and tone"—Anonymous.

A few IAS Director-Generals helped give a new lease of life to the ASI. They brought new energy and vigour and opened the doors of the ASI to private players such as NTPC, Indian Oil, etc. With Ajay Shankar, IAS, a very noticeable change had resulted, as he promoted all the ASI activities with great enthusiasm. His untimely death in an accident proved to be a shocking setback to the ASI. While Ajay Shankar used to work as a statesman, the day-to-day administration at the Delhi Main Office was handled by another competent officer, SB Mathur, IAS. After Ajay Shankar's death, the position of Director-General was assumed by another IAS officer, Komal Anand, who distinguished herself by taking quick decisions and implementing them. During the operation of the removal of encroachments from Tughlaqabad, Madam displayed extraordinary courage. Officers such as Gauri Chatterjee and Anshu Vaish carried out their responsibilities with dignity and impartiality. It was during their tenure, sensitive projects such as the excavations at Ayodhya and Ram-Setu took place. They dealt with all the complicated issues of the turbulent days with remarkable composure and sagacity. Among the Additional Director-Generals, mention must be made of Vijay S Madan, Praveen Srivastava and Juthika Patankar, who ran the department with remarkable diligence. In Delhi, when I had started a drive to collect and distribute old clothes to the poor, especially in winter, Smt Patankar, who came from a distinguished family and took a special interest in the upliftment of the poor, used to donate generously. Madam ensured that all the clothes were dry-cleaned before donating them. Mrs Patankar was quick to realise the problems of the ASI and was full of sympathy with the organisation and its officers.

The most distinguished IAS Director-General was KN Srivastava, who served the ASI with passion and commitment. Unfortunately, his term in office was very short. I still remember the clarity with which he presented to the Delhi Chief Minister, Sheila Dikshit, the case against a few Muslim groups who had forcibly encroached and started offering *namaz* in four historical mosques under the ASI's protection. And that too when the legislator and his group, who had masterminded this illegal act, were seated next to the Chief Minister. Shri Srivastav's arguments were so coherent and reasonable that Chaudhary Mateen Ahmed, the MLA, could say nothing, and the Chief Minister, who had a soft corner for the *namazis* due to political compulsions, had to change her mind. Since I was the Superintending Archaeologist of Delhi at that time, I had become the target of the Muslim group's ire. A similar encounter took place with another group of Muslims in front of Shafi Quraishi, the Chairman of the Delhi Minority Commission. By the time the meeting came to an end, the other members of the Minorities Commission and the *Imams*, who came with many complaints against the ASI, were totally silent.

Within one year, Mr Srivastava completely galvanised the organisation and also ensured the timely promotion of all. Since he was widely well connected, the interdepartmental relation before the Commonwealth was also very smooth. If Srivastava had continued in the ASI for two more years, he would have certainly revamped it and taken it to greater heights. But fate decreed otherwise. Even after his departure, he is still being fondly remembered by all the staff members in the ASI.

Some of the prominent Secretaries from the Department of Culture, notably, RC Tripathi, BP Singh, VV Ayyar, N Gopala Swami, Dhanendra Kumar and Jawahar Sarkar realised the difficulties of the ASI and extended their full cooperation to it. Jawahar Sircar was a man of innovative ideas, but the department lacked the funds or the human resources to implement many of them. He wanted that some of the monuments like the Qutub Minar and Humayun's Tomb to be opened for the public during the night also. But the ASI suffered from the acute infrastructural and manpower shortage. The ratio of monument versus monument attendant was shorter than 1:1. Every monument has to be opened from 6 am to 6 pm, which makes it twelve hours. As per labour law, one can take eight hours' job from an employee. Occasionally, one can take over time from an employee, but it cannot be an everyday affair. While an employee can avail of earned leave, casual leave and weekly holidays, a monument enjoys none of it. So, the question was about how to stretch the available workforce? Somehow, the ASI was managing it with private security. But it was not possible to entrust the full security of the monument to a private agency. The idea of opening it for the public during the night, where there are no sculptures, is a good proposal, provided there is enough manpower and security personnel. Some European countries have night tours like Paris by night where few of the monuments can be viewed from outside in a restricted way. They also do not permit viewing the monuments from inside. An exception is the Eiffel Tower. But in the case of the Archaeological Survey of India, there were neither funds nor the infrastructure for all these extra works. No government wanted to strengthen the ASI and expect it to perform extraordinarily well with rickety infrastructure. Fortunately for me, when the issue of night opening was taken up with the Delhi Police for security clearance, they refused to support it from the security angle due to the situation prevailing in Delhi. That was a great relief for the beleaguered office of the ASI.

The archaeologist community has had a long-standing demand that the organisation should be headed by an academic person rather than an IAS officer. This demand could have been perfect till 2000. However, in recent years, the administrative work has increased so much that an academic DG would find it difficult to run it unless he is exceptionally competent due to his preoccupation with academic subjects. People of the academic bent of mind with few exceptions apart are not that fast in taking decisions.

Before 2000, it might not have mattered much. But in the post-2000, in a fast-moving world, the dynamics have changed, and new management mantras have emerged. An ordinary IAS officer also cannot run it as it requires firmness, persuasive qualities, and openness to new ideas and a willing mind to support excavation and academic activities. He should also be endowed with vision, dynamism, and a passion for the country's cultural heritage. The DG should directly be in contact with the Superintending Archaeologist (SA), who is the real implementing authority.

A Superintending Archaeologist (SA) is always bogged down with enormous weight imposed by the responsibilities. As the heritage administrator, he has a whole state to look after with fragile infrastructure. As an estate officer, he is directly in charge of the removal of encroachments and demolitions. I have carried out several such demolitions in different parts of the country. Often, it is an unequal fight as the SA has to fight with the powerful real estate sharks. As an archaeologist, he has to conduct both exploration and excavations to stay afloat. With all the odds against him, he would still be transferred every three years. (In a bizarre order earlier, the tenure of an SA was for two years.) In the meanwhile, if he does not complete the excavation report, he would be held responsible for that also. He has to fight with powerful religious groups, as every community would try to convert the non-living monuments into living monuments. He also has to prove his academic worth if he has to remain in the field of archaeology. In short, he is a beleaguered officer who has to wear so many hats with alacrity.

There were few Secretaries and Director-Generals who sympathised with this dignified Tahsildar. It is time that the syllabus of the Institute of Archaeology is revamped to include heritage management, crisis management and marketing heritage as course material. It is also necessary to have periodic in-service courses to upgrade the quality of the serving officers. Along with it, his designation from the Superintending Archaeologist should be changed to the Director to give respectability to the post. Once in a meeting of the ASI officials, I had taken up the issue with then Minister of Tourism and Culture, Jagmohan.

The founder and chairperson of Swayam, Ms Sminu Jindal is a charismatic and inspirational leader whom I had the privilege to meet and interact with during my posting in Delhi. If it has now become possible for the tourists with reduced mobility to visit historical monuments, such as the Qutub Minar, Red Fort, Taj Mahal and the Purana Qila, the full credit for it goes to Sminu Jindal. Owing to Madam's untiring efforts and persuasive skills, the officials of the Archaeology and Tourism Departments have become aware of the need for 'accessible tourism' and the importance of having ramps in tourist places and public places, like the Taj Mahal, Qutub Minar, etc. Once this facility is introduced, people with reduced mobility and senior citizens can also access every nook and corner of our monuments.

When this idea of accessible monuments was first brought to my notice, there were many financial difficulties. Nevertheless, I decided to implement it and made Qutub Minar India's first barrier-free monument. Before Swayam sensitised us with the idea of 'accessible monuments,' the subject had never occupied an archaeologist's mind space. But once it was implemented in Qutub Minar, even people without disabilities often used the ramps, which was originally designed with differently-abled people in mind.

The ramps have also given rise to a sense of discipline, which was not present earlier in the monuments. This is clearly visible, especially when busloads of school-children come to see the monuments in large numbers. Earlier, they used to run everywhere in the monument, but now they have a ramp to lead and guide them. Once aware of the silent discipline factor in the monuments, the ASI, which was earlier a reluctant supporter of accessible tourism, now became the most vociferous and active supporter of it. Impressed by this turnaround, the Tourism Department of India announced an award for the Qutub Minar, which was shared by the ASI and Swayam, the organisation founded and nurtured by Sminu Jindal.

Ms Jindal is one of the most inspiring young leaders I've ever met. At the age of 11, she met with an unfortunate accident, which changed her life forever. Ms Jindal turned this adversity into an advantage by springing from the wheelchair into the business world by running India's steel, oil and gas industries. Ms Jindal is the only differently abled business leader in the world to feature in the Fortune Five hundred list. "We cannot always choose the music the life plays for us, but we can choose how we dance to it." This is exactly what Ms Jindal has done. As the Managing Director of Jindal SAW Ltd., she pays equal attention to Swayam also.

In Delhi, the Indian National Trust for Art and Cultural Heritage (INTACH) and the Agha Khan Trust for Culture (AKTC) are quite active in the conservation field. INTACH, under the dynamic leadership of Major General LK Gupta, has diversified its activities into various fields. Apart from conservation and preservation, it has substantially contributed to making the general public aware of the country's rich heritage. Its heritage walks and interaction with various schools have been hugely popular. Since its various wings and chapters such as natural heritage, intangible heritage, heritage tourism and heritage academy are headed by highly experienced officials, INTACH could make a visible impact in the field of culture.

The AKTC, where I worked after retiring from the ASI, has done excellent work in repairing and conserving Humayun's Tomb. Some of my colleagues from the ASI including Dr Jamal Hasan and Dr SB Otta, are very critical of this kind of conservation, whereas another group, which includes RC Agarwal and Dr BR Mani, among others, endorses it strongly. I stand with the

AKTC and so some part of the conservation was approved and carried out while I was the Superintending Archaeologist. Well, a difference of opinion among those who are all practitioners of conservation is understandable as they are learned and have genuine differences.

The CEO of the AKTC, Ratish Nanda, has built the Indian branch of the AKTC virtually from scratch. With rare far-sightedness, he has collected all the conservation materials, which would be difficult to get after a few years, as various courts have imposed prohibitions on their mining. After ten years, it would be difficult to collect many of the conservation materials that the AKTC has already used to repair Humayun's Tomb. The critics of the AKTC should bear in mind what a vital service the AKTC has rendered in giving a new lease of life to Humayun's Tomb. Perhaps history would judge the contribution of AKTC to Humayun's Tomb and Nizamuddin better after 25 years. Presently, we are too close to the work carried out, and it may not enable us to evaluate it objectively. The question of over-conservation and under-conservation is an issue that should be taken up by the AKTC when it comes from the practitioners of conservation. But when it emanates from the tribe of conservation illiterates, hailing from Aligarh, it is always advisable to ignore it.

The lime-mortar workshop, conducted by the AKTC at Humayun's Tomb, revived a dying tradition and imparted training to many aspiring conservationists. Now, the AKTC is building an Interpretation Centre, a museum, a parking area and a cafeteria near Humayun's Tomb-Sundar Nursery area, and it would dramatically change and enhance a visitor's experience at the site.

Even when I worked in the ASI, I did not believe in the principle of minimum conservation or minimal intervention in the Indian context. I always recommended the restoration of monuments to that level which would enable a tourist to imagine and visualise how the structure stood in the bygone era. In the East, where the climate is very harsh, it is not appropriate to use

Western methods, no matter what the armchair conservators sitting in five-star hotels think, nor is it feasible to follow in letter and spirit whatever John Marshall wrote several years ago, based on his understanding a century ago. Time is moving ahead. And the conservators also should move ahead to stay relevant with the time.

Dr Nizamuddin Tahir, who calls himself a traditional and in-situ conservationist, thinks that the methods and the philosophy behind the techniques used should be site-specific. There are several sites where restoration is required, and in pre historic and proto historic places, one should stick to minimum intervention. If we know about art, architecture, plaster and building materials used, then what is the harm in restoring a structure that lies in ruins with its own architectural members lying all around it to its original form? That gives a tourist a better idea of how it must have looked when it was standing in its original grandeur. I have already dealt with temple No 3 in Nalanda, which has been caught in the cross-currents of excavation and conservation principles. Alas! Now the most prominent *stupa* of Nalanda looks more like a Christian cemetery steeple than a Buddhist *stupa* or temple.

When *stupas* No 2 and 3 were located in Sanchi near the main *stupa*, both of them were nothing more than a heap of scattered stones piled up. Had it been left without restoration, both of them would have disappeared without leaving behind any trace. In his enormous wisdom, John Marshal restored and reconstructed it along with its gate by the side of the main *stupa*. The fact that the restored *stupa* right from scratch eloquently speaks against all those teachers and preachers of conservation who emphasises minimum intervention quoting from John Marshal and others' manual. Needless to say, our perception often changes when we work in the field and gain more insights into the problems. In the same way, the early explorers saw Satdhara *stupa,* as another massive heap of stones with many thousands of stone pieces scattered all around. It was Dr RC Agarwal who took up the conservation of it as a UNESCO-sponsored project. The project progressed very well under Dr AK Sinha, PK Mishra and SB Otta. It was during my period that a major part of the conservation was completed. As it was a UNESCO-sponsored and funded project, an international UNESCO team periodically visited the site to monitor the conservation and restoration. None of them found anything objectionable in fully reconstructing the *stupa* or the restoration work against any of the international charters. Dr Rekha Radha Vallabhi, Dr Manual Joseph and Dr Dileep Kamari effectively monitored the work at every stage.

In the in-situ conservation, the fallen structure is conserved at the same site, as it is in an upside-down manner, without interfering with it in any way, as a temporary measure. In Goa at St. Augustin, Dr Tahir preferred the in-situ conservation method and has accomplished it by adding a new direction to archaeological conservation. But such conservations have many practical problems as it does not allow the visualisation of the site. Of course, it could be adopted as a temporary measure for a limited period. But the final solution is to resort to proper conservation by reusing the available material. The Satdhara example shows that UNESCO has no objection to large scale repair and reconstruction as some conservative conservators may make us believe.

In Sikandra, the tomb of Akbar in Agra, few of the fading paintings were retouched and restored by the ASI. But it was stopped as there were objections against it. Over the years the paintings that were retouched are still there for all to see and the part that was not retouched has almost been lost. What is the best method of preservation? The preservation that allowed it to be preserved or that led to its total loss? Often the critics without any experience behave like a legless coach who trains athletes for the next Olympics.

While restoring, one has to be very careful and only traditional and skilled painters should be permitted to retouch such paintings. This problem will assume a bigger dimension in places such as Ajanta, Bagh, etc. At Sikandra, the paintings and some of the fallen minarets have been restored or reconstructed during the British period. One could have asked why the fallen minarets of Sikandra were restored? The broken minarets were not creating any structural problem. Similarly, in the ASI, many other monuments all over the country have been reconstructed or restored. Those who actually work in the field of conservation know very well that the principle of minimum intervention is the *mantra* of those who preach and teach conservation but not of those who practise it. Practising conservationists learn how to overcome their difficulties and often find solutions different from those suggested in the manuals and books.

However, it is also true that those who practise restoration and reconstruction do not speak openly in favour of the restoration, so as not to invite criticism from preachers of conservation. They wanted to take a line of least resistance. The time has come for the practising conservationists to stand up and speak out their minds openly. It is heartening to observe that in a clear change of attitude, the ASI has changed its policy and now has no hesitation in approving the restoration works. But I had started taking up restoration and reconstruction works at many monuments where architectural members were lying down, much before the Archaeological survey of India changed its policy guide line and the best example is Bateshwar in Morena. Mr Janwij Sharma, Add-Director conservation, who had earlier looked at Bateshwar restoration and reconstruction with much reservation, was a completely changed man when he actually visited the site.

□

With Barack Obama: An Unforgettable Moment

During the preparation for the Commonwealth, while moving from place to place, I saw many child beggars near the crossroads. They were present at every traffic signal or during traffic jams. On inquiry, it was found that they were the children of daily wage labourers engaged by various government offices such as the CPWD, PWD, MCD, NDMC, and the ASI. After a little more investigation, I found out that migrant workers from various parts of India had come to the capital city to work at Commonwealth related jobs. They were workers chiefly from Uttar Pradesh, Madhya Pradesh, Bihar, Jharkhand and Bengal. Although the migrant labourers help in building establishments in large cities or work in big factories, textile mills, brick kilns and agricultural fields, on completion of the structure, they get driven out from the very city they have helped in building structures. At home, they don't figure in the social initiatives and Below-Poverty-Line surveys due to their absence at the time of the survey owing to seasonal migrations. They find no place in the smart city solutions. Since they never enter the consciousness of the urban planners, they are treated as part of the problem once the township is ready and the construction is over. Being very poor and having none to look after their children at home, these children migrate with their families and never get a chance to go to school. They are never at a place for more than a few months. The slightly older children, between the ages of six and ten, have all become beggars. It is calculated that six million school-aged children are affected by migration every year. The UNESCO Global Education Monitoring (GEM) is of the opinion that most countries are far from guaranteeing education for migrant children. Although our National Education Policy (NEP) envisaged the universalisation of Elementary Education (UEE) and Right to Education (RTE) in 2009, there is something wrong at the implementation level as it hardly reaches the real beneficiaries. The universalisation of primary school education is one of the Millennium Development Goals (MDGs). There are flexible schooling options for the migrant groups in the form of the Education Guarantee Schemes (EGS), and the Alternative and Innovative Education Schemes (AIE) under Sarva Shiksha Abhiyan (SSA), but rarely do we find the benefits trickling down to the migrant workers. Under such conditions, my wife, Mrs Rabiya Muhammed and I decided to start 'Canvas Schools' in 2008 for the migrant workers' children, who have been working at various ASI sites in Delhi. This was both a slum school and a crèche. Earlier, infants of working mothers were kept in a cloth cradle, hung up on nearby trees, often exposing them to sunlight. Our school was a great relief for mothers as their infants and children were taken care of. The importance of this crèche and Canvas Schools can be appreciated when we realise the fact that the Right of Children to Free and Compulsory Education Act was passed on 4th August 2009. The actual implementation might have taken after many more months. Naturally, in a government system, the implementation process takes a lot of time. Even after that, whether such arrangements are supervised by the right-committed management is the biggest question.

Initially, the students did not show much interest in the schools, so we had to provide refreshments, uniforms, warm clothes and develop toy-and-fun parks. Soon, it started picking up and sometimes, students from the neighbourhood also joined. The school had no restrictions in any manner. Eventually, support came from the ASI contractors who undertook a substantial part of the expenditure. Pawan Jain, a businessman in Delhi, gave blankets at a cheap rate and sometimes even free. We did not collect any funds from anybody but merely created an opportunity for any person desirous of offering financial help to give it directly to the children. Soon it started picking up steam. Our five Canvas Schools at Red Fort, Purana Qila, Siri Fort, Qutub Minar, Tughlaqabad and Adilabad were a great help for the 'Children of a Lesser God.' In the meanwhile, the *CNN-IBN* channel representative Neenaz, who came to Tughlaqabad to see our conservation work, was fascinated by the Canvas School. Similarly, *Loksabha TV*, who came to the Red Fort to report on the conservation work, was also impressed by our school within the Red Fort. They gave extensive coverage to it as it was an initiative by a Government Department much beyond their official mandate, and that too while we were racing against time because of the Commonwealth Games deadline. A few days later, I received a phone call from the *CNN-IBN channel,* informing me that I had been selected as one of the nominees for Citizens Journalist Awards. It attracted a lot of attention as the award was distributed by the celluloid king, Amitabh Bachchan.

It is my submission that at every project site, big or small, the migrant labourers should be provided with adequate washroom facilities and Canvas Schools plus crèches for their children. The Ministry of Women and Child Development should issue the necessary orders to the departments that are employing migrant labourers in their various works. I further followed it up by writing to the Director-General that there should be a provision for schools of migrant children and toilets for the labourers. It evoked no response. Often laws and rules are being framed by people who are not aware of the ground realities. Even if there is a suitable law, if the implementing agencies comprise people who have no social commitments or love for the downtrodden, then the law cannot bring any change in the society.

In the meanwhile, the American President, Barack Obama had come to India on an official visit. I had the privilege to be his guide. Naturally, the American Embassy must have done an investigation on my background. Perhaps the Embassy learned about our 'Canvas Schools,' and President Obama expressed a desire to spend some time with the children at the school. Earlier, there was some opposition to the school. While we were discussing this, Ms. Sweta from the *Indian Express* happened to hear about it, and the next day it was published in the newspaper. Soon a show-cause notice was issued to me for running schools in the monuments. I explained that these were tented temporary schools and the expenditure was being met from my salary and the voluntary donations of a few persons. Gradually, all opposition to the school died down.

Mrs and Mr Obama were the happiest when they met the children. Both of them literally sat down on the floor to interact with the children as they were tall and the children were tiny tots. They had brought special gifts for them, which were distributed personally by Obamas. He told them: "I know you have faced many problems in your life, and you may face many more. However, you have to study hard despite all the hardships. Education is the only way to be successful in life." I translated these words for the children's benefit. The children, of course, did not know that they were face to face with the most powerful man and woman on the earth.

On their arrival, a boy received them by addressing them: "Welcome, Mrs and Mr Obama." President Obama was impressed by the boy. He asked the boy: "What is your name?"

"My name is Vishal," replied the boy promptly. That further impressed the President, who had visited India in 2010.

Five years later, in 2015, President Obama returned to India as the Chief Guest for the Republic Day, at Prime Minister Narendra Modi's invitation. Five days before the President's second visit, I received a phone call from the American Embassy, with a strange message asking if it was possible to trace the boy Vishal, who had received Obama in 2010. By that time, I had retired from the ASI, and our Canvas Schools had also stopped functioning. I had forgotten Vishal, but the US President had not. I expressed my helplessness as Vishal had neither an e-mail nor a mobile. As it was an embarrassment for the Embassy, they persuaded me to locate Vishal. Then I remembered that I had the mobile number of Ramdas, Vishal's father. Immediately, he was contacted, and it was learnt that Vishal was now studying in St. Columba's School. What a brilliant transformation! There was no facility at all in our Canvas School at Tughlaqabad. But what was needed was a little push at the right time. That was provided, and the rest had been accomplished by the children themselves.

On 26 January 2015, Obama was the Chief Guest at the Republic Day parade. On 27 January, he was scheduled to address a distinguished gathering of industrialists at Delhi's Siri Fort. Here, the American President Barack Obama introduced the boy Vishal and said: "India's young generation is promising. The children I had the occasion to meet at Humayun's Tomb in 2010 are a good example of it. All of them were eager to learn and make their contribution to the growth of the country, and Vishal was one of them." He spoke not only of international trade relations and nuclear weapons but also reminded us of how to bring about transformation in society by uplifting the poor and the marginalised.

Of all the appreciations I received for the social upliftment of the downtrodden, this was the most significant recognition. Earlier, Obama had sent me a letter of appreciation with his signature for making his visit to India a memorable one. It was not a lifeless email, but a letter signed by his hand and delivered through an official of the American Embassy. We all have a responsibility towards society. We must also spare time for such work and promote it, or at least, not oppose it or create impediments to it. Let us remember and act according to the *Shanti mantra:*

Om sarve bhavantu sukhinah
Sarve santu niramayaah
Sarve bhadraani pashyantu ma
Kaschid dukha-bhaag bhavet
(May all be happy
May all be free from illness
May all see what is auspicious
May no one suffer.)

The recitation of this *mantra* is not going to bring mental peace to anybody, but certainly, when we act according to this *mantra*, it would bring peace to the individual and be powerful enough to change the world slowly.

In 2016, when Mata Sundari College in Delhi invited me to deliver a lecture on archaeology, I took Vishal also and introduced him to a large gathering of college students as an inspirational youngster whose example could be emulated by the younger generation. The students and the teachers, mainly professors such as Shabnam Suri, Amarjeet Kaur, Lokesh Kumar Gupta and Deepankar supported me financially, in helping Vishal. This was a spontaneous reaction. Anybody can serve a needy person or donate to a worthy cause. As Martin Luther King, Jr said: "You don't have to know the second theory of thermodynamics in physics to serve. You only need a heart full of grace. A soul generated by love."

□

Are Qutub Minar and Taj Mahal Hindu Temples?

The second byproduct of the unholy alliance of the *extremist Muslims* and Marxists is the outlandish claim of Hindu fundamentalists for all the important historical monuments of medieval India. A section of Hindu scholars led by SK Bhatnagar, PN Oak and DS Triveda has argued that most of the Muslim historical structures of Delhi, Agra and Fatehpur Sikri are originally Hindu structures. For them, the Qutub Minar was a Hindu astronomical observatory (Dhruva Stambha or Vijaya Stambha) of Varahamihira and the Taj Mahal was the Tejo-Mahalaya temple of Lord Shiva. They also claim that invading Muslim armies appropriated and converted them into *minars* and mausoleums. What is the truth? It is to be admitted that wanton destruction and appropriation happened in the case of the Quwwat-ul-Islam, by the side of the Qutub Minar. It was the earliest mosque built in north India by destroying and reusing the temple parts, but a study of the architecture of the Qutub Minar and Taj Mahal reveals that neither of them is Hindu in conception or in execution.

Those who propagate a Hindu origin for both these structures are not aware of the architectural principles and evolution of the construction of arches, domes, *minars* and the development of decorative arts of medieval India. They are also blissfully unaware of the architectural evolution of various Sultanate and Mughal monuments and yet come out with such irrational theories. In their effort to prove that these were Hindu structures, they associate the destruction of 27 temples with the 27 stars (*nakshatras*) of Indian astronomy and the 12 points of Qutub Minar with the 12 signs of the zodiac. Had there been such a big astronomical observatory in Delhi, it would have been mentioned by astronomers such as Aryabhatta (476–550 CE), mathematician Brahmagupta (598–668 CE) or Varahamihira (505 CE).

The Qutub Minar complex has two parts—the Quwwat-ul-Islam mosque and the Qutub Minar proper. The mosque is undoubtedly constructed out of the spoils of twenty-seven Jain and Hindu temples, and the Qibla wall is the only Islamic structural component and that was too forcefully placed after the demolition of temples. Many idols and sculptures in highly damaged condition have been reused for constructing the Quwwat-ul-Islam mosque. Apart from reusing temple parts, Hindu masons have been employed for converting the temple into a mosque. This is indeed the case with Quwwat-ul-Islam, but not with the Qutub Minar.

The Qutub Minar is entirely Islamic in origin and concept. Although Hindus and Jains built *kirti stambhas* (c 1179–1191) and *vijaya stambhas* (Rana Kumbha in Chittorgarh Fort, c 1448), all of them are square with typical Hindu carvings and embellishments. Indian architects did not construct circular, cylindrical or tapering minarets like the Qutub Minar. The stalactite pendentives below the balconies, which look like hanging beehives, known as *muqarnas*, was one of the well-known decorative features of Islamic decorative vocabulary. The Circo stellate plan with alternate circular and angular fluting was not known in India. It was widely practised in the *minars* of Persia, Central Asia and Afghanistan, especially the minarets of the Ghaznavid ruler, Mas'ud 111 (1030–1040) originally measuring 144 ft in height with semi-circular flutings over a stellate base. His son Bahram Shah (AD 1084–1157) built another *minar* like this, 600 metres away from Masud's *minar* in Ghazni, from where the early invaders, notably Mahmud Ghaznavi, came to India.

The minaret of Jam in Firozkoh, the capital of the Ghurid kingdom in Afghanistan, was built in 1190 by Ghiyas-ud-Din

Ghori (1173–1202), brother of Muhammad Ghori, who conquered India in 1192. This minaret marks another important stage in the development of minaret architecture in India. The Jam minaret has intricate brick, stucco and glazed tile work, consisting of calligraphy and geometric patterns, showing a close affinity with similar decorative works in the Qutub Minar. The other prominent minarets of Central Asia are Kalan Minar (1127), Web Kant (1141)—both in Bukhara—and the Jarkurgan in Uzbekistan. There were more than 60 such *minars* and towers between the 11th and 13th centuries in Central Asia, Iran, Iraq and Afghanistan, well before the construction of the Qutub Minar in India. In short, the Qutub Minar is Islamic, both in concept and in execution. However, since Hindu masons had worked on it under Muslims, Hindu art forms have tremendously influenced the artwork on the Qutub Minar.

PN Oak and some others often claim that the Taj Mahal has many underground chambers, which enshrine the Tejo Mahalaya or a Shivalinga. They are ignorant of the fact that there are underground chambers in Humayun's (1565–1572) and Abdul Rahim Khan-i-Khana's (1627) tombs also and both of them were built before the Taj Mahal. In the Humayun's Tomb, a number of chambers are occupied by the graves of later Mughal princes. The most important among them is the grave of Dara Shikoh, the eldest son of Emperor Shah Jahan, who would have been the next emperor. But in the war of succession, he was defeated, met a violent death and then buried in one of the chambers of Humayun's Tomb. Recently, in a remarkable discovery, Sanjeev Kumar, an engineer by profession, identified this grave with the help of historical references and grave iconography. It also has the graves of Murad and Daniyal, the second and third sons of Akbar. After the Taj Mahal, many prominent tombs such as Bibi ka Maqbara in Aurangabad (1668) and Safdarjung (1754) also have underground chambers below them. For a magnificent structure like the Taj Mahal with a height of 243 feet and situated on the banks of River Yamuna, the well foundation and underground chambers are required as structural components.

Similarly, the octagonal structural form (Musamman Baghdadi) of the Taj Mahal is significantly influenced by the Subz Burj (1530–1540), Afsarwala Gumbad (1566–67), Nila Gumbad (1560), Humayun's Tomb (1558–1572) and the tomb of Abdul Rahim Khan-i-Khana (1627).

The evolution of the double dome of the Taj Mahal with its cylindrical drum can be traced back to the dome of Subz Burj (1530–1540) and Humayun's Tomb (1565–1572), both in Delhi. Even in Central Asia, where the double dome with cylindrical drum originated, the earliest such domes appear in Gur-e-Amir (1404) built by Timur, followed by Ishrat-Khaneh (1460–64), both in Samarkand and the shrine of Abu Nasr Parsa in Balkh (1460).

It can be noted that all the domes of the Sultanate period (1192–1526), notably Ala'i Darwaza (1311) in Qutab complex Ghiyasuddin Tughlaq's Tomb (1321–1325), Firoz Shah Tughlaq's Tomb at Hauz Khas (1390) and tombs of the Sayyids (1414–1451) and Lodhis (1451–1526) have single domes. The technique of double-dome construction had not registered its presence in India during the Sultanate period (1192–1526). However, the Taj Mahal (1632–1652) flaunts a perfectly developed lofty double dome as its crowning glory. If double domes are dated to the 15th century even in central Asia, which is the place of its origin, how could they be dated in India to a much earlier period, as some over-zealous people want us to believe in the case of the Tejo Mahalaya Mandir which, according to them, was built in 11thcentury? It is often difficult to discuss such issues with closed minds, who have no knowledge of the evolution of architecture in India.

Along with the above-mentioned three structural components (underground chambers, octagonal structure and double dome), the minarets of Akbar's tomb at Sikandra (1605–1613), the perforated screen of Salim Chishti's mausoleum at Fatehpur Sikri (1606) and the inlay work of I'tmad-ud-Daulah's mausoleum (1622–1628) are the other architectural and decorative features that have influenced the Taj Mahal in its making. The octagonal bastions of the Taj compound wall are from Sher Mandal (1540–1545) of Purana Qila of Sher Shah Suri. If the above-mentioned architectural components from the aforesaid structures, built a few years before the Taj Mahal, are placed at the end of a four-square garden (Char Bagh), another Taj would stand up for all to see. In order to understand the architectural evolution of the Taj Mahal, a chronological study about its various architectural components and its introduction to the structures built before the Taj Mahal is essential.

What are the Hindu structural and decorative elements visible in the Taj Mahal? If two cultures live side by side, both would influence each other. The inverted lotus (*urdha padma*), the vase pinnacle (*kalasha*), kiosks (*chhatri*), etc., are from Hindu architectural vocabulary. The lotus and vase (padma, *kalasha*) have no importance in Islamic architecture. In Hinduism, Vishnu is Padmanabha, one from whose navel the lotus sprang up and Brahma is Padmasambhava, the one who was born on a lotus.

Similarly, the *purna kalasha*, also known as *mangala kalasha*, is a symbol of prosperity in Hinduism. Inside the tomb, the corners of the exquisite marble screen have been decorated with *amalka*, an important temple decorative feature in North Indian temples. All these motives are taken from Hindu architecture due to cultural assimilations and exchanges.

Most of the Mughal structures were placed by Mughals in the centre of a garden. In such cases, both the foreground and the background is the garden. But most innovatively, Shah Jahan placed the Taj Mahal, not in the middle of the garden but on the end of it, on the bank of the river Yamuna, harnessing the magnificent view of an ever-changing sky and horizon as Taj's backdrop. Since the horizon is changing with every passing hour, waxing and waning, in accordance with the sunrise and sunset, the Taj changes its moods from morning to evening. Every day, the rising, the midday, the afternoon and the setting sun play with its myriad rays on the white marble dome and the arches of the structure reflecting its subtle changes. "Thus, responsive to the faint shift of the light and the play of the clouds, the Taj changes its mood with every passing hour." The setting sun with its play of colours on the western horizon is a treat for a tourist. If the horizon was not harnessed as the backdrop and the reflective marble was not used as a building material to reflect, refract and retain the light, the Taj would not have appeared as beautiful as it looks now. This manipulation of light is known as the 'alchemy of light' or chemistry of light.

The change of mood varies not only in accordance with the timing of the day but also with the change of seasons such as the summer, the rains, the winter, the spring and the autumn. During the change of the seasons, the colours of the flowers in the lush green landscape also change. The Taj is at its melancholic and sombre best when it is about to rain, and the dark clouds are hovering over the sky. At that moment, it evokes a feeling of a broken-hearted person at the loss of his beloved, and the Taj is about to weep. The red sandstone enclosure walls, the lush green landscape and the white marble mausoleum against the ever-changing blue sky offers a contrast of colours and make it a breathtaking experience.

It is to be noted that four square and terraced gardens, which are different from the *amravana aramas* of the ancient period, were introduced in India by Babur. The *pietra dura* (inlay work) of flowers such as lotus, lily, narcissus, iris and tulips in multicoloured semi-precious stones add charm and beauty to the structure. According to Abu Talib Kalim, a contemporary writer, these stone flowers surpass the real flowers in beauty but what they lack is their fragrance. The pietra dura work, a European technique of ornamentation, originated in Florence in the 16th century, reached India in the 17th century. Although it was introduced in the Jahangir's tomb in Lahore (1628–1636) for the first time in India, it flourished as one of the best decorative art in the Taj Mahal.

Thus, the Taj Mahal is an attempt at synthesising and collating the best examples of architectural inheritance of the Mughals from India, Persia, and Europe. Taj assumes golden proportions, a mathematical ratio, which denotes the perfection of proportion, symmetry, harmony and balance in physical form. This mathematics of harmony is the most visually satisfying form.

Francisco Pelsaert, who was in Agra and wrote a book, described the palaces owned by various Mughal nobility but has not spoken about the magnificent white marble palace which belonged to Mirza Raja Man Singh. Certainly, Raja Mansingh and later on Jai Singh had a haveli made of brick and red sandstone which by no stretch of the imagination could be made of white marble and with the present architectural features. The site was purchased from Raja Jai Singh in place of four other properties for which the royal decrees issued by Shahjahan still exists in Rajasthan Museums and archives. It is well known that Akbar had married the sister of Mansingh, from the Kachwaha family of Rajputs of Amber. Emperor Jahangir was not only born in this union of Mughal Rajput wedlock, but he, in turn, married some more Rajput ladies. Shajahan was born in the marriage of Jahangir and Jagat Gosain, another Rajput lady from the Rathor house of Jodhpur. Both Shajahan and Raja Jaisngh were blood relations, and the Jaisngh's family was given the title of Mirza Raja Jai Singh, a title reserved only for the royal family members. Similarly, orders issued for the marble for Taj Mahal from the Makrana quarry are also available in the archival records of Rajasthan.

Peter Mundy, the English traveller who visited Agra in 1631–32, speaks explicitly about the beginning of the construction thus: "The king, now building a sepulchre for his late deceased queen, Tage Moholle, whom he dearly loved, intends that it shall excel all others." Jean Baptiste Tavernier, the French merchant traveller, who visited Agra in 1640–41 and again in 1665, says that it was being built at a great expenditure. Neither Francois Bernier, the French physician and traveller who stayed at Agra in 1656 nor Niccolo Manucci (1639–1717) speak about the conversion from the temple to the tomb.

It is sometimes claimed that historians of the Hindu school have secretly taken samples of the wood from the doors of the Taj Mahal and had it carbon tested privately in some research institutions. They found that the wood dates back to the 11–14th centuries. This is an outlandish claim which cannot be endorsed by anyone who has an understanding of carbon testing. Many valuable doors of the Taj Mahal, covered with silver and other valuables, were looted during the declining years of the Mughal Empire. Most of the present-day doors of the Taj Mahal were made during the days of Lord Curzon. How could the doors, made in the 20th century during Curzon's period, be dated to the 11th–14th centuries in the C-14 test? Moreover, the surreptitious sample collection, unauthenticated private research lab and dating from 11–14th century make the conclusion questionable.

I have already made a passing reference to the royal decrees (*farmans*), issued by Emperor Shah Jahan to Raja Jai Singh for the exchange of sites and supply of marble for the construction of the Taj Mahal. The first decree, dated 20 September, 1632, housed in the Rajasthan State Archives at Bikaner, talks of expediting the shipment and instructs him to extend full co-operation to Muluk Shah, who had been deputed to Amber to this effect. The second decree, dated 3 February, 1633, again instructs him for a large quantity of marble from the quarries of Makarana. This *farman* also speaks about the deputation of Sayyid Ilahdad to Amber for the arrangement of 230 carts for transportation of the same to Agra. A third *farman*, dated 30 June, 1637, admonishes Jai Singh to desist from allowing his agents to quarry marble as that was resulting in a short supply of the marble to Agra. The fourth *farman*, housed in Kapad Dwara collection in Jaipur, dated 28th December, 1633, names the four properties, which were given to Jai Singh in place of the property taken from him for the construction of Taj Mahal.

Those who promote such claims regarding the Hindu origin of the Taj Mahal behave like their colonial cousins, the *jihadi* Muslims. It can be pointed out that Hindu architectural texts such as '*Mānsārā*,' *Māyāmatā*, and *Samarāṅgaṇa Sūtradhārā* make no mention of *minars*, arches, domes, perforated screens, inlay works, glazed tiles, etc. It would be worthwhile to ask them whether the Tejo Mahalaya has been mentioned in any of the Hindu Shilpa texts? If so, what are the iconographic specifications and attributes of such a diety? Do we have any Tejo Mahalaya temple in any other part of India?

Sometimes, even some of the liberal Hindus get swayed by these unreasonable arguments due to the fact that in north India, especially in Delhi, Agra, Jaipur and other tourist sites, one does not find ancient temples that constitute the 'marvels and mysteries of Indian architecture.' No doubt there were many beautiful pieces of ancient Indian architecture in north India, especially in and around Delhi, Agra, Jaipur and other places, but all of them were thoroughly destroyed and taken over during Muslim invasions by iconoclasts with religious zeal. It is but natural that the aggrieved Hindu community would nurse a grievance against the tribe of iconoclastic Muslims. Such people fall easy prey to the arguments of people such as DS Triveda and PN Oak, who claim the Qutub Minar, Red Fort, Taj Mahal and various other historical structures as Hindu monuments.

Extremist Hindus have made many wild claims regarding the Hindu origin of Kaba (in Mecca), the Vatican (the headquarters of Pope in Italy) besides the usual claim of the *pushpak vimana*, Sushruta's surgery, internet, missiles and other such discoveries mentioned in the Mahabharata, Ramayana and various other mythologies. For them, India is the centre of the world and the pre-Islamic idols and the black stone of Mecca (al-Hajar-al-Aswad) were taken from India. Some argue that Mecca's black stone is a Hindu shivalinga.

Sculptural art started in India from the period of Ashoka (268–232 BCE), but authors of these arguments are blissfully unaware of sculptural art and idol worship in the Egyptian, Mesopotamian, Akkadian, Assyrian and Babylonian cultures of the Middle East. All these cultures had highly developed sculptural art many centuries before it started in India. The Great Pyramid of Giza, rising to a height of 481 ft in height, dated to 2600 BCE was the tallest manmade structure from 2600 BCE to 1311 CE, till it was surpassed by Lincoin cathedral. Temple of Amun, Karnak (1312–1301 BCE, temple at Luxor (1408–1300 BCE) temple of Abu Simbel (1301 BCE) are few other structures and rock cut caves in ancient Egypt that are awe inspiring in grandeur. Abu Simbel has six colossal statues rising to a height of 33 ft representing king Rameses and queen Nafertari. Tereh, father of the Biblical Patriarch Abraham, was a master sculptor in the city of Ur. The huge archaeological wealth of gold, silver, precious stones and sculptural wealth of lion's head and bull's head discovered at Ur in the Royal Tomb

(2550 BCE) in Mesopotemia is only second to that of Tutankhamun (1332–1323 BCE) in Egypt. Tutankhamun's mummy was adorned with gold mask inlaid with lapis lazuli, carnelian, quartz, obsidian, turquoise and faience and weighs 11 kilograms. It contained more than 5000 catalogued objects of exquisite beauty and took many years for the documentation and cataloguing it. What our overzealous and overnationalist advocates of Bharatmata should understand is that carving of sculptures and idol worship was not an exclusive cultural expression of India. Many such parallel thoughts and cultural and religious expressions existed all over the world, much before they started in India.

□

Marketing the Indian Heritage

In-depth knowledge of one's own culture is a prerequisite for developing self-confidence and encouraging the growth of new ideas. A comparative study of other contemporary cultures would help one get a better understanding of our position in the past and in a proper perspective. Every student of history knows that after the Second World War, Japan and Germany were literally razed to the ground. However, they managed to rise from the ashes like the proverbial Phoenix. This was possible because the general public was made aware of their glorious past. A new generation born with such a realisation can give a country and society a new sense of direction and take the community to new heights of progress. The post-World War Japan and Germany were borne out of this realisation and consequent remedial action. Similarly, a study of Indian heritage can also rejuvenate the dormant spirit of Indians and awaken them to their glorious past by showcasing the country's rich heritage. The culture and civilisation of a country are like oil found in the desert, provided it is polished, showcased and marketed. The oil reserves decrease the more they are exploited, whereas the cultural heritage gets further enriched and replenished with renewed splendour if appropriately utilised. The more it is used and rubbed, the more facets emerge in sparkling colours. Apart from that, understanding its greatness awakens the dormant soul, uplifts the spirit, and prepares one to encounter seemingly insurmountable tasks. Such an awakening is imperative in rejuvenating the present society and creating a new generation.

On account of its glorious past and rich culture, India once enjoyed the prestigious position of a 'universal teacher.' It tremendously influenced Central Asian, South Asian and Far East Asian countries. We must learn to recognise our inner strength.

When Hanuman was made aware of his boundless energy, he shook off his languor and worked miracles. Similarly, our youngsters are capable of great things when made aware of their rich culture handed down the generations. But care should be taken to see that whatever we speak is validated by science and technology. Trumpeting unscientific myths at science congresses will make the country a laughing stock to others. All ancient civilisations and religions have their own set of mythologies, but none declares them as scientific facts as we do in the annual sessions of the Indian Science Congress. Myths and legends have their different domains.

The government can make the ASI one of its most important and income-generating departments, provided it is run with a vision and its heritage is marketed intelligently. It would be desirable to have two divisions–the Archaeological Survey of India (ASI) and India Heritage Development Corporation (IHDC) to make it efficient and competitive. The latter can deal with the ASI's entire revenue, such as ticket collection, issuing various licences, conducting auctions, running cafeterias, selling mementoes, running bookshops, etc. It should also take over the sound and light programmes, which the Tourism Department handles. The guide and photography licences were sometimes with the ASI and at times with the Tourism Department. In any case, the ASI suffered due to mishandling of issues by the Tourism department when various individuals in different state courts contested it. The Tourism Department did not show the same efficiency that the ASI displayed in the innumerable court cases as they were short of staff to handle such cases. It would be in the interest of the ASI to hand over such powers to the IHDC.

The licence fee from the feature filmmakers was only Rs. 5,000 till a few years ago. Now it has been enhanced to Rs. 50,000, but even that is a paltry amount for maintaining the ambience of a monument, which is shown in feature films. Once, an agent who had approached me for a licence on behalf of the film company informed me that while the ASI was collecting a mere Rs 5,000 (five thousand only) as licence fee, he, as an agent, was charging Rs 1,00,000 (one lakh) from the filmmakers. This revelation brought into sharp focus how the ASI had failed to market and profit from the heritage sites. I believe that a fee of Rs 3,00,000 (three lakhs) per day is reasonable for permission to shoot a feature film in a monument. However, for documentary films, it should not be more than Rs 5,000. Presently, there is no distinction between a feature film and a documentary film.

Once a corporation is formed in the ASI, like the ITDC and IRCTC, income generation would get a proper place in the ASI scheme of things. Presently, no such thought as 'income generation' has entered into the mind space of ASI management. The new thought process would enable the ASI to come out of the woods, stand properly, make an image changeover, and earn its own reputation. When the ASI changes itself from a department that is fully dependent on the government's mercy into a revenue-earning department, both its own self-esteem and its image in the eyes of others would also change. This changeover of the image is essential for a respectable and meaningful existence.

Starting Heritage Consultancy Services is another lucrative business where India Heritage Development Corporation (IHDC) can engage itself. By joining hands with the National Cultural Fund, it can take up the conservation and preservation of monuments on a larger scale. If there is a credible agency like the IHDC, many private organisations with heritage properties would prefer to seek help from the ASI rather than approaching any of the private organisations that charge exorbitant amounts. Several religious trusts, universities, High Court buildings, etc., are housed in such heritage structures, and all of them are receiving government funds for their conservation. Sadly, untrained persons from CPWD and PWD are taking up inappropriate renovation work in the name of conservation and destroying these heritage structures. Once, a Central Government university approached me for conservation of its heritage structure. But by the time I reached there, the CPWD had taken up the repair work without any expertise and destroyed it. Universities prefer to entrust such works to the CPWD or PWD to overcome audit objections. If the IHDC had taken up such specialised work, both the engaging institution and the Indian heritage would have benefitted. The audit also would not have had any objection as IHDC specialises in heritage conservation. The Tourism Departments of various states would like to take up environmental development works in the periphery of monuments but cannot undertake it due to heritage laws. Such works could also be entrusted to IHDC as it has heritage experts and is part and parcel of the ASI. Due to the absence of such an agency and mechanism, most departments are going to private players, who charge exorbitant amounts. IHDC would be able to do more work of better quality with the same amount than many private organisations.

Another area where the ASI can do a profitable monument-related business is by selling memorabilia, such as pens, marble pen stands, T-shirts with the photograph of the monument engraved or embossed upon it. I had developed some very good memorabilia by using the image of the relic casket of the Buddha, excavated at Piprahwa. After the death of Buddha, his mortal remains were enshrined in eight places. Of them, a few have been excavated and displayed at the Indian Museum in Kolkata and National Museum in Delhi. Fortunately, the Piprahwa relic casket made of soft stone has an inscription in the 5th century Brahmi script, stating that this relic belongs to the Buddha and his family members. It struck me that if similar caskets were made with Brahmi inscription engraved on it with a few grains of holy soil taken from Bodh Gaya, Nalanda, Sarnath and Kushi Nagar kept in it, then tourists from Buddhist countries would purchase it as the most precious item and keep them in their puja room for daily worship. I made several pieces and gifted them to distinguished persons who visited the country, including Barack Obama, the American President. The production cost was Rs 400, but any Buddhist would be happy to purchase it from a government outlet for Rs 5,000. It is an item that China could never replicate as they cannot replicate the soil of Bodh Gaya, Nalanda, Vaishali or Sarnath. Many such items could be marketed through IHDC from its authorised outlets at Nalanda, Bodh Gaya, Sarnath, Vaishali and Kushi Nagar.

Although the ASI is issuing non-antiquity licences to various antique shops which are making huge profits, it is sad to note that the ASI is charging absolutely nothing for such licences. In the present-day world, if any agency issues licences without charging even a single rupee, it is the ASI. On the other hand, it is spending money from its own limited budget to organise such licence meetings. The payment to experts for serving on the board of such committees is very poor. Often we found it below our dignity to pay such a paltry amount to the participants with such in-depth knowledge on the subject. The experts still obliged the ASI due to their attachment with the department. The antique dealers are making enormous profits based on these licences issued by the ASI. It is high time that both the government and the ASI changed their attitude and explore the infinite possibilities of business diversification and converting the ASI into an income-generating department.

Many private business groups such as Taj Mahal Tea, Ajanta Watch, Char Minar cigarettes use the names of the World Heritage Monuments and national monuments for branding and selling their products. Why shouldn't the ASI charge these companies for using its photo and brand name? Copyright laws are applicable worldwide, so why can't the ASI use it profitably and plough back the same amount into the conservation of the monuments? Is there any other country where a company uses a monument's name for selling its product free of cost? One has yet to hear of brand names like Pyramid tea, Eiffel Tower watches, or Great Wall cigarettes. Would the owners of Burj Khalifa permit anyone to use its name? A counter-argument is that these companies are popularising the monument, but I beg to differ because national monuments do not require publicity, and often the footfall is much more than its carrying capacity, which is now actually damaging the monuments. Once a Heritage Corporation is formed, many such avenues can be explored to augment the corporation's revenue.

Egypt is opening its first archaeological factory in the industrial zone of Obur city named Qualyubia, as part of its attempt to fight the spread of Chinese-made products in the local markets. Recently, Mustafa Waziri, the Secretary-General of the Supreme Council of Antiquities, said that the factory would protect intellectual property rights for Egyptian antiquities. It is learnt that the factory, which costs about 100 million Egyptian pounds, is equipped with the latest technology and has manual and mechanised production lines for casting metals. According to *Amr al-Tibi*, it is done as part of the amendments made in 2010 to the Antiquities Protection Law No. 117 of 1983 to protect the intellectual property rights and trademark of the Supreme Council of Antiquities products. Their feasibility study says that their profit will touch ten million pounds within less than three years. Their product will carry a special stamp, barcode and a certified certificate. It is high time India also enacted a similar Antiquities Protection Act as the Egyptian government did.

When I was posted in Delhi as Superintending Archaeologist, the annual revenue amounted to Rs 30 crores. I did a 'prospective calculation exercise' to increase the revenue from Rs 30 crores to Rs One hundred crores by increasing the cost of the entry tickets, photography and filming licence fees, etc. Following this calculation exercise, it was not difficult for the ASI's Delhi circle to increase its revenue from Rs 30 crores to Rs 100 crores. It was a simple hypothetical study and calculation exercise. It is admitted that other circles are not as revenue-earning as the Delhi and Agra circles are; some of them, like the Ranchi Circle, has very few ticketed monuments. Despite this, there are ways to convert one's assets from dead sites and monuments into vibrant cultural and revenue-earning products. All that is required is a few imaginative, ignited and fertile minds, a mindset ready to change, and a dynamic minister and DG to push the department's transformation. By carefully protecting and ticketing many non-ticketed monuments, the revenue collection can be increased several times without much difficulty. Even now, many monuments can be ticketed. If the monuments are non-ticketed, apart from losing revenue, they are devalued by the public and reduced to serving as an easy meeting place for anti-social elements. One cannot stop them from entering and misusing the area, as there is no ticketing system. The ASI is also prone to neglecting such places as there is an acute shortage of manpower and the management of such places usually involves a daily fight with the local trespassers. Based on my experience, I am confident that if a definite plan is drawn up and implemented, the ASI's income would increase, thereby paving the way for making it an autonomous organisation.

The Akshardham temple in Delhi is an excellent example of how the authorities have artificially marketed the Indian heritage. The question is not about whether the heritage they are selling is real or artificial, but a lot of it depends on how they market it. Once a tourist or a pilgrim completes the visit to various temples and pavilions of Akshardham, he leaves the premises highly impressed by Indian culture and tradition. Does a visit to any of our monuments leave such an impression in our mind? Perhaps not, but I was highly impressed when I visited Akshardham on an invitation from the temple management committee. Their presentation of India's heritage was superb and unmatched.

Of all the programmes, the best I enjoyed was the Sanskriti Vihar boat ride. It was a 12-minute boat ride through 5,000 years' heritage of the country through life-size sculptures and robots to portray life from Vedic India to the modern era. During the ancient period, one can watch India's scientific achievements and meet illustrious figures such as Aryabhatta, Brahmagupta, Varahamihira, and physicians such as Jeevaka, Sushruta Charaka, Patanjali and others. Similarly, other figures who contributed to the culture and civilisation of the country are also represented there. After this enjoyable boat ride, one disembarked from the boat, proud of one's heritage and fully charged with national pride.

Similarly, in Kolkata, a time machine, a 30-seater motion simulator, provides a virtual experience of a space flight journey into an unknown world, run by the hydraulic motion-control system. The same 'time machine' can be taken as a model, and the journey to different worlds could be modified into different cultures, such as Harappan, Vedic, Buddhist and other dynastic periods. There are many ways to showcase our heritage to the world. Of course, there would be problems in having such programmes within the monuments, but one can always think of having it within the regulated area of the monument. The 'time machine' idea can also be incorporated in museums as it does not require much space or large construction.

By introducing such innovative programmes with the help of modern science and technology, each monument can be turned into a learning centre and a powerhouse, where the next generation's mind can be ignited. Along with it, the government can take steps to educate and improve the tourists' outlook. A historical monument is usually emblematic of the place where it is located. Most visitors to the monument are not well informed about its historical significance. Some people visit the monument only to satisfy their curiosity, and very few visit them out of a genuine interest in the history and culture. But once at the site of the monument, both the historical site and the guide should be able to trigger the visitors' minds. Qualified guide-cum-photographers should be stationed in the monuments to interpret the history of the monument for the general public. Good guides are an asset to every monument, and they can make the monument speak for the visitors.

Countries like Greece and Rome conduct short-term courses in exploration and excavation. Such courses give an opportunity to learn about the culture, art and architecture of the country. Greece and Rome have their attractions as they are the cradles of the European civilisation. They also offer an opportunity to participate in exploration and excavation. Such courses are attended not only by youngsters but also by senior citizens. If the International Nalanda University or Archaeological Survey of India were to organise such courses in or around Nalanda, Rajgir, Bodh Gaya, Vaishali, etc., there would be several participants from Buddhist countries, both students and senior citizens, ever ready to join in and spend a few months in such places.

When senior citizens spend one or two months in India, the revenue the country earns is much more than what they might have spent if they come as a tourist for five days. If youngsters join this course as part of their degree examination, the seniors could join for intellectual and spiritual satisfaction. While serving in Bihar and elsewhere, I had several discussions with tourists about such short term courses. For them, such an opportunity would have been a dream come true. How lucky they would be to consider themselves part of an excavation in the holy land where Buddha once walked! To top it all, such courses should be combined with medical tourism, Ayurveda, Siddha and modern massage therapy for various ailments as these have caught the imagination of the West. Nalanda, Bodh Gaya, Rajgir, etc., are such holy places and cultural mines that no country can steal them from India. After taking due permission from the Ministry of External Affairs, universities in Bihar could enter into an exchange programme with similar institutions in Buddhist countries. But Indian politicians and heritage managers have to package and market it to the emerging new world. IHDC can play a meaningful role in all these areas and prepare the ASI for a great leap forward.

It is a matter of regret that the authorities have made no sincere attempt to turn our historical monuments into channels of cultural regeneration. Every historical monument needs interpretation centres and qualified guides to explain its significance of the monument. Most of the guides are indeed knowledgeable and capable, but quite a few have weak backgrounds in history and resort to embellishing their talk with popular stories. It is, therefore, imperative that all tourist guides be given proper training by the government in institutions like the IITM. In many of the non-ticketed monuments of rural areas, there are no guides. Such places need to be identified and trained guides deputed to them. This will provide rural employment to the educated youth. Such local guides are the stakeholders and also serve as the protectors of the monuments against vandalism.

The ITDC has done a remarkable job by introducing light-and-sound programmes at monuments in different parts of the country. Such programmes, apart from recreating the vanished culture, transport a person into the distant past. It is the need of the hour to introduce more such shows in many more monuments. As a nation, we must educate, inform and awaken the *kundalini* of the visitors and ignite the mind of youngsters.

Often, the budget allotment to the ASI is very poor. At the same time, the Tourism Department gets liberal allotments even though 90 per cent of Indian tourism is heritage tourism. However, the tourism budget could be utilised for the environmental development of the monument, provided there is proper coordination between the Tourism Department and the ASI. Individually, at many places, I have been successful in persuading the Tourism Department to carry out works that are essential for the development of the surroundings of the monument. This was more on personal initiative and coordination, but a policy decision and coordinated efforts are required to create a new benchmark. In a fast-changing world, the ASI has to think aloud, change its myopic vision, rethink and chart its functional and business strategies.

The commercial potential of many historical monuments has not been tapped largely on account of the indifference of the archaeological Survey of India. Most of the ministers and officials are unaware of the commercial potential of monuments and are least interested in developing them. It is here that a Heritage Development Corporation can play the role of a game-changer. It is always advisable to combine the tourism and culture ministries under the supervision of a single minister for coordinated development. The ministers and the secretaries can be appointed only on the basis of their interest, passion and familiarity with the subject. Inputs should be invited even from retired officials in order to profit from their vast experience. Followers of the BJP and the RSS are quite eloquent about the 'glorious civilisation of India' but have miserably failed in projecting a vision.

Naturally, when the BJP came to power, those associated with culture expected a quantum leap forward. Of course, during the period of Atal Bihari Vajpayee, the situation prevailing during the

Congress period continued unabated, as Murali Manohar Joshi and Ananth Kumar were at the helm of affairs. Although there was no expected quantum jump, the department did not register any decline either. Ananth Kumar raised the revenue of the ASI by increasing the entry ticket prices and charging enhanced ticket charges from foreigners. That was a big positive step in the right direction.

When the late Jagmohan was appointed as Minister of Tourism and Culture by Atal Bihari Vajpayee, he injected new vigour and vitality into the department and galvanised it through conservation, preservation, and land acquisition activities. He strengthened the department by creating new posts, new circles and increasing the budget. Owing to the all-round development, it was considered to be the 'golden period' of the ASI. He himself used to attend the meetings of the Superintending Archaeologists and give necessary directions as he knew all the important monuments. Sometimes he would directly ring up the Superintending Archaeologists to enquire about the position of the ongoing work. Such all-consuming interest by a Cabinet Minister in the ASI was never seen before.

Even while he was the Minister of Urban Development, the ASI was often invited and I remember attending two meetings at Benares and in Delhi. Jagmohan was the driving force for removing slums from various parts of Delhi, especially the Turkman Gate area, Jama Masjid, Humayun's Tomb and Tughlakabad. Those who had seen these areas before the removal of slums knew what a great service he had rendered to the city. It is a tragedy that Jagmohan's tenure as Minister of Tourism and Culture was cut short as he lost the election in 2004. Had he continued for two years more, the fortunes of the department would have taken a different turn.

When Dr Manmohan Singh took over as the Prime Minister, the ministers in charge of Tourism and Culture, namely Ambika Soni, Narayanswami and Kumari Selja maintained the tempo of the activities of the department in all the spheres. Both Ambika Soni and Kumari Selja did not feel offended even if the departmental officials differed from them on issues. I have already cited the example of Ambika Soni in the chapter of Amarkantak that how madam supported the ASI even when there was both political and religious pressure on her.

Once at a meeting specially convened by Ms Kumari Selja to iron out an issue, I expressed my grave concern in front of my senior officers, as that was against the agreement by the ASI and the second party concerned. Although the minister was visibly annoyed as the case was referred to her by another minister, Selja Kumari did not press for it. Later on, she was so impressed by my stand that when I retired from ASI, I was immediately appointed as a consultant despite my not wanting it, as I was getting another very good assignment. I reluctantly joined just to honour the minister's order, and once the minister was transferred to the Women and Child Welfare Department, I immediately tendered my resignation as the consultant.

This shows the quality of the ministers that even when you differ from them in front of other high officials, the minister is prepared to honour your intellectual integrity. After Selja Kumari, Chandresh Kumari Katoch took over as the Minister of Tourism and Culture. During her period, the ASI suffered a severe setback to its prestige when an excavation was carried out at Unnao in Uttar Pradesh as per the dream of a temple priest, who had seen buried treasures near a temple. It brought disrepute to the scientific department.

When Shri Narendra Modi came to power, riding on the wave of popular sentiments, what the general public expected was a repeat of what they had seen during the period of Jagmohan. Culture lovers all over the country were hoping to see a sea of change in the field of culture, but it proved to be a magnificent illusion because the financial power of the Superintending Archaeologist was reduced from Rs 25 lakhs to Rs 3 lakhs and the rest of the powers were concentrated in the central office at Delhi. This concentration of power in the hands of a few in the Delhi office brought the entire Archaeological Survey of India to a grinding halt.

Earlier, with the financial powers of Rs 25 lakhs, most of the officers carried out conservation works in different parts of the country. The entire task of reconstructing 80 temples at Bateshwar in a hostile terrain was carried out successfully by using this financial power of Rs 25 lakhs. But once that financial power was withdrawn and all the powers were concentrated in the hands of a few at Delhi, the ASI became a wholly paralysed body, especially during the period of Dr Mahesh Sharma (Minister), NK Sinha (Secretary) and Rakesh Tiwari (Director-General, ASI). I thank my stars for having retired from the ASI before being a silent witness to this 'dark age' of the ASI. It is a strange irony of fate that the Archaeological Survey of India was suddenly pushed into this state of paralysing paranoia during the period of the BJP, which used to boast of the glorious civilisation of the country.

Let me record with all humility that even if I were there in the ASI during this period, I too would not have dared to think of starting the conservation of Bateshwar temple. It is painfully noted that during the last seven years of the BJP rule, not a single temple has been reconstructed at Bateshwar.

A few months back, Prahlad Patel, Minister for Tourism and Culture, visited Bateshwar and was impressed at the reconstruction. He was shown the photographs of the site when it was in total ruins. In front of each reconstructed temple, the earlier photos revealed what a Himalayan task had been undertaken to reconstruct the temples. There were none to remind him that all such reconstruction had taken place during the Congress party's rule. He was disgusted when he was told that the reconstruction estimate had been rejected on flimsy grounds and that Bateshwar stands, less than half completed, for all these years as a testimony to the BJP's total failure and mismanagement of the ASI. Even after one year of Prahlad Patel's visit, nothing has happened.

While structural conservations and temple reconstructions were reduced to a minimum, toilet complexes consisting of a ticket counter, cafeteria and souvenir shops at exorbitant costs were constructed in many monuments where such amenities were not required at all. In Nagpur, the Old High Court building has been provided with such a high-cost toilet complex where the number of visitors is very low. I have pinpointed the case of Nagpur toilet as it is not far from the RSS headquarter and anybody associated with Sangh can verify it. But many such toilet complexes have come up in many parts of the country, obviously not to serve the public. Then, whom? The omnipresent and most powerful contractor lobby.

The Archaeological Survey of India has its own engineering wing which carries out both structural and non-structural works. Structural work includes work related to the monument proper, such as the actual conservation of various temples, mosques, churches, palaces, forts, etc., whereas non-structural works include construction of boundary walls, pathways and toilet blocks, ticket counters and cafeteria etc. Earlier, the ASI had been doing both these works very economically on a shoestring budget. Under the new dispensation, all these non-structural works were assigned to a few organisations, such as Telecommunications Consultants India Ltd (TCIL), Water and Power Consultancy Services (WAPCO), National Projects Construction Corporation Limited (NPCC), at a much higher rate than what the ASI had been doing. While the ASI has its engineering wing, to carry out all these works cost to cost, what was the need of assigning these works to outside agencies at such an exorbitant cost? Happy to note that the present Director General Mrs V Vidhavathy has realised the gravity of the problem and started taking initiative not to allow these organisations to further exploit the Archaeological survey of India.

The toilet movement initiated by the Prime Minister Shri Narendra Modi was a revolutionary one after the first movement started by Rajeshwar Pathak of the Sulabh group. But in the case of the Archaeological Survey of India, the well-intentioned toilet project was hijacked by a few interested organisations and individuals. An inquiry into the necessity of such toilets, where the number of tourists is very few, such as Nagpur, Tughlakabad, St Augustin (drinking water facility), Kodumbalur and many other monuments in different parts of the country, is absolutely necessary. This period would go down into the history of the ASI as the most unfortunate period during which all those who imposed these "toilet complexes) knew the cost of toilets and cafeterias but not the value of temples and monuments." (With due apology to Oscar Wilde)

Realising that the most important reason for this 'downfall of the ASI was due to the reduced financial power of the Superintending Archaeologist, I complained to one of the Sangh Parivar's top leaders in 2018. (I had retired from the ASI in 2012) After the Ayodhya verdict in November 2019, one more complaint was made orally. I even sent the points in writing, and on 31 December 2019, the ministry concerned issued an order restoring the Superintending Archaeologist's financial powers, which had been withdrawn in 2016 with certain ulterior motives. Like me, many other senior officials had tried their best to restore the financial powers of the Superintending Archaeologist.

I knew that even though the ministry issued the order, there would be organised attempts by various forces at many levels not to implement it. In February 2020, I took up the issue with Prahlad Patel, the minister in charge of Tourism and Culture, when I met him in Jabalpur, where he had come to inaugurate the World Ramayana Conference. During the discussion, I enlightened him on the deplorable state of affairs at the ASI. I specifically pinpointed that one of the main reasons was the reduction of the Superintending Archaeologist's financial power. He informed me that orders had already been issued for restoration of the financial powers of the Superintending Archaeologist. I brought to his attention that based on the ministry's orders, another order had to be issued by the Director-General to make it operational, which had not been done even after two months.

The minister assured me that as soon as he got back to Delhi, he would see to it that the Director-General of the ASI, issues the necessary orders, but the order did not come, as assured. Finally, after much pressure, the order was conveyed to the ASI's various offices in the month of August 2020, eight months after the first order was issued by the ministry. What was the reason for delaying the implementation of such an important decision?

This period created one more danger, which is looming large on the future of the ASI. The ASI had carried out excellent works in many foreign monuments like Angkor Wat in Cambodia, often competing with European and Far East Asian countries. Similarly, the ASI had restored the 5th century Wat Phou temple complex in southern Laos. In Myanmar, the ASI is taking up the restoration of five pagodas in Bagan, a UNESCO World Heritage monument. Earlier, the ASI had carried out similar exploration, excavation and conservation works in Afghanistan (Bamiyan), Nepal, Angola, Bahrain, etc. These stellar performances in foreign lands were mainly on the basis of excavation and conservation experience gained in India. Unfortunately, presently the structural conservation experience has been reduced to the minimum. Funds are being spent on building large toilets, pathways and boundary walls through TCIL, WAPCO, NPCC and some other organisations.

As a result a new generation of conservation assistants and engineers are coming up in ASI with no experience with structural conservation problems. They would not be able to handle the complex problems of conservation in any of the foreign countries, leave aside, compete with other nations, as India had done in Cambodia. If the present situation continues, the day is not far off, when none would even mention the name of the ASI in the conservation field. The space vacated by the ASI would be taken over by some private players and contractors.

Presently, self-evaluation and weeping over the present deplorable condition of the ASI is going on within the organisation. Officers also fondly recall the condition of the ASI before the BJP deconstructed the ASI. Of course, those who are in the service cannot speak out, but the retired officials of the ASI, who have seen the earlier regimes and the present pitiable condition of the ASI, should take up the issues wherever they deem fit.

During the last seven years, apart from the ASI's systematic structural deconstruction, the department has been managed by the wrong people at the right places. Dismayed and disappointed by the performance of their dear institution, some officials preferred to opt for voluntary retirement and migrate from the

ASI to other departments. The first to opt for voluntary retirement was N Tahir, Director and the man who had discovered the relics of Queen Ketavan of Georgia at St. Augustin Church. It was this relic that was gifted by the Government of India to the Government of Georgia on 9 July, 2021. It is a grave reflection upon the ASI that such a person had to opt for voluntary retirement during this period. The second to leave the ASI was Mrs Sathyabhama, another Director and a very intelligent officer. Dr Nambirajan, the present Joint Director General, although opted for VRS, later on, withdrew it when there was a change of DG at the Delhi Headquarters. Dr Prabhakar, the former Director of the Institute, preferred to leave the ASI and join IIT Gandhinagar. This brain drain and exodus is a poor reflection on the performance of the ASI and the ruling BJP.

□

The Lessons of Experience: Pakistan, the Curse of Indian Muslims

What did I get from my years of government service in the Archaeological Survey of India? It is difficult to answer this question in one sentence. Being an archaeologist, I had a ringside view of the civilisational clashes and consequent wounds to Indian history, which were not very glaring and conspicuous to history students. The latter read about conflicts and dialogues but seldom have the opportunity to feel them from close quarters. Having been posted in many historical places of clashes and dialogues and personally dealing with and excavating many such historical remains, I had a better view of history.

This closer view forced me to speak out some unpleasant truths, which were gall and wormwood for some and music to some others. While the 'civilisational clashes' (Samuel P Huntington) have left festering wounds, they have also provided an opportunity for 'civilisational dialogues'(Hans Kochler). Clashes and dialogues are part and parcel of every evolving society. Nobody can keep man away from such forces of history in a living community, howsoever hard he may try.

The basis of the cultural identity of every Indian is his heritage. All the cultures, notably the Harappan, the Vedic, the Maurya, the Gupta, the Gujjar Pratihara, the Rajput, the Sultanate, the Mughal and the European, have been responsible for the creation of India's vibrant ethos, culture and civilisation. A man is physically and culturally the by-product of all these assimilative cultural forces that subtly and silently work within him. During the course of day to day life, every religion influences the other. Several such cultural exchanges and sharings have gone into the creation of our composite culture. Firaq Gorakpuri has aptly summed up this process:

"Sar zameine e Hind par aqvam e alam ke 'Firaq'
Qafile baste gae Hindostan banta gaya"

On the soil of Hindustan, o Firaq, caravans from all over the world kept coming, and so was Hindustan made.

Those who deny such exchanges are ignorant of the silent forces of history. Even a puritanical protagonist of a single culture or religion cannot shake off all these influences. Without them, we cannot be complete Indians.

A Muslim who refuses to acknowledge Lord Rama and Lord Krishna as his cultural and national icons because of his religious beliefs cannot be regarded as a true Indian. Likewise, a Hindu, who disowns Sultan Iltutmish or Akbar, cannot be a real Indian either. Similarly, British and other European heritage and values run in the veins of every Indian.

In India, during the invasion of Islam in the Middle Ages, many excesses were committed by the rulers. Sacred temples were destroyed, and mosques were erected in their place. Every invasion resulted in a mass-scale massacre, uprooting of villages and towns, large-scale violence and forced conversions. The Islam that came to India through Afghanistan during the 11th century along with Mahmud Ghazni (971–1030 CE) and Muhammad Ghori (1173–1206 CE) was not the Islam of Prophet Muhammed. Arab Muslims had come to Kerala and the western coast as traders. The local Hindu rulers extended them full support. There were instances when the Hindu rulers encouraged fishermen to convert to Islam to serve in the Muslim navy that supported the Hindu rulers of Kerala.

The conquest of Sind by Muhammad bin Qasim in 712 CE also did not cause the kind of violent upheaval as did the Afghan Islamic conquest by Mahmud Ghazni (971–1030 CE) and Muhammad

Ghori (1173–1206 CE). The selective readings of the Quran, relevant when Muslims were victims, were now indiscriminately applied by Afghans when they were the rulers.

This indiscriminate use of Qur'anic verses not relevant to the context, provided fire and fangs to an uncompromising Afghan Islam. Ghazni and Ghori's Islam was the fierce *jihadi* Islam where they demolished temples, looted the population, killed thousands and caused untold miseries. Even in modern times, Afghanistan is in perpetual turmoil. Neither the Persians nor the Greeks nor Islam could civilize them. It was only Buddhism that could pacify the ever-turbulent Afghans during their long history.

Afghanistan is at the crossroads of caravan routes and civilisational exchanges. Ideally, the region should have been a crucible of various cultures and civilisational strands. Such a geographic situation would have naturally broadened their outlook, but instead of becoming a synthesis of various cultures, why did it opt for the fundamental and *jihadi* form of Islam, defy all historical analysis. The fact that Pakistan has become a centre of all types of Muslim *jihadism* with every ruling government's active support is another disgusting story. In the Middle East, Syria is entirely under the grip of extremist ISIS forces. The conversion of Hagia Sophia from a museum to a mosque in Turkey and the recent attacks in Paris and Vienna are alarming trends.

It is high time that the Muslims revisited their reading of selective verses from the Quran, which have been appropriate only for a fledgling Islam when they became the victims and were driven out of Mecca. But as time progressed and situations changed, Muslims should have reconsidered the relevance of the same verses and realigned their thought processes in the light of the emerging world. It is here that the Muslims have faulted and opted for a suicidal course. There is hardly any thinker who could influence their thought process. *The Missing Introspection,* a book written by Sultan Shahin about the total lack of introspection by the Muslim community, is revealing in various ways. He blames the petrodollar Islam for radicalising the Muslims and keeping a separate identity by keeping a beard and veil.

While the Indian Muslims want religious freedom as a minority community, even after the creation of Pakistan, they shudder at the prospect of similar freedom being granted to minority communities of Hindus, Sikhs, Buddhists, Christians and Ahmedias in Pakistan, Afghanistan, Bangladesh and other countries. The Ahmedias have suffered more persecution than any other community in Pakistan since 1974 by being declared non-Muslims. All the minorities in Pakistan, mostly Hindus, Christians and Buddhists, are victims of continuous persecutions and forced conversions. Blasphemy rules are blatantly misused against minorities, but the Indian Muslims are not bothered about the sufferings of non-Muslim minorities in Islamic countries.

Ironically, Indian Muslims are concerned more about the Palestinian cause and the American attack on Iran and Iraq than the plight of the Ahmedias, Hindus, Buddhists, Sikhs and the Christians of Pakistan. It is time for Muslims to spare some time for self-introspection, reset their mindset, and engage in course correction. They are still busy blaming the Hindus for all their misery without any introspection.

Where have the Muslim countries, their leadership and Muslims in general gone wrong? It is primarily the fault-line of all the Semitic religions, notably Judaism, Christianity and Islam, born and brought up in the arid, hostile and desert area. Nomads and culturally backward as they were, fought with highly evolved cultures flourishing around them and grew up uncompromising. The Jews, who were a microscopic minority, survived many savage attempts of their ethnic cleansings and violent upheavals in history. Since they were not political power, they did not indulge in any forced conversion. Even otherwise, conversion is not generally encouraged in medieval and modern Judaism. Although an accidental development, it has served Judaism very well.

All three religions are strongly monotheistic in which 'only their God and religion' is the only true and right one, and all others are false. It does not end here; it goes to an extreme extent. Every believer has to convert the idol-worshipper to their true faith and religion. When this strong belief and political might is combined, it assumes a highly frightening proportion. Both Christianity and Islam suffered from the monstrosity of these two strange, heady, cocktail ideas.

Christianity in Spain and Portugal introduced inquisitions and imposed inhuman punishments on Jews and Muslims. The inquisition in Goa constituted one of the darkest chapters in Indian history. The worst part was that the neo-converts, even after their conversion, were suspects and were easy targets for the inquisitors. Fortunately, it is to the credit of the Muslim clergy that it did not develop an institution like inquisition in Muslim countries. Neo-converts were neither suspected nor did they suffer due to their previous religious history.

A very bold attempt to bring Christianity and Islam together was made at the initiatives of His Highness Sheikh Mohammed bin Rashid Al Maktoum, UAE Vice President and His Highness Sheikh Mohammed bin Zayed Al Nahyan, the Prime Minister and Ruler of Dubai. In their distinguished presence, His Holiness, Pope Francis and the Grand Imam of Al Azhar, Dr Ahmed Al Tayyeb, signed the historic Abu Dhabi Declaration—a document on human fraternity in the United Arab Emirates. This document seeks to encourage stronger relationships between people to promote co-existence among peoples and confront extremism and its negative impacts. It was the first Papal visit to the Arabian Peninsula, hosted by the UAE government. Recently, in the month of March 2021, the Pope made another historic visit to Iraq to meet the Shia religious head Ayatollah Sistani. It was the first meeting in history between the head of the Catholic Church and the head of the Shia Islamic establishments. What Pope stand for is not simply peaceful coexistence but also 'active fellowship' so that different religious groups can participate in the organised worship of the other groups. This concept of active fellowship will go a long way in bringing the world together. Pope Francis reminds one of St. Francis of Assisi (1183–1226), who had met Sultan Al Kamil of Egypt (1177–1238) with a peace message while the Crusades were waging war between Christianity and Islam. The need of the present world is the emergence of Universal religious and political leaders with mass appeal like the Pope, the UAE ruler Mata Amritanandamayi and Shri Shri Ravi Shankar.

The agreement signed to construct a Swaminarayan temple at Abu Dhabi between Prime Minister Shri Narendra Modi and Sheikh Mohammed bin Zayed Al Nahyan is another such historic agreement. It is heartening that the temple's foundation laying ceremony (shilapujan) took place on 11 February 2018. As part of its Year of Tolerance programme, the UAE government allocated 14 more acres of land to the temple in January 2019. The temple celebrated Krishna Janmashtami on 24 August 2019 with traditional fervour. It is hoped the path illuminated by the enlightened ruling dynasty of Abu Dhabi would be followed by other Arab Islamic countries also.

During their conquests of Syria, Egypt, Iraq, Persia, Central Asia and Afghanistan, Muslims completely wiped out all indigenous faiths and religions. The Jews, the Christians and the Parsis were given some concessions and freedom due to their status as *dhimmis* (protected), a higher position granted by Prophet Mohammed and the second Caliph, Hazrat Umar. After the conquest of India by Muhammed bin Qasim, the Hindus of India were also granted the status of *dhimmis*. That position continued only in Islam, which came through Sind. When the same Islam reappeared in India through Afghani conquerors, the status of Hindus was changed from *dhimmis* (protected) to that of idolaters (*mushrikun*) and *kafirun* (infidels). Once their position changed, nothing could prevent the invaders from their temple-demolishing spree.

It is to the credit of India that when the rich and strong Egyptian, Byzantine, Persian and Roman (Syria) civilisations succumbed, India alone could offer resistance and refused to be submerged in the Islamic deluge. Of course, India was politically conquered, but its spirit was always head and shoulder above the all-consuming Islamic whirlpool. Although Indians suffered heavily and were put to untold misery, they refused to bow spiritually to the uncompromising form of Islam, which displayed its violent streak.

Marxist historians come up in defence of Islamic atrocities

with some strange arguments. In a blatant attempt to defend Islamic fundamentalism and reduce the gravity of violence unleashed by them, the Marxists argue that all the violence, destruction of temples and iconoclasm, etc., were primarily due to the Muslim forces' greed for gold and silver stacked in the temples. Had it been so, they could have looted the temples of their valuable treasures, but what one finds is not only looting but also wanton destruction and iconoclasm in which all idols were mutilated. That exhibits the Muslims' uncompromising mind against all forms of idol worship and ensures its destruction as their religious duty for being the victor.

A cursory look at the images reused in the Quwwat-ul-Islam mosque in Delhi and Adai-din-ka-Jhonpda in Ajmer would make this point amply clear. There, one can see mutilated Hindu and Jain idols and structures reused in various parts. In front of the Quwwat-ul-Islam mosque, an inscription eloquently speaks that twenty-seven temples were destroyed to construct this might of Islam (Quwwat-ul-Islam). This has been further attested by Hasan Nizami in *Taj-ul-Maasir*, a contemporary work.

This *jihadi* spirit is further strengthened by the conviction that even if he is accidentally killed in the temple-destruction spree, would directly ascend to the promised heaven where every luxury awaits him. What more allurement is required to prepare a *jihadi* mind? While heaven is being furnished for him by angels after martyrdom, the Marxist historians of Aligarh Muslim University (AMU) and the Jawaharlal Nehru University (JNU) are there in the terrestrial world to defend them!

Without reducing the importance of gold and silver in military marches, it is submitted that the overpowering urge of Afghan jihadis was the destruction of 'false gods' and cessation of idol worship. The economic interpretation cannot be treated as the prime cause of temple destruction from a *jihadi,* who is a radicalised human bomb. Penetrating into the psychology of a *jihadi*, Rajat Mitra, the psychologist, says: "When he is possessed of the *jihadi* spirit, a mere stone in his hand turns into a veritable missile."

Another strange argument of the Marxist historians is that

it was not only the Muslim invaders who had destroyed temples, even the Hindu kings indulged in the destruction of temples of the enemy kings. They quote Raj Tarangini of Kalhana, in which King Harsha (1089–1111) of Kashmir is said to have destroyed temples. Without questioning the authenticity of the information, may I ask them, how far is it justifiable to use this isolated example to counter the series of wanton destruction of temples over centuries, the mutilation of idols or throwing them under the pavement of Jami mosques so that believers could tread over them?

The communist historians also point out the cases of the presiding deities of the enemy country being taken to another territory to be installed in another temple. In all these cases, idols were appropriated and installed but never mutilated or desecrated. The isolated incident of Kashmir's Harsha or appropriation of few gods should not be used to whitewash the misdeeds of the medieval temple-destroyers.

While the economic interpretation and the example of Kashmir's Harsha have miserably failed to convince the liberal Hindus, due to its flawed logic, it has provided an all-powerful weapon to the *jihadis*. They quote Marxists profusely to justify the violence and barbarity of their ancestors. The unholy alliance of the intellectual Marxists with *jihadis* is still the support base for *jihadis* in various universities and academic forums. By analysing temple destruction purely from an economic point of view and minimising the Jihadi spirit behind it, the Marxist historians have directly and indirectly helped Muslim fundamentalists. No Marxist historian in AMU and JNU thinks about the damage they have already caused to the country.

On the other hand, this approach of the Marxists has provoked a strong reaction from the right-wing Hindus. This strong reaction is not only from extremist Hindus but also from the non-denominational Hindus, who otherwise do not entertain any hardened posture. How long are the Hindus going to put up with the indignities and humiliations? The pent-up feelings sometimes erupt when they see the sites of religious humiliations, such as Ayodhya, Mathura, Kashi and many others. The 'transgenerational trauma is further aggravated when a Hindu visits such places and learns their history.

By economic interpretation and the justification of medieval barbarity, the Marxists are leading the Muslims to a dangerous suicidal path, which closes all the doors and windows of self-introspection and repentance. The Marxist interpretation prevents even educated Muslims from introspection and the necessary course correction. Introspection is required not only by Muslims but also equally by the Marxist historians who are misleading them. Ghalib is entirely relevant for the Muslims and Marxist historians in this hour of crisis.

'Umar bhar Ghalib yahi bhool karta raha
dhool chehre pe thi, aur aina saaf karta raha'

(All through my life I kept on making the same mistake. The dust was on my face, but I kept on cleaning the mirror).

Who can predict, when, into that heaven of freedom and introspection, our historians at AMU and JNU would awake!

The descendants of medieval temple-destroyers are now active in committing acts of collective killing in the name of Islam in Pakistan, Afghanistan, Syria, Yemen and elsewhere. It is a matter of regret that even while committing acts repulsive to the human conscience, they take the name of Prophet Mohammed, the messenger of peace. These activities will obviously bring disrepute to Islam.

The biggest enemies of Indian Muslims are not the Hindu extremists but the extremist Muslims themselves as also the Afghani and Pakistani extremists. Both these countries are not only at the bottom of development indices but also hamper the growth of Indian Muslims. A visit to the Wagah border of India and Pakistan and the evening flag ceremony between both the countries would clarify how India is ahead of Pakistan in various fields, although both the countries got freedom from the British on the very same day.

Indian Muslims should openly condemn international Islamic terrorists and Pakistani terrorist organisations such as the ISIS, the Taliban, the Al Qaeda and the Jaish-e-Mohammad. Afro-

Asian countries such as Nigeria, Egypt, Syria, Yemen, Iran, Iraq, Afghanistan, Bangladesh and India are the worst affected by these groups' toxic ideology. Since 2000, many countries such as the USA, UK, France, Germany, Spain, Belgium, Sweden, Russia, Australia, Canada, Sri Lanka, Philippines and Indonesia have been affected by various versions of jihadi Islam. A study of terrorism by a German newspaper, *Welt am Sonntag* says that from 2000–2019, terrorist attacks have killed 146,811 people. As per the *Global Terrorism Index 2016 Report*, in 2015, four Islamic extremist groups, namely ISIS, Boko Haram, the Taliban and Al Qaeda were responsible for 74 per cent of all deaths. According to Daniel Byman, Professor in the Walsh School of Foreign Service, Pakistan was probably the most active sponsor of terrorism in 2008. Pakistan's sponsorship role in the attack on the Indian Parliament in 2001 and attacks in Mumbai, Varanasi, and Hyderabad are well known.

The *US Country Report* on terrorism describes Pakistan as a 'terrorist's safe haven.' Satellite imagery from the FBI suggests the existence of several terrorist training camps in Pakistan. The bloody hand of Pakistan in Kashmir is known to the entire world. They sponsored the ethnic cleansing of Kashmiri Hindus. Unfortunately, Kashmiri Hindus have become refugees in their own motherland. The book *An Infidel Next Door,* written by Rajat Mitra, gives an insight into the real condition of the Kashmiri Hindus, who were driven out of their own homes. For a radical Kashmiri Muslim, his neighbour is either a *kafir* or a Muslim.

The Muslim *ulemas* should also seriously think about revising the syllabus being taught in various religious institutions, especially where priests are being trained. The syllabus designed for an Islamic country is not suitable for a secular country like India, where the majority consists of Hindus. The fault lines of the earlier syllabus should be identified, and remedial measures are taken to make it relevant to a secular society. It is the teaching of this wrong syllabus that is at the root of all problems that Muslims face all over the world. The ISIS, the Al Qaeda, the Jaish-e-Mohammad, the Houthis in Yemen and many other *jihadi* organisations are the products of this wrong syllabus. Sufi Islam, on the other hand, is more accommodative of indigenous thoughts and can play a leading role in Islam's transition from an uncompromising one to a liberal Islam.

Fortunately for Muslims, the Hindus, who constitute 80 per cent of the population, are tolerant and broad-minded despite their persecution at the hands of the medieval Muslims. Tolerance is ingrained in Hinduism and the Indian way of understanding the world. The Indian *Upanishads*, the zenith of Indian wisdom from which Sanatana Dharma emanates, admits all forms of faiths and beliefs into its vast repertoire. Neither does it think that it is the only true religion, nor does it assume any hard posture. It stands for the welfare of the entire human race, as stated in the *Brihadaranyaka Upanishad:*

'Om sarve Bhavantu sukhinaḥ
Sarve santu nirāamayāah
Sarve bhadraani pashyantu
Ma kashcid dukha bhaag-bhavet'

(May all be happy,
May all be free from illness
May all see what is auspicious.
May no one suffer.)

Equally, it craves for new world order as quoted by *Bhagavad Purana* from *Maha Upanishad* and popularised in *Hitopadesha*:

'Ayam nijah paro veti ganana laghu chetsam
Udara charitanam tu vasudhaiva kutumbakam'

(Only narrow-minded people divide this as one's own and that as others. But for the broad-minded one, the entire world is one single family.)

In this context, it is pertinent to recall the speech delivered by Swami Vivekananda on 11 September 1893, at the First World's Parliament of Religion which I have quoted in the chapter of the "Tragic story of Queen Ketavan." Muslims should take cognizance of the existing realities and come closer to the Hindus to create a united India. Hindus have forgotten and forgiven everything despite having suffered seriously. Creating a congenial atmosphere for reconciliation and helping to heal the Hindus from transgenerational trauma is an initiative that is required to be taken more by the Muslims.

Whenever there were opportunities for settling issues, Muslims have blatantly refused to accept such opportunities. They have found more comfort in the suicidal trap prepared by the community's fanatical elements and the communist historians of Aligarh and JNU. In matters like this, Indian Muslims would do well to emulate the Christians of Goa. For six years, from 1991–1997, I worked in Goa, especially in Old Goa's churches. During the first few years, I stayed near the Church of St. Francis of Assisi. My children grew up playing in churchyards. In Goa, the Portuguese had destroyed several Hindu temples and persecuted the Hindus. Muslims also suffered heavily at the hands of the Portuguese. However, Christians do not regard the medieval barbarity of temple desecration as right. No Christian scholar has justified the medieval cruelty of the Portuguese. I was in close contact with the priests. I have not seen any priest justifying the wrongs committed by their ancestors; on the contrary, they condemn what their ancestors had done. It is perhaps for this reason that in Goa, healthy Hindu-Christian relations exist. Muslims should learn from Christians and reset their mindset.

□

The World Teacher that India Was

In the ancient times India was always looked upon as a spiritual guru by the rest of the Asian countries. India was connected to China, Central Asia, Southeast Asia and the Far East through the Chinese silk route. In the Arthashastra, written by Chanakya, there is a reference to Chinese silk, a significant indication of the connection between the two countries. From the 1st century CE to the 8th century, China looked towards India for knowledge and philosophical ideas. It is said that Buddhism was for the first time introduced in China in 68 CE at Luoyang, during the period of Emperor Mingdi of the Eastern Han dynasty (25–220 CE). Two Indian monks—Kasyapa Matanga and Dharmaratna—went to China along with the scriptures, perhaps at the invitation of the Emperor Mingdi (58–75 CE). They lived there and translated the Buddhist sacred books into Chinese. Thus, an active era of cultural and intellectual exchange took place between India and China. India had started assuming mythical proportions in China, and the Chinese were looking at Indians with esteem and respect. Fahien (337–422 CE), the celebrated Chinese traveller, has left a vivid account of India in his travelogue. Emperor Wu of Liang (502–549 CE) of the Liang dynasty regarded Emperor Ashoka as his ideal ruler and icon. Although he followed Confucianism in the beginning, later embraced Buddhism and banned the sacrifice of animals, very much like what Ashoka did on becoming Buddhist. This attachment with Buddhism earned him the nickname Bodhisattva. In 527 CE, he spent three days in the Tan

Tai Buddhist monastery and in 529 CE, stripped off his imperial clothes, donned a Buddhist monk's dress and spent a few days performing monastic work, including giving a lecture on the '*nirvana sutra.*' In 546 CE, he spent more than one month at the Tang Tai Monastery. This emperor is also credited to have written a major Buddhist repentance service litany, titled 'Emperor Liang's Jeweled Repentance.' This is why many Chinese travellers, such as Xuanzang (602–664 CE), and Yijing (635–713 CE), came to India in search of knowledge. When Yijing studied at Nalanda, there were 56 international students at the university, and a majority of them were from China.

In China, thousands of people accepted Buddhism in preference to Confucianism and Taoism. Xuanzang established a translation bureau to translate Buddhist scriptures from Sanskrit to Chinese. The Chinese Emperor, Taizhong (626–649 CE) immensely, helped Xuanzang in spreading Buddhism all over China.

One day, the Chinese Emperor, Taizhong (626–649) requested Xuanzang: "Master, You and your disciples have translated many Sanskrit texts to Chinese. May I request you to translate at least one book of the Chinese thinker Lao-Tsu into Sanskrit?" The fact that Xuanzang politely declined the Chinese Emperor's request with a smile demonstrates India's greatness in the field of culture and philosophy.

Buddhism spread from China to Korea and from there to Japan. It is said that a princess, Suriratna, also known as Heo Hwang from Ayodhya in India, married a Korean King, Kim Suro of Geumgwan about 2,000 years ago and started the Karak dynasty. An ancient Korean text, Samguk Yusa speaks about the wife of the King who came from Ayuta.

In Japan, both Hinduism and Buddhism profoundly influenced the way the Japanese worshipped. In his book, *Indian Deities Worshipped in Japan*, Benoy K Behl has made an in-depth study of the subject. In Indian architecture, the gateway of a stupa is known as *torana* and in Japan, they still call it as '*tori.*' The most popular gods and goddesses of Japan, notably Benzaitensama (Saraswati) Baishaman (Kubera), Daikokute (Shiva), Kichijoten (Lakshmi),

Enma (Yama), Karura (Garuda), speak volumes about the Indian influence on Japanese culture. Although the Siddha script has disappeared in India, it is still alive in Japan. According to Haji Nakamura: "Without Indian influence, Japanese culture would not be what it is today."

Borobudur, the Buddhist *stupa* in Central Java, built by the Sailendra dynasty belonging to the 8th century, is the largest Buddhist temple. It has six squares and three circular platforms topped by a central dome. It is adorned with 2,672 panels and 504 Buddhist statues. It seems that it is directly influenced by the Kesariya *stupa* in Bihar, built probably by king Harsha (606–647 CE), which has also six circular platforms, two hundred years before Borobudur. The Prambanam temple dedicated to Shiva in Java, measuring 154 feet in height and built by the Sanjai dynasty in the 9th century, also displays a pronounced Indian influence.

Angkor Wat in Cambodia, dedicated to Lord Vishnu and built by Khmer king Suryavarman (1113–1150), is another great temple that shows the extent of Indian influence. This Mahameru, situated within a moat of more than 5 km and an outer wall 3.6 km in length, is three storied, one on top of the other. Towards the later period of the 12th century, it was transformed into a Buddhist centre of worship. The other Southeast Asian countries such as Burma, Thailand, Malaya, Philippines and others are strongly attached to India both culturally and religiously and look upon India as their spiritual preceptor.

Although racially, most of the Central Asian and South Asian countries are Mongoloids and physically look more like the Chinese, from religious and cultural point of view, they are more Indian than Chinese. While the Southeast Asian, Central Asian and Far East Asian cultures have the historical structures of only one or two cultures, India has a bewildering variety of Hindu temples, Buddhist *stupas*, Sultanate *minars*, Mughal tombs, Jewish synagogues, Portuguese, English, French and Dutch churches and forts. As a country, we have stopped short of celebrating this bewildering variety of heritage and marketing it the way it should have been.

But despite this unique heritage, where do we stand today? By conserving and rejuvenating our cultural heritage, we can restore the lost glory of the past. For this, we require ministers and bureaucrats who are endowed with a vision and passion for the country's rich culture. We should also be able to market our heritage in an attractive way.

Buddhism is one of the primary religions of China, Japan, Korea and South-East Asia. However, we have not been able to use this to our advantage, as we have failed to present our cultural heritage to the world in an appropriate way and make it a focus of attraction. Today, countries such as Sri Lanka, Burma, Nepal and others have closer relations with China than with India. Similarly, there has been a great deal of influence of the Ramayana and the Mahabharata in Malaysia, Indonesia (Bali) and Cambodia (Angkor Wat). However, India has not been successful in using these emotional bonds as soft power in its foreign policy.

No matter whichever government comes to power at the Centre, there is a shortage of ministers, bureaucrats and officers with a positive cultural outlook. We imitate the West in most matters, but when it comes to proper conservation and marketing of our culture, we seem to forget their example. The conservation of historical monuments and their marketing is a very lucrative industry in the West. We must learn to emulate them. If we succeed, we can earn more than the West and reap greater rewards. The revenue will be capital for the nation's development. Our ruling class conveniently forgets this simple truth. Our ministers and bureaucrats need to understand that our heritage is not a financial burden on the government exchequer but a source of income, if used properly. We need to turn these resources into revenue and plough back the revenue earned for the conservation of monuments. If this is done for ten years, a time may come that the ASI would be self-sufficient and may not have to depend upon government funds. It would be able to run on its own steam.

When India has failed in marketing heritage by appointing wrong persons at the right places of heritage institutions, China is making giant strides and relegating India by founding a duplicate

Chinese Nalanda University, at the Nanshan mountains, spread over 618.8 acres. The Chinese have named their university as Brahma Pure Land, a concept borrowed from Yoga Vasistha and Mahayana Buddhism. They are offering courses in Buddhism, Tibetan Buddhism and Buddhist architectural design and research. This university is running these courses in association with the Buddhist centres in Thailand, Sri Lanka, Nepal and Cambodia.

To sideline Buddhist places in India such as Bodh Gaya, Rajgir and Vaishali, the Chinese are aggressively promoting Lumbini, the birthplace of Buddha. Since 2010, Yin Shun, the Dean of the Chinese Nalanda University, has been advocating a South China Sea strategy and has closely worked with Thailand and Nepal to create a Buddhist 'One Belt and One Road' (OBOR). Ultimately the plan is to connect Wuxi and Hainan through the Buddhist OBOR by usurping the legacy of Buddha. While China is marching ahead with its duplicate Nalanda University, India's real Nalanda started in 2014 with 14 students has many miles to walk.

By developing the silk route, China has attempted to draw all channels of commerce towards itself. On the other hand, India is unable to do anything remotely similar. The silk route is a pathway not only for culture, but also for commercial transactions. On 14 May 2017, the One Belt One Road initiative was inaugurated, adding 40 more countries, which include China, Russia and Pakistan. Simultaneously, the Chinese are actively engaged in aggressively expanding their maritime silk route and bringing all the neighbouring countries within its orbit. While China is marketing its heritage attractively, many of our policymakers still consider our heritage to be a burden, which should be dismantled at the earliest opportunity, so that new structures can be constructed in its place.

The Travel and Tourism Competitiveness Report 2019 ranked India 34th among 140 countries, which is a poor show for a country with such highly rated and unique cultural heritage. Spain tops the list, followed by France, Germany, Japan, the United States and the UK. In Asia, while Japan is on the fourth position, China is the largest travel and tourism economy in the Asia Pacific and

13th among the top travel destinations. Many small countries, such as Thailand, Malaysia, New Zealand, Singapore, Korea, Hongkong and others, are ahead of India, even though they don't have such a rich cultural wealth, which India boasts of. While travelling in the European, South Asian and Far East Asian countries as a tourist and comparing them with the Indian tourism, one really feel they are much ahead of India.

In this context, it is better to recall Mark Twain, "Twenty years from now, you will be more disappointed by the things that you did not do." Let us change our mindset. Dream big and act without losing time.

□□□